Pétanque:
The Greatest Game You Never Heard Of

B. W. Putman

No part of this book may be reproduced, stored in a retrieval system or transmitted by any means without the author's written permission.

The author is committed to support the international Pétanque training and education community. But be forewarned, you may not post any <u>written or graphic</u> information excerpted from this book on your personal or club's website or photocopy it for training purposes without the author's explicit written permission.

Regardless of what Grace Hopper reputably said, <u>it is not</u> "easier to ask for forgiveness than it is to get permission."

To Kris
In gratitude for indulging my plunge into yet another frivolous and meandering journey, even more thanks for joining me in the process - also for being my favorite doublettes partner.

Table of Contents

Chapter 2: Skills, Strategy & Etiquette 23

Chapter 3: Throwing Techniques 43

Chapter 4: Throwing Mechanics 73

Chapter 5: Competition Boule Selection 101

Acknowledgements

This is where I'd usually acknowledge the generous support and assistance proffered by the U.S. Pétanque Federation (*FPUSA*) and the rank-and-file players. But I quickly discovered that the American Pétanque community is not only content, but seriously committed to maintain its virtual invisibility. Apparently they fear that Pétanque will be hijacked by the masses and pursued as a competitive sport rather than the traditional French Expat approach as a leisure-time activity practiced by an elite few within a French cultural context. This mindset is aptly illustrated by the *Portland Petanque Club* whose solitary annual membership recruiting effort is a one-day booth at the Bastille Day celebration. **The message is clear, Pétanque is first and foremost a French pursuit – only Francophiles are welcome into our privileged community.**

While doing research interviews at a major club in the San Francisco Bay area I was antagonistically confronted by several French-American players and accused of being a "typical American, turning Pétanque into an engineering project." When I asked why there are dozens of wonderful French Pétanque books, but none have been translated into English their collective response was delivered with a classic Gallic shrug, "We French understand Pétanque; Americans have no need of that knowledge." I also find American players equally closed and defensive. For the record, during my Pétanque travels through Belgium and France I never encountered those attitudes. European players are delighted to speak of their love of the game. Most were amused at the prospect of a clueless American undertaking the daunting task of writing the first comprehensive English language Pétanque book for an unreceptive and virtually non-existent audience.

I must confess ambivalence about bringing the good news of Pétanque to mainstream America. When a sport is embraced by the masses it undergoes a dramatic transformation. I personally observed this phenomenon during the halcyon days of disc golf. Until the late 1980s disc golf was an odd and arcane activity practiced by a few thousand laid-back ex-hippies at fewer than 150 courses. It was "discovered" by the public in the early 1990s and within a few years became a mainstream mania. You can imagine the spike in techniques and expertise as the sport was assaulted by bloodthirsty competitors who left us (the mellow pioneers) in the dust with nary a thank-you. As of 2010 there were over 3,000 disc golf courses in the U.S. of which almost 90% are hosted in free-use, public spaces. Although I love the number and variety of courses and the availability of inexpensive, high-tech golf discs, I often reflect fondly on the days before the invasion of the great unwashed masses. But that's the nature of change; one must accept the bad with the good or find another sport.

To provide perspective on this tale of two sports consider *La Boule d'Or*, America's oldest Pétanque club founded in 1959. The terrain is located in San Francisco's Golden Gate Park. A five minute walk from *La Boule d'Or* is Marx Meadows, the site of the *Golden Gate Park Disc Golf Course*. On several occasions I've had the pleasure of playing 18-holes of disc golf followed by a few hours of Pétanque underneath *La Boule d'Or's* fragrant eucalyptus trees. **But the astounding fact is in terms of popularity, on a typical Saturday or Sunday more people play a round of disc golf at Golden Gate Park than throw Pétanque at La Boule d'Or for the entire year!**

I absolutely love both sports. Why over the past two decades has the popularity disc golf exploded, while U.S. Pétanque is static or in decline? ***The answer is obvious; it's a function of the collective attitudes of each sport's national association, the local clubs and the typical player.*** I acknowledge with respect, affection and admiration Pétanque's great obligation to the French, but if the U.S. game is to survive and prosper now is the time to let the genie out of the Bordeaux bottle. Like its astoundingly popular Italian cousin Bocce, Pétanque's future success in America is predicated on shedding its ethnic shackles; it must be promoted based on virtues, rather than pedigree. I ask of the Pétanque player who takes umbrage to that contention to please enlighten me, "Why is American Bocce (a grossly inferior sport by every conceivable measure) tens-of-thousands of times more popular than American Pétanque?" I've asked that question dozens of times and have never received a coherent response.

In terms of the actual acknowledgements, my two grassroots Pétanque startup groups provided the ideal "proof of concept" laboratories to determine Pétanque's appeal beyond its highly constrained and self-imposed demographics. I thank the following guinea pigs for their assistance and comradely in accompanying me on this fool's errand. Like life it was always about the journey, never the destination.

- Kris Martens our resident artist provided the cover artwork, performed the photo editing and enhancement and created the artwork, business cards, banners, car door magnetic signs, T-shirts, hats and other promotional items that helped make La Boule du Bono and Pig Iron Petanque such tremendous successes. Not to mention my favorite doublettes partner infusing all with her élan vital!
- Kathi Garcin, the cover and throwing mechanics model, is an endurance athlete, cyclist, kayaker, yoga practitioner and inveterate gym rat. She's Pétanque's new demographic. Kathi also recruited many accomplished, fit athletic couples to prove the assertion that Pétanque is a great complement to physically demanding sports. Couples really can play together – whether they prefer to be teammates or opponents is a different dynamic and well beyond the scope of this book.
- Jan Kirtland was one of the few U.S. players who supported this project. We played together in the 2011 **Portland Pétanque Club Mixed Doubles Championship** in which half of the teams that we competed against were composed of two men! (*Talk about a club that just doesn't get the concept at a multitude of levels*.) She copyedited much of the book and provided invaluable feedback on drills and training ideas. She was also a regular participant in my summer Pig Iron Pétanque group. Jan just kicked off a *Pétanque for Kids* program. If you have young children you should visit her website.
- Philippe Boets of *Pétanque America* provided technical editing on the boules chapter and offered invaluable insight. Although we have extremely different perspectives and attitudes, we agree that the future of Pétanque in America is best served by grassroots, community-based organizations playing in non-dedicated public spaces.
- Loren Schneider provided the brunt of copy and technical editing for the final draft. He also attempted to keep my *FIPJP* and *FPUSA* polemics focused and productive (sadly, to no avail.)
- A special thanks to Ron and Shirley Gerhart who brought years of European and American experience to our terrain and provided novices with support and focused tutorials.
- To Smudge Martens, furry and ferocious, providing equal measures of recreation and irritation.
- I also thank the dozens of people in the U.S. and France that I interviewed and ruthlessly hounded about their techniques and strategies (often, lack thereof), and general perceptions regarding Pétanque's miserable failure in the U.S. and its medieval sexist underpinnings. I quickly discovered that the fastest way to shut down a conversation was to mention that I was writing an English language Pétanque book, which I learned to keep to myself. I apologize for that omission, but not for my modus operandi as agent provocateur; "warm and fuzzy" didn't cut it. I knew that I had to crack a lot oeufs to make this French omelet.

Finally, thanks to all of the regulars of our winter Palm Springs group at *La Boule du Bono* and our summer *Pig Iron Pétanque Club* in Lake Oswego, Oregon. Between the two groups we introduced Pétanque to over 120 people. Some threw only a few times, but many stayed the entire season.

Introduction:

It's simply Un-American!

Have you ever discovered an activity that was so exhilarating that it compelled you into an evangelical frenzy and upon bringing the good news to family, friends and occasional stranger, your revelation was greeted with nothing more than an uncomprehending stare? ***Welcome to Pétanque.***

Perhaps the problem is that just about every aspect of Pétanque is un-American. It violates the expectations of what constitutes an acceptable sport or leisure time activity. It's simple to play, yet difficult to master; the strategy is utterly obvious, yet it's superbly subtle and multilayered. The equipment is inexpensive and lasts for years; it's the lowest of low tech, nothing but a few baseball-sized steel boules (balls). And the game imposes terribly unreasonable constraints; a player can't instantly improve by upgrading to the latest titanium oversized driver or tungsten ceramic racket frame – the only path to improvement is via an antiquated ritual called "practice." I have no doubt that when Pétanque is finally embraced by mainstream America that the rules will be expanded to allow boules with integrated GPS guidance systems.

What really keeps Pétanque from being embraced by Americans is that it reeks of egalitarianism. Sure the great unwashed masses now even play golf, but their high-tech clubs and Tiger Woods fashion accessories let them dream, at least for a fleeting moment, that instead of a déclassé Muni course they're actually on Pebble Beach. There's no such escapism for Pétanque, which doesn't even require shoes with cleats, pleated knickers or high-tech wicking fabric. Although it may sound ghastly, I've even seen people play in flip-flops, but they had better not drop a boule on their foot. Even in international and professional tournaments participants are usually clad in cheap polo shirts with cheesy logos; one would expect haute couture from the French. But fear not, the egalitarianism is tempered by blatant sexism that permeates Pétanque's very core. To ensure that the fairer sex is suitably handicapped, the smallest official boule size was purposefully chosen to be too large to fit the average woman's hand. (Didn't I say that Pétanque strategy was subtle and multilayered?) But as many American and French players have confessed to me on the sly, Pétanque is where they escape women in general and their wives in particular.

Nonetheless, at least functionally, Pétanque is equally accessible to men and women and the young and old. Granted forearm and shoulder strength are assets, but a delicate touch and merciless cunning usually vanquishes unbridled brute strength. And forgive me for being indelicate, but a calorically challenged person with a BMI of 35 can directly compete with an ultra-marathoner with 5% body fat. There's nothing quite so satisfying than to see a couple of old fat guys dispatch a team of young gym-rats with six-packs (and I'm not talking about beer.)

And don't get me started about where it's played; there are no lush fairways, sparking blue waters or veranda bars with bistro tables and lazily swirling ceiling fans. Pétanque terrains (even for the professionals) are small patches of dirt and gravel, indistinguishable from the typical unpaved parking lot; in fact, although I should be loath to admit it, I regularly play on public walking paths, gravel parking lots and even empty fields – that's why we call it a "terrain" and not a court, to signify the lack of grooming. Pétanque terrains don't require water, fertilizer, pesticides or maintenance. They are an environmentalist's dream and a capitalist's nightmare.

But worst of all, and perhaps most offensive, is the language used by the typical Pétanque player. The terms that describe the terrain, equipment, techniques and strategies are French! And that's extremely confusing to the average American, because as Steve Martin so keenly observed, "It's like those French have a different word for everything."

I'm an inveterate wonk compulsively driven to undertake a comprehensive analysis of every new interest. The day I picked up my first boule I performed an exhaustive Internet search with the quest to assemble an inventory of English language reference and instruction materials. Although completely unfamiliar to America, Pétanque has a substantial U.K., Australia and New Zealand following, but to my astonishment there wasn't a single English language Pétanque book currently in-print! There are dozens of great French language Pétanque books written by generations of masters, but to the best of my knowledge none have ever been translated into English – can you say, "Conspiracy Theory?" In desperation I purchased an out-of-print U.K. book and was given a fairly recent Australian book by a friend in the business, but both were little more than beginner's pamphlets which I consumed and disposed of in less than thirty minutes.

There are many English language websites with Pétanque information, but they aren't comprehensive, coherent or consistent. The information which is not contradictory is highly derivative; like so many Internet-based resources, most sites replicate hollow clichés and urban myth. So, as I have done several times in the past, I girded my loins, rolled-up my sleeves, stocked up on caffeine infused beverages, bid my normal life goodbye and committed to write the book I wish was available when I started my Pétanque journey. To prepare for this miserable feat:

- I traveled to Belgium and France to observe Pétanque in its natural habitat, understand its cultural underpinnings and learn native French pointing and shooting technique.
- Visited seven West Coast Pétanque clubs to interview players, observe casual play and watch sanctioned tournaments from the club level through national championships.
- Analyzed dozens of hours of live and recorded professional play to perform analysis of the complex throwing motions and to derive competitive strategies
- Using only hand tools and no water, transformed a large empty desert field into a multi-tiered, world-class terrain for less than $125 in materials.
- Started two successful grassroots organizations to prove that current American Pétanque demographics are an aberration. During the season we introduced over 120 people to Pétanque, of which over 65% were women. Many of our regulars were accomplished elite athletes who view Pétanque as a complement to their otherwise physically demanding sports. They loved the socialization, strategy and vicious competition. It also enabled athletically mismatched couples to compete as peers. Much of the information in this book regarding novice through intermediate play was derived during this rich and rewarding experience.
- Developed novice training drills and alternative games for weekly club training sessions
- Played on every conceivable terrain and returned to conclusion that I first sensed in Belgium. You don't need a club house with fences and a locked gate. *Pétanque is best enjoyed in non-dedicated, public spaces that are available in almost every community in America. A patch of dirt and gravel or the infield of a baseball diamond provides a fantastic terrain.* (Restrooms are also an asset.)

I've always learned technique oriented sports by taking group or private lessons. Having a trainer and a coach is the difference between quickly mastering technique and spending years hacking away in frustration. When I started playing Pétanque at the well regarded Portland Pétanque Club I inquired about training sessions and hiring a coach for private lessons. I was told, *"Be nice to some of the guys and maybe they'll give you a few tips."* That's the American Pétanque training philosophy in a nutshell. And that's why serious American athletes don't consider it a worthwhile pursuit.

Pétanque as Techniques Orientated Sport

A novice can learn a basic demi-portée (half-lob) pointing throw in a few minutes after which they can play in a live game and have a terrific time. Often (unfortunately) such a great time that they'll never be compelled to practice and improve their game – why complicate things when you're already having so much fun? But there are "athletes" among us; people that pursue sports whose complex movements require years to master. They are only interested in activities that challenge their body and mind. I contend that Pétanque can do that.

I designed this book to be all things to all people. My goal is to provide current players with a structure to formalize their command of throwing techniques, strategies and competition boule selection; while the novice receives a comprehensive introduction to techniques and strategies. The book is predicated on Pétanque throwing mechanics evolving from simple-to-complex. It provides the swing components: ready positions, backswings, shoulder rotation, torso torque generation, forward swing, release with rétro generation and follow-through. You practice and integrate the components into your kinetic chain - Simple-to-Complex, Novice-to-Expert; as is true in all techniques orientated sports, you determine the expertise that you wish to achieve and the consequent complexity that must be embraced.

Chapter and Appendix Summary

Chapter One: The French Game of Boules (Photos: 12, Diagrams: 0)
The first chapter is the "Who, What, Why, Where and How" of Pétanque. Including a section that addresses the most common question, "Why Pétanque instead of its popular Italian cousin Bocce?" We also examine the organizations that oversee playing rules and sanctioned competition; and why, from my perspective, these organizations are the root cause of Pétanque's dismal U.S. status. The good news is that 90% of the U.S. population resides far from an existing club. Good news you say? Think of it as an opportunity to start your own group; a process that is so cheap and easy that you can be playing Pétanque and having a fabulous time in a matter of days! The Chapter concludes with a *Petanque in Two Minutes Quick Start* guide.

Chapter Two: Skills, Strategy and Etiquette (Photos: 2, Diagrams: 17)
This chapter examines game flow, scoring, strategy, rules and etiquette all within the context of playing the first end (initial twelve throws) of a new game. Each throw is captured in a technical diagram and you are lead step-by-step through game flow and strategy. Understanding the immutable connection between etiquette, strategy and victory is paramount to becoming an accomplished player. If you aren't captivated with Pétanque by the end of the chapter, you'd be better off taking up Bocce!

Chapter Three: Throwing Techniques (Photos: 6, Diagrams: 26)
This chapter is a comprehensive examination of pointing and shooting throws, terrain analysis and rétro (backspin) control techniques. Strategic concepts are integrated throughout the technique descriptions. Twenty-five technical diagrams enhance the text and provide a features quick reference. The novice and intermediate player will return to specific sections from this long and intense chapter for many months.

Chapter Four: Throwing Mechanics (Photos: 25, Diagrams: 7)
To the best of my knowledge this is a ground breaking chapter. Information at this depth and scope has never appeared in any English language forum. Although it starts at the novice level, some of this material is so biomechanically complex that one may have to train several months before attempting to implement some of the details. This chapter describes the mechanics of every type of throw that was introduced in the previous chapter. Employing 25 photos and detailed text it provides analysis of novice pointing throws, advanced squat pointing techniques and flat trajectory shooting, including torso torque generation. As in previous chapters, a tremendous amount of strategy is integrated throughout the material in the relevant context. The chapter concludes with training drills, alternative training games and a quick word on warm-ups and strength training.

Chapter Five: Competition Boule Selection (Photos: 17, Diagrams: 4)
Almost everyone starts with cheap, generic one-size-fits-all boules as suggested in the first chapter. Players who have developed sufficient technique are motivated to acquire a set of competition certified boules to complement their hand size, strength, throwing style and preferred role. Boule manufacturers and club websites usually provide a useless cliché riddled and myth-centered one page document with purchasing advice. This twenty page chapter provides a comprehensive analysis of competition boules. I started my boule research on a fall afternoon in Paris at the Obut concept store, followed by a weekend at the fabled Jardin du Luxembourg Pétanque terrain. For several months I acquired and tested nearly every major boule technology: including different types of steel, hardness, finish and striations. I have owned or personally thrown every boule described in the chapter. With this information you will save time, money and frustration by purchasing the ideal set of competition boules to complement your physicality and preferred playing style the first time.

Appendix A: Rules to Remember
There's no need to slog through the nearly undecipherable bureaucratic-speak of the English translation of the official rules. The meaningful rules are interpreted and presented within the context of game play in Chapter 2. This appendix is a quick and approachable rule reference.

Appendix B: Pétanque Quick Start
This is a reprint of the "Pétanque in Two Minutes Quick Start" from the end of Chapter1. It is also available as a download from my website.

Appendix C: The Art of Placing the Jack
More than you really need to know about making a strategic jack toss. We prefer angled and oddly shaped public spaces where jack tossing is an art that sets the tone for the entire end. This thoughtful appendix is definitely worth a peek for any competitor looking for an edge.

Appendix D: Cutthroat: A Game for Three
This is a two page summary of the mystifying rules of our favorite training game called Palm Springs Cutthroat. It's also available as a PDF download from my website. Along with the "Pétanque in Two Minutes Quick Start" you'll want to keep several copies of this document with your gear.

Index:
This index provides contextual references including French language terminology.

Total: **Photos: 56, Technical Diagrams: 53**

Chapter 1: The French Game of Boules

Imagine a few thousand years ago that two bored soldiers are standing watch. Looking for a diversion to pass the time they improvise a simple game. In a moderately flat clearing they find a couple of hand-sized relatively round rocks. The object of the game is to roll or toss a rock toward a designated target such as a tree or another rock. The stone that comes to rest closest to the target wins. That ancient game has evolved into many popular European bowls games in which balls (aka bowls or boules) are rolled, tossed, lobbed or lofted at a small target ball called a "jack."

Lawn Bowls, usually associated with the English, is played with slightly asymmetric balls (bowls) on a long, beautifully manicured bowling green. Bocce is by far the most popular outdoors bowls game in the U.S. It uses 107mm (a little larger than a soft-ball) 920g (2-lb) balls. In both Lawn Bowling and Bocce the ball is typically released after a multistep run-up similar to American ten-pin bowling. The goal of ten-pin bowling is to knock down the target pins; the goal of other bowls sports is to bring the boule to rest in close proximity to a target jack – not necessarily to hit it!

The "Birth" of Pétanque

Pétanque was created in 1907 near Marseilles. The existing game was Boules-Lyonnaise. Like Bocce it featured long courts, large and heavy boules and a multiple step run-up. The legend asserts that a revered Boules-Lyonnaise player crippled by arthritis could no longer stand and deliver the boule with the traditional run up. Aggrieved at seeing the former champion sidelined, his fellow players carried him (in his chair) onto the playing surface. They drew a circle in the dirt around his chair and proclaimed that everyone must now throw from within the circle with both feet on the ground. To compensate for the absence of run-up the court length was reduced by half. Thus Pétanque, from the Provencal "*pèd tanca*" or "anchored feet" was born. Like most legends one can find dozens of variations on the Internet. The story reveals Pétanque's two definitive characteristics: *short terrains and a static throw with anchored feet.*

The basic rules and game flow of Pétanque are similar to Bocce. Despite their obvious similarities, and with due respect to its impressive U.S. following, Bocce is to Pétanque what checkers is to chess. Bocce employs large, heavy boules rolled on long, smooth, level groomed courts. **Pétanque uses smaller, only slightly lighter steel boules on short, ungroomed, unleveled dirt and crushed gravel terrains which encourage tossing, lobbing and soaring rather than bowling-style rolling.** To evade Pétanque's sloping and rocky terrains accomplished players throw high graceful lobs which slam into the ground in close proximity to the target jack; aggressive Pétanque shooters remove opponent's boules from play by striking them through the air rather than rolling into them bocce-style. When a shooter fires the perfect shot which dispatches the opponent's boule and replaces it with his own, spectators may cry out "carreau, carreau" in appreciation of Pétanque's equivalent of a home-run.

> Large boules and a level, groomed court make Bocce a bowling-style, rolling game.
>
> Pétanque's smaller, denser boules and short, ungroomed terrains favor aerial and savagely aggressive play.

The greatest attraction of Pétanque is that it can be all things to all people. Like a Renoir painting it is subtle, multilayered and complex. It may be savored by a casual novice through the most rarified connoisseur. Bocce claims strategy and complexity, but Pétanque (to use a Bridge term) "delivers in spades!" Its facade of simplicity evaporates as players develop skills which reveal its myriad of subtle layers.

The Essence of Pétanque

It's A Tough Sell

The first time I saw a boule hovering at apex, a moment before crashing to the terrain, I became interested. A minute later hearing, almost feeling the rifle-like crack of a boule shot by an opponent I was smitten. After a few hours of play I was compelled to

bring news of this life changing discovery to friends and family - their reaction was a collective thud. It wasn't as if I hadn't done a fine job of communicating the wonders of Pétanque, but it was like bringing vintage French wine to a Monday Night Football crowd of Miller Lite drinkers. They'd recognize the stuff in the bottle was potable, but it's the wrong color, isn't carbonated, doesn't come in a six-pack and isn't advertised by cheerleaders.

When it comes to sports most Americans believe that "if it wasn't invented in the U.S., then it's not worth doing." Even soccer, by far the world's most popular sport, has taken decades to achieve a modest toehold among U.S. born participants and spectators. Compounding the issue is the currently unfavorable (and usually ill-informed) opinion that so many Americans have of the French.

Why should a player be concerned with Pétanque's popularity? If your reason for playing Pétanque is to enjoy a beautiful summer day tossing boules with family and friends, then your only concern is finding a place to throw in a pleasant park with picnic tables, shade and restrooms. On the other hand, if your primary interest is to pursue Pétanque as a competitive sport; to master skills and strategies and play in tournaments, then having a pool of serious competitors and training partners is mandatory. A significant increase in Pétanque's popularity as a competitive sport would benefit players at all levels:

1. High visibility, low maintenance terrains would become common in parks and other public venues.
2. Parks departments and community colleges would offer Pétanque classes, support local venues and use this book as the required text.
3. Hotels, resorts, wineries, campgrounds, restaurants and pubs would provide Pétanque facilities for customers and guests.
4. It would be possible to find venues and partners when traveling for business or leisure.
5. Boules and accessories would be carried in brick-and-mortar stores providing hands-on evaluation, instead of having a limited selection available only via the Internet.
6. Maybe one day in addition to Golf and Tennis, there might be a Pétanque channel!

Easy to Learn, Difficult to Master

The rules are learned in minutes (see *Pétanque in Two Minutes* at the end of the chapter) and the novice can immediately play games. Unlike most sports, novices aren't quarantined until they develop sufficient skills to merge with the herd. Pétanque newcomers are immediately (often against their wills) compelled into playing games with experienced players; from day one the novice is exposed to techniques and tactics through conventional game play.

But that's also a problem because it diminishes the value of training and rote practice drills. Most American players spend 95% of their time on the terrain playing games; little time or effort is invested in experimentation, perfecting techniques or constructing strategy scenarios. Because it is so easy to learn, Pétanque lulls players into thinking that they don't need to practice – that they can just play games; consequently their skills and command of strategies plateaus very quickly.

Last summer I introduced several friends to Pétanque by having them play games with members of an elite West Coast Pétanque club. Within a few weeks it was difficult to distinguish the quality of play between my novice friends and club members who had been playing for many years. This troubles me because it implies that Pétanque is such a simple game that it can be mastered in a few weeks. It is somewhat true that short distances and the random nature of ungroomed terrains make the difference in novice and intermediate quality of play essentially a matter of consistency; but that diminishes Pétanque's appeal to athletes who prefer technically demanding sports with a skills and strategy learning curve that takes years to plateau.

> If one only plays games and doesn't work on mastering fundamentals, developing new challenging techniques and implementing strategy scenarios outside of the context of game play, then you may have a great time but never become an accomplished player.

Pétanque's essence is social - not the type of social interaction that precludes intense, hard-fought competition, but social in terms of team interaction, specialization, strategies and respect for opponents. In tennis singles is king; doubles is only for those that can't excel in singles or can no longer cover the entire court. It's the opposite in Pétanque; doublettes (doubles) and triplettes (triples) are preferred. Tête-à-tête (singles) is usually only played in special training games (*see Chapter 4*) because it is one-dimensional and boring.

- In singles each player throws three boules, which puts a total of six boules into play.
- In doublettes each player also throws three boules with a total of 12 boules in play. Doubling the number of boules increases game complexity and resultant strategies.
- In triplettes each player only throws two boules, also with a total of 12 boules in play.

Like most team sports doublettes and triplettes support specialized players roles. Everyone initially learns to be a pointer. In simple terms the pointer's role is to throw the boule so it stops closer to the target jack than the opponent's best boule. After a player has game experience and has mastered basic pointing throws he may decide to become a shooter. The shooter's function is to strike the opponent's boule to knock it out of scoring position. The pointer isn't constrained to only point, nor is the shooter constrained to shoot; these are only player specialty designations. When there aren't any strategically important boules to shoot, the shooter makes a pointing throw. If the shooter is out boules and it is critical that an opponent's boule be shot, although he may not prefer to shoot, the pointer will give it a try. When two novices are teamed together, usually neither player is comfortable shooting. However, it is important that a player assumes the shooting role if for no other reason than to learn to consider and attempt to apply standard strategies.

Pointers and shooters use different throwing techniques which impose different mindsets. Pointing is a matter of getting close to the target jack (in French called the "cochonnet" or piglet); the operative word is "close." Shooting is a hit-or-miss proposition. After the shot is thrown if the target boule is still resting peacefully in its original position, the shooter didn't do his job. The shooter must shake off a miss and not let it erode his confidence. Not to diminish the role of pointers, but shooting dominates advanced competition. A team without a shooter may throw beautifully precise points, but those boules will be immediately removed from play by the opponent's shooter.

In triplettes the third role is the *milieu* (middle-man) or all-purpose player. A milieu is comfortable pointing or shooting as the situation dictates. The milieu plays under a different type of pressure. He never knows what kind of throw he will be required to attempt and is often called upon in critical situations when the pointer or shooter is out of boules.

In triplettes each player only throws two boules. When it is a team's turn to throw they carefully consider the match score, the position of the boules and the skills and reliability of the team members with boules in hand (boules left to throw). Then decide who should throw and what type of throw will be attempted. Understanding the strengths and weakness of team members and opponents is the key to successful play.

A simple pickup game with randomly chosen teams doesn't have the capability to leverage player synergy to invoke subtle and complex strategies. Once you have committed to a regular doublettes or triplettes team and get to know your teammates strengths and limitations, you can start to implement complex strategies.

Men and Women Should Compete as Equals

Most couples are athletically mismatched, whether due to evolution or social programming the average U.S. male is much more athletically skilled and experienced than the average female. However, obesity rates are much higher in American males so one may argue that men are more likely to be in poor cardiovascular condition, but that's a discussion for a different forum. The point is that Pétanque is a great sport for athletically mismatched couples – whatever direction that mismatch may occur.

> Pétanque is a great equalizer where style and tactics usually triumph over brute strength and unbridled aggression. It is an ideal activity for you and your to partner to play as teammates or compete as opponents.

The object of American ten-pin bowling is to roll a large heavy ball down a smooth, fast ally and knock down pins. It doesn't demand exceptional strength, agility or speed. Bowling balls are manufactured in sizes and weights appropriate to most adults. Nonetheless even in recreational leagues, male bowlers typically have 20% higher averages than females.

There are many theories why female athletes don't perform as well males even in sports where strength, size, speed and cardiovascular fitness don't provide a significant advantage. Some theories are sociological, speculating early stage competitive orientation. Most young boys are initiated into games with a primary focus on competition; females sports often focus on socialization and peer support with competition as a secondary consideration. Other theories speculate brain differences affecting three-dimensional spatial awareness.

From evolutionary and childhood development perspectives men usually have a significant advantage in throwing games. Most U.S. boys regularly play throwing orientated games, but only a small percentage of girls play competitive baseball or basketball. Pétanque's short terrain and lighter boules minimize the advantage of previous throwing experience.

- The average boule is the size of a baseball: 72mm (2.8") and five times heavier: 720g (25oz)
  - ❖ A bocce ball is the size of a softball: 107mm (4.2") and 920g (32oz)
- The distance from the rond (throwing circle) to target jack is 6m (19.6ft) to 10m (32.8ft)
  - ❖ An official international bocce court is 27.5m (86.92 ft) long
- The Pétanque player is stationary and both feet must stay in contact with the ground.
  - ❖ In other bowling sports allow a multistep run-up prior to release

That's not to say that having strong forearms and shoulders don't benefit a Pétanque player. There are many advantages to point from a squatting stance, similar to a baseball catcher. The pointer's graceful soaring high lob (portée or plombée) can be physically demanding. Depending on the height and distance, a high lob requires considerable strength, especially when thrown from a squat. In au fer (on iron) shooting the shooter's boule travels the entire distance to the target boule through the air. Au fer shooting requires precise and consistent body mechanics which takes years to master. In researching this book I attended several West Coast Pétanque tournaments. Many times I asked why U.S. women shooters are so rare. The usual response (provided equally by men and women) was that most women aren't strong enough to shoot, especially au fer. **That's nothing but ignorant, sexist nonsense**. Although it may appear physical, accurate and consistent au fer shooting is predicated on precise technique, flexibility and subtle torso torque. Strength is an asset, but flawless technique is always more effective than undisciplined muscle.

It is true that well-developed forearm and shoulder strength enable a player to make a wider variety of longer throws from more advantageous postures with greater endurance and consistency. On the other hand, shoulder flexibility which enables an effortless, high backswing is a key to consistent shooting and women typically have much greater flexibility and shoulder health than men.

I am not aware of any physical reason why men and women can't compete in every Pétanque role as peers. Strength issues can be overcome by flexibility, precise technique and rote drilling. To say that traditional French Pétanque is male dominated is an understatement; 95% of registered French players are male. In the U.S. things aren't a much better. Regardless of misleading club membership statistics, less than 15% of regular U.S. players are female. I've been told many times that the Pétanque terrain is a sanctuary from women in general and wives in particular. My Pétanque startups have over 60% women; 66% of our original members were couples. *Recruiting women and couples is critical to gaining community support.*

> Most Pétanque strength limitations can be overcome by mastering precise throwing techniques. And precise technique is only mastered through repetitive practice.

A Game for the Ages

Players who learn Pétanque in childhood or early adulthood naturally modify their game as they age. As physical skills diminish, compounded by shoulder injuries or knee/hip limitations that make squat pointing uncomfortable, the seasoned player focuses on the cerebral aspects of the game. People introduced to Pétanque at middle-age or beyond embrace it within the limitations of their current physical state. Those who can comfortably squat and wish to become accomplished pointers will learn to squat point; those with knee or back issues will point standing or crouching.

Players with rotator cuff injuries learn to throw with an abbreviated backswing and follow-through. Those with lower back injuries, hip problems or hamstring limitations may use magnets to retrieve boules without stooping. Older shooters throw higher trajectory shots instead of drilling opponent's boules with line drives. Aging is tough, but with a little compromise one can stay at the top of their Pétanque game well into their seventies and beyond.

The Best Bargain in Sports

A casual golfer spends over a thousand dollars a year on green fees, driving ranges, balls, clubs and a collection of bizarre accessories and training aids. Not to mention the de rigueur $15 cigar and outrageous drink prices at the clubhouse. Avid, yet frugal tennis players rely on free public courts but still may spend several hundred dollars a year on shoes, stringing, over-grips, balls and occasional indoor court fees to escape inclement weather.

Pétanque is one of the best bargains in sports. The initial cost to outfit four people with generic boules, target jack and cheap metric tape measure is less than $75. A set of three competition certified boules starts at $70. A typical set of boules has a lifetime of 5 to 15 years.

Club membership is only required to play in sanctioned tournaments. Typical annual U.S. membership dues are $25/adult and $45/couple. Entrance fees for club and regional tournaments are equally reasonable. Plus, Pétanque doesn't require special clothes or shoes. Come as you are, but don't forget sun block, wide brimmed hat and insect repellent.

The Ideal Sport for an Environmentalist

A typical Pétanque terrain is hard packed dirt with a thin layer of crushed rock and it shouldn't be table-top level! My Palm Springs terrain is an empty field in the desert. We have no water source to periodically wet the surface so it does get a wee bit dusty between rains.

> My typical monthly maintenance routine is to take a few minutes to drag a landscape's rake over the terrain to redistribute gravel and rake out ant hills.

Pétanque is so committed to natural surfaces that once a game is underway it is forbidden to groom the terrain; which includes removing any natural object such as leaves, acorns, twigs, bark and rocks. They are part of the terrain and represent essential random components. Just across the wash from my Palm Springs terrain is one of several hundred lush desert golf courses. The sprinklers run several times a day, guzzling scarce water; the monthly application of fertilizer and pesticides has significantly damaged our valley's ancient aquifer and every week huge riding lawn mowers suck fuel and expel toxic fumes and ear splitting noise. **The typical sounds generated on a Pétanque terrain are the melodious clack-and-clang of boules and an occasional unrestrained squeal of delight.**

Pétanque and golf are two environmental extremes. **The sad truth is that Americans rarely consider ecological issues in choosing leisure time activities.** But if you prefer a bicycle to a car, a kayak to a jet-ski and you'd rather cross-country ski or snowshoe rather than tearing up the woods in a snowmobile, you and Pétanque may be simpatico.

It' Not a Workout

Pétanque is competitive, but it's not a workout. In fact, there's an ongoing joke about the Professional Pétanque Players diet which consists of huge amounts of highly caloric foods washed down with the consumption of vast quantities of adult beverages. Pétanque won't whip you into shape – it's not that kind of sport. But neither are golf, bowling, horseshoes and many other beloved American sports. Non-physically demanding sports have one redeeming characteristic - your friends and family won't have any excuses when you try to drag them out onto the terrain!

Low Injury Risk Potential

Even compared to other bowls games Pétanque is considered static and not physically demanding. But there are a few issues that can make throwing a boule uncomfortable. Hand

> A structured warm-up enables a player to throw their best and it also minimizes the potential of developing overuse injuries.

or wrist conditions such as arthritis, bursitis or carpal tunnel syndrome may impede the back-handed grip and wrist snap rétro (backspin) generation.

Preexisting shoulder and rotator cuff injuries are a major concern. Most pointers, whether standing or squatting use a shoulder high follow-through. The shooter's follow-through is typically a little lower at just about chest level. Pain induced by lifting the hand of a straightened arm above shoulder height is an indication that the throwing motion and follow-through may need to be modified.

Why Pétanque Instead of Bocce?

One of my goals in life is to convert Bocce players to Pétanque. Bocce is the most popular outdoors bowls sport in the U.S. because it successfully severed its ethnic ties. Bocce is of Italian origin, but it is not controlled by an Italian organization.

Bocce Myths

Like most Americans when I decided to learn a bowls game I looked first to Bocce. As part of my research I purchased Mario Pagnoni's *The Joy of Bocce (3rd Edition)* and read it cover-to-cover. **Almost everything I learned about Bocce was**

> Pétanque is not played on a court; it is played on natural terrains, or piggybacks on public facilities such as baseball fields and dirt/gravel walking paths.

grossly disappointing. A great myth is that Bocce can be played on any surface, including lawns. In reality any play more serious than at a family picnic must be played on a dedicated, groomed court enclosed in side and end-boards. Bocce courts are expensive to construct and require significant maintenance. **Over 25% *The Joy of Bocce* book is dedicated to court construction techniques and a pictorial review of the author's favorite courts.**

The most amazing information in the book was that there are no standardized rules defining how Bocce is played, what types of throws are legal or even the basic dimensions and geometry of a court! The book showed Bocce courts ranging from 48ft to 86ft long. Sideboard and backboard bank shots are legal in some areas, in other areas only the sideboards are used, but backboard banks are either illegal or dampened. In some areas 45° angled corner boards are installed. U.S. rules differ significantly from International rules. **Two chapters and *another 25% of the book* are**

> *Vive la Lack of Différence*!
>
> It's reassuring to know that every type of throw you practice and every skill you develop may be applied to any Pétanque competition in the entire world.

dedicated to explaining rules; one chapter for U.S. rules (and regional variations) and another for International rules. Even within the International rules some standard throws are only legal on certain types of courts in certain circumstances.

Imagine that you are an American tennis player vacationing in France and you head down to the local courts to hustle a game. You start to play and discover that local rules allow the ball to bounce twice, the server gets three faults and bank shots off the side and back fences are legal! It wouldn't be tennis as I know it. **The Bocce community celebrates different rules, courts and techniques as self-expression and regional diversity; I find it to be a confusing mess. Bocce definitely isn't for me.**

Pétanque is the Antithesis of Bocce

This morning I met five friends and we played a couple of games of triplettes. But the amazing thing is, other than the lack of an arbiter (umpire) and 60-second clock, from the initial coin flip to match point every aspect of our casual game was identical to those played at international and professional events. French is the lingua franca of Pétanque. When you have mastered the French Pétanque terms used throughout this book you can play anywhere, confident that the game you play on your home terrain is identical to the game that's played in every farflung corner of the world.

Pétanque Organizations

The FIPJP and FPUSA: Lip Service and Failed Missions!

The *FIPJP* (Fédération Internationale de Pétanque et Jeu Provençal) is Pétanque's international governing body. Only boules produced by *FIPJP* certified manufacturers may be used in sanctioned competition. The *FPUSA* (Petanque Federation of the U.S.A.) is the U.S. contingent of the *FIPJP*. It is the liaison between U.S. member clubs and the international Pétanque community. According to its website *the FPUSA's objectives are*:

1. To grow the sport of Pétanque in America and raise the awareness of the American public to the sport, and to stimulate creation of new *FPUSA* clubs, individuals and independent members.
2. To introduce Pétanque to public and private educational institutions throughout the nation.
3. To promote competition and championships at all levels; Regional, State, National and International. For all men and women; young, juniors, and senior citizens.
4. To encourage community groups, the U.S Park Service and the Park and Recreation Departments of cities to develop Pétanque courts in their parks.
5. To publicize Pétanque in magazines, radio and television, local newspapers and special videos.

Unfortunately, other than objective #3 (supporting sanctioned tournaments) the only successful mission of the FPUSA is to enforce all FIPJP proclamations without question and ensure that the French International Organization controls and monopolizes every aspect of Pétanque.

> The only reason an independent, grassroots Pétanque club should join the *FPUSA* is so that it can hold sanctioned competitions and its members can compete in regional, national and international *FIPJP* competitions.

The other FPSUA objectives are nothing but lip service. There are local clubs, such as the successful mega-style *Fresno Pétanque Club* that embrace several of these goals and do a fine job of community outreach. But clubs like Fresno are the exception, not the rule. At last count there were only approximately 50 *FPUSA* member clubs with less than 2,500 members. *Australia, with only 6.5% of the U.S. population, has the same number of clubs and more registered players!*

For most readers the question of whether you should join a local *FPUSA* member club or start a new grassroots organization is moot. By conservative estimate over 90% of the U.S. population doesn't live within a reasonable distance of an existing club. The most successful Pétanque tournament held in the U.S. is the annual **Pétanque America Open** sponsored by Philippe Boets. It speaks volumes that this tournament is not *FPUSA* sanctioned – it is open to everyone. Another irony is, although Pétanque America is the exclusive source of certified boules in the U.S., Philippe doesn't appear to care what kind of boules you throw! **He just wants everybody to show up, throw Pétanque and have a great time – wouldn't that make a perfect *FPUSA* mission statement?**

The Official International Rules of the Game of Petanque is a ten page document produced by the *FPUSA* which may be read online or downloaded from their website. Instead of dedicating an entire chapter spewing pages of meaningless rules, I've worked the most common rules into the context of game play, starting with *Chapter 2: Let's Play Pétanque*. For a quick reference see *Appendix-A, Rules to Remember*.

FPUSA Membership and Competition Eligibility

Only *FPUSA* members may play in sanctioned tournaments. You may join a federation member club or acquire an independent (individual) membership. A minimum of eight members is required for a club to apply for *FPUSA* membership.

To apply for an *FPUSA* independent membership you must live more than *100 miles from an existing member club*. **That's right – One Hundred Miles!** That presents two issues. The notion of regularly making a 200 mile round-trip drive to play the world's most ecologically responsible sport is incomprehensible. You would be nothing but a statistic used to prop up membership numbers. Second, you may live near a club that doesn't meet your needs. Pétanque is social and one of its great joys is interacting with teammates and competitors. There are many justifiable reasons why you would choose not to join an existing local *FPUSA* club. It may be a French culture club that uses Pétanque as an excuse to hold elaborate pot luck meals, drink fine wines, speak French and perhaps roll a few ends of Pétanque when the mood strikes. It may be a good ole boys club that detests or minimizes women, or simply advocates politics or policies that you find repugnant.***

> The *FPUSA* has revoked your right to choose; if you want to play sanctioned tournaments you must hold your nose and join a local (100 miles distant?) club.

Finding Petanque Players in Your Area

The first step is to visit the *FPUSA* website and follow the *Locate a Club* link to find the nearest member club. As previously mentioned, 90% of the U.S. population doesn't live near an existing *FPUSA* member club. If you're a 90%er don't despair, I can practically guarantee that there several publically available locations in your community that will make fine Pétanque terrains. And there may even be closet Pétanque players lurking nearby just waiting for someone to kick-start a grassroots club.

I have had no luck in pursuing members of French clubs or French language groups to become regular players. Initially they love the idea; after all, it's so French! But after a session or two the honeymoon is over. The reality sets in that hanging out in dirt and gravel fields tossing heavy metal balls doesn't seem nearly as French as sipping Café au laits at the local bistro. However, depending on your level of desperation, it may be worth your time to contact a local French culture group. Although most Francophiles haven't actually thrown Pétanque they may have spent many pleasant hours watching locals play in quaint village squares. Members of the group may know of local Pétanque opportunities. The easiest way to find a French club is to visit your community college, visit the world-wide Meetup Group at http://www.meetup.com/ or search your local Craigslist with keywords *French* or *Petanque*.

As a long shot you can drive around looking for mysterious 50cm circles draw in the ground on dirt and graveled areas (think miniature crop circles). They are called ronds (circle in French) and designate the playing circle in which a player stands to throw a boule. A rond is a sure sign that someone in the area has recently played Pétanque! Roaming the Belgium and Normandy countryside we discovered many undesignated terrains by spotting ronds. We would stop and start throwing; almost magically locals materialized at the sound of boules clanging and happily played until they drank all of our beer.

Start Your Own Pétanque Group

The only way Pétanque will grow in the U.S. is for motivated people to bootstrap the process and start grassroots organizations; it is cheap and easy, and may be one of the best investments that you'll ever make. Let's assume that you've come up dry on your local searches and are yet to find a single person who would recognize a Pétanque boule as anything other than a ball-bearing on steroids. You could build a terrain in the middle of a corn field and wait for disembodied Frenchman to materialize to throw petanque, smoke unfiltered cigarettes, and bemoan the state of the world. But there are more reliable methods which are explained in a three-step process in just a few pages.

How Many People Do You Need to Play Pétanque?

Solo practice is great, but socialization and competition are Pétanque's major attractions. Be flexible and you'll be able to accommodate any number of players.

- ✓ **One Person**: skills practice
  - Requires extra set of boules for pointing and shooting scenarios. Solo practice provides focus and intensity. It enables you to work areas of your game independently of other player's demands.
- ✓ **Two People**:
  - Play singles (usually the last choice), run drills, or play special training games. These games are such effective training tools that sometimes we break into groups of two instead of playing standard doublettes or triplettes. Our favorites, Eight-Ball and Poison-Ball, are described near the end of *Chapter 4*.
  - *Six-Ball*: Each player throws six boules. This has the complexity and strategy of doublettes or triplettes and each player must assume the roles of pointer and shooter.
- ✓ **Three People**:
  - *Cutthroat*: A variation of singles with a third person as a designated shooter. The complete description of this complex game is in *Chapter 4* and Appendix-D.
  - *One-on-Two*: The singles player throws six boules and the doublettes team has three boules each.
- ✓ **Four People**:
  - Standard doublettes with each team has a pointer and shooter
- ✓ **Five People**:
  - *Two-on-Three*: A doublettes team (3 boules each) plays against a triplettes team (two boules each).
- ✓ **Six People**:
  - Standard triplettes where each team designates a pointer, shooter and milieu

A game consists of a minimum of three ends. An end is complete when all of the boules have been thrown and points are allocated to one team. An official game is played to 13 points; but accumulating

13 points can take a long time. If you want to rotate team members quickly to ensure that everyone gets a chance to play together, or if time is short you can make several variations:

- Play a game to 5 or 7 points
- Play a fixed number of ends (5 ends typically takes 20 to 25 minutes to play)
- Play for a fixed time period

Can You Learn to Play Competitive Pétanque From a Book?

With the information in this book and a bit of focus, discipline and a couple thousand throws you can become an intermediate-level, competitive Pétanque player. Not to flog a dead horse, but the majority of clubs do not approach Pétanque as sport in any American sense of the concept. Sports are predicated on mastering a basic set of skills. Once those skills are mastered the participant may start playing games. Even then the majority of time is spent drilling

> You're likely to learn to play better with a more comprehensive skill set and at a faster rate on your own, then if you joined the typical U.S. club.

to perfect current skills, learning and mastering new skills, and practicing game scenarios and strategy implementation. This is true for most skills-based sports including baseball, basketball, soccer and tennis. I've played competitive tennis for twenty-five years and the majority of time I spend on the court is hitting serves, practicing groundstrokes and volleys and running agility drills. Likewise, the majority of the time I spend on the Pétanque terrain is shooting practice, hitting données (more about that in *Chapter 3*) and working through pointing scenarios.

The fact that Pétanque is so easy to play is also its greatest weakness. Within minutes of your first visit to a club you will be playing a game. It's Pétanque's version of OJT (On the Job Training). Few U.S. clubs support a regular structured training program or periodic skills practice sessions. Typically you show up on a regular club day and everybody is teamed up for doublettes or triplettes. Techniques and strategies are allegedly learned in the context of play. This is a feeble attempt at mimicking the way that Pétanque was once taught in France through cultural transmission. If you learn Pétanque by only playing Pétanque your skills quickly plateau and you will have a mediocre game for years. Contrary to the U.S., in France Pétanque is taught as a true sport employing unrelenting, repetitious drills with special apparatus and video recording for feedback and analysis; similar to the way that most competitive sports are taught in the U.S.

> If all of your time is spent playing games when the pressure is on you'll make the safe throw - the one you know. *The very structure of a game precludes experimentation and innovation.*

Since Pétanque can be all things to all people, if your goal is social and you have no competitive aspirations then club play provides a gentle venue. But most club play is detrimental to skills development. Although the competition may be casual, you'll still feel self-imposed pressure not to let your teammates down. Even if you try a new or challenging shot, you get one chance – you can't suspend the game and repeat the throw until you get it right – and that doesn't address the requirement of programming muscle memory through intense consecutive repetition.

There's no doubt that skills are only truly tested in pressure packed game conditions, but muscle memory is only obtained through grueling repetition. If your desire is to embrace the essence of Pétanque, then it must be approached as a competitive sport.

Do It Yourself: Grassroots Petanque in Three Steps

Starting a grassroots Pétanque organization is *cheaper and easier than you imagine.*

1. Find a place to throw with a minimum area of 12m (40 ft) by 3m (10 ft)
2. Purchase <u>two sets</u> of *Play-a-Boule* generic boules online. Each set has six boules, a target jack and measuring string. The total for two sets with shipping is about $72.
3. Recruit three to five adventurous and dependable friends, with the emphasis on "dependable." Make a pact and then sign it in blood by the light of the full moon.

That's it - you're on your way. With eight members you can go legitimate and apply for *FPUSA* Club membership. But there are plenty of independent groups that believe Pétanque shouldn't be constrained by arbitrary rules and bureaucratic regulations. It's your group, do what you want!

1) Finding a Local Terrain

Although you probably don't live near an existing club it's likely that a nearby location, with little to no modification, will make a fine terrain. Imagine a hard-packed dirt village square in the south of France. It's relatively flat, but far from tabletop perfect as it slopes gently toward the edges to facilitate drainage. Ground settling and wear-and-tear has produced contours and depressions. The surface is covered with a thin irregular layer of crushed rock, pea-sized pebbles and even occasional larger chunks of stone. Perhaps there's a fountain in the middle and trees scattered about drop leaves and seeds which commingle with the dirt and gravel. Benches and tables around the perimeter are occupied by locals and tourists enjoying a drink, conversation or reading the newspaper. I've just described my summer terrain, but it's not in France; it's Millennium Park Plaza in Lake Oswego, Oregon. In a typical two hour session we interact with dozens of people who are using the restaurants or cafes, or just wandering through the park. It's a perfect community based activity, accessible for all to watch or join in by throwing one of our many sets of guest boules.

An additional appeal is that village squares often have odd meandering shapes. Traditional Pétanque is freeform, play radiates in any and all directions. On tournament days when the terrain must host many simultaneous games it can be efficiently subdivided with long galvanized nails and string into individual rectangular pistes (lanes).

Boules are too heavy and dense to play on a grass lawn. ***Playing Pétanque on a lush lawn is like trying to swim in Jell-O***. Dead lawns which are essentially hard packed dirt work well, just as long as there is enough dead grass or grit to provide friction. Playing at the beach sounds like great fun, but it's difficult to find hard-packed sand that isn't steeply sloped. Think hard packed dirt and gravel. Throw everywhere and you'll soon know what makes an interesting and practical terrain.

Many formal club terrains look like a lightly graveled parking lot. It's impossible to control boule rollout on a smooth hard surface without friction provided by gravel or grit. Imagine rolling a bowling ball on a tile floor with the intent of making it come to rest at a precise location in the center of the room. Gravel, crushed rock, rock dust or DG (decomposed granite) provides friction which enables a skilled pointer to consistently stop their boule within 25cm of the target jack. The picture at the bottom of the previous page is a gravel parking lot. It has a compacted dirt surface with a fine layer of crushed rock, rock chunks, several pot holes, many bumps and a few small gullies. Sounds terrible right? On the contrary, it's one of our favorite downtown Palm Springs terrains. It provides a controlled, yet randomly irregular surface that demands multiple types of throws, touches and strategies. **Many of the best terrains are just plain ugly and that's one of Pétanque's greatest beauties.**

Your Local Baseball Field is Often the Best Place to Start

At least 80% of the U.S. population lives within six miles of a publically accessible baseball field. A typical dirt or clay composition baseball infield is a fine terrain. Some are all dirt and others only have dirt base paths with grass filling in the rest of the area. I prefer all dirt infields which allow unconstrained, freeform play.

Often the dirt surface is extended beyond the fences which provide off-field play when the field is in use. Many baseball fields have gravel parking lots which are another usable terrain. Playing at public sports venues also provides Pétanque recruiting opportunities.

The first time I played on a baseball field I assumed that the groomed surface would be monotonous and too fast to control boule rollout. Much to my surprise the entire group had a great time. The light layer of sand and grit provided sufficient rollout control, the drainage contours and slightly worn base paths made interesting and frustrating challenges. I now throw baseball Pétanque several times a month because it complements traditional rough, ungroomed dirt and gravel terrains.

Look Around, Terrains Are Everywhere

I keep a couple sets of cheap boules in the car so I can stop whenever I spot a potential terrain. If I had a bumper sticker it would say, *"Caution: I Stop at the Sight of Hard-Packed Dirt."* One of the fastest ways to develop your game is to play on a variety of surfaces. You'll discover in *Chapter 3* that there are many types of pointing throws. The type of throw is dictated by the speed and complexity of the terrain and the configuration of boules in play. A few weeks ago I interviewed several competitors at a regional triples tournament. Among my list of questions was to describe their favorite terrain. Most of the top players simply said, "Whatever terrain I'm playing on."

> Think: Non-Dedicated, Public Spaces!
> A Pétanque startup doesn't need a dedicated terrain. The most enjoyable places I've thrown were never intended to host Pétanque.

I've thrown on walking paths in the middle of large cities including San Francisco, Portland, Paris, and Brussels, on the dirt patio of an ancient Normandy farmhouse, in a desert wash ten miles from the nearest road, in the outdoor dining areas of restaurants, wineries and pubs, alongside a horse corral in a high mountain valley under towering Ponderosa pines and at the base of giant boulders in Joshua Tree National Park while taking a break between rock climbs. These terrains are just as enjoyable (and even more challenging) than most U.S. and European clubs that I've played. Search Google Images and you'll be rewarded with a fascinating collection of terrains.

Philippe Boets of Pétanque America authored a paper called *Pétanque in Public Parks* which provides suggestions on where to play in public areas and how to work with local authorities to create *non-dedicated, multi-use terrains*. Integrating Pétanque into the public infrastructure is a brilliant way to generate community goodwill. The future of Pétanque is not a few exclusive mega-clubs, it's thousands of micro-groups distributed throughout local public venues.

Pétanque is an ideal activity for an ecology-oriented resort. On the right is the beautiful jungle piste at Thailand's **Phanom Bencha Mountain Resort**. Only France has a greater number of licensed Pétanque players than Thailand. Below is one of two Pétanque pistes at the luxurious **Parker Palm Springs Resort**. ("Pétanque" and "luxurious" rarely collide in the same sentence.)

You can build your own terrain as described at Petanque.Org and many other websites, but remember *the key to pointing proficiency is regularly playing on a variety of surfaces*. If you always play the same terrain you'll quickly memorize every rock and contour which leads to lazy habits (as specified in the next chapter). Don't depend on a home field advantage; perfect your skills on any and every terrain available. And don't forget your local ballpark. On the other hand, there's nothing like having your own terrain on which to hone au fer shooting skills. Although the terrain plays a role in every Pétanque throw, *the essence of au fer shooting (which is entirely through the air) can be practiced on any hard terrain.*

2) The Gear: Equipping the Petanque Enthusiast

Now that you know how easy it is to find a local terrain, you need to get the gear.

1. **Boules**: (12) Twelve boules support standard play and training drills
2. **Jacks** (cochonnet): 30mm target balls; keep a couple on hand.
3. **Measuring Device**: To determine which team is holding the point and point allocation at the end's completion. A metal metric tape is best, but it's OK to start with a string.
4. **Rond** *(Optional)*: Initially use your finger, toe or a stick to draw a roughly 50cm diameter throwing circle in the dirt. For many reasons which will be cited in the book, I always use a prefabricated rond. They cost about $10 + shipping online or a simple plastic tubing, rope or wire cable rond can be fabricated for one to three dollars.
5. **Scorekeeper** *(Optional)*: In competitive Pétanque the current score is etched into every player's head. In recreational play it's easy lose track because everyone is having so much fun. Typical cost is about $12.

Chapter 5 is an in-depth tutorial on selecting competition certified boules. Understand throwing techniques and strategies, and a couple of months of experience are prerequisites to understanding the technical aspects of boule selection. To get started I suggest that you purchase an inexpensive set of generic, non-certified boules. You can't use them in *FIPJP/FPUSA* sanctioned competition, but you'll always need generic boules for loaners, shooting practice and pointing scenarios. At the time of this writing Play-a-Boule (http://www.playaboule.com/) is the only reliable U.S. source for inexpensive generic, yet regulation size and weight boules.

I suggest that you purchase **two sets of six boules**. One set of groove options 1&2 and one set of groove options 3&4. Among other functions (as discussed in *Chapter 5*) grooves help novices identify their boules. Each set of six boules comes with a basic zipped carrying case, a jack and a simple measuring string. For less than $75 (including shipping) you've got enough equipment to kick-start your group.

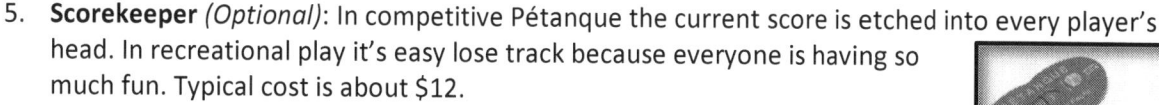

The *Petanque-America* online store is the only U.S. source of certified boules. They might start carrying high-quality, generic boules in the near future. I suggest you always check their website before buying from *Play-a-Boule*.

Play-a-Boules are shiny chrome. Regardless of the number of stripes they all look alike to me. I periodically shoot them with a quick burst of metal spray paint using a different color for each set of three. Use restraint, you're giving the boules a few subtle I.D. spots not a total make-over.

If money isn't an issue, forego generic boules and immediately purchase competition certified boules from Petanque America - also give me a call to schedule private lessons.

3) Recruiting Players to Build a Diverse Base

A sincere commitment from three to five friends is enough to get started. But once things are rolling you'll want to expand the group and continually bring in new recruits. Here are a few suggestions:

- ✓ Start a Meetup group at http://www.meetup.com/ . Within a few hours you'll have a great website explaining all about Pétanque. It's easy to post photos, schedule sessions, start discussions and post new ideas. Write a short persuasive description of your group which makes the reader's feel that without Pétanque's gentle embrace they are destined to lead a drab and wretched life. Post several photo albums of club throws which depict well-adjusted people having the time of their lives standing in a dirt field throwing metal balls high in the air. Peruse other Meetup Pétanque groups (including mine) and see how they've approached marketing and recruitment issues.
- ✓ Make a free posting at Craigslist in Community/Activities. Make sure to include lots of keywords like: Pétanque, bocce, croquet and horse shoes. My perpetual Craigslist listing has the title: **Play Pétanque - A Bocce, Croquet, Horseshoes Alternative** and a brief description of the group and a link to our Meetup Site.
- ✓ Even if you want to start a competitive gonzo Pétanque group you still might consider tapping into the local French culture or language groups and even having a presence at your local Bastille Day celebration. *Unless you want French culture issues to eclipse competitive Pétanque as the group's mission, this should only be a minor part of your marketing strategy.*
- ✓ *Order full color high-quality business cards* with information about your group, including your website URL. Almost every day curious people walking or biking along our terrain stop to watch us play. I immediately break from play for a quick word. After they are informed that, "No, we are not playing Bocce" I give them my standard thirty-second sales pitch, a handful of business cards and encourage them to visit the website and read about Pétanque and the group's goals. They might instantly join or at least show up at your next scheduled session.

> Assume that every hundred cards you handout will elicit less than five responses and ultimately, only one or two new members. Focus on reliable quality players rather than bloated membership numbers

- ✓ Create a full color brochure about Pétanque with the group's mission statement. Include contact information tear-offs. Post them on bulletin boards in libraries, colleges, community centers, fire stations, supermarkets, coffee houses and pubs. *Talk a pub owner into believing that a little Pétanque tossing on his dirt back patio area will increase beer sales and he'll be on the phone ordering a couple of tons of gravel before you ask for a refill.*
- ✓ Find a terrain that's near a busy location like a swap meet or farmer's market. Be playing and yelping with unbridled joy whenever the venue is teeming with people and you'll get attention.
- ✓ We have business cards, T-shirts, hats, posters, bumper stickers and our club banner produced by Vista Print (http://www.vistaprint.com) Great selection, high quality and reasonable prices.

Pétanque Quick-Start Guide

Having taught over 100 people to play in the last six months I analyzed typical questions and misconceptions to create a one page *"Pétanque Two-Minute Novice Quick Start."* To minimize confusion standard French terms were replaced with English equivalents. A printable PDF version is available for download from my website.

Pétanque in Two Minutes Quick-Start

Equipment 12 boules, target jack and tape measure (or a long piece of string)

Petanque means "anchored feet". The thrower stands inside a circle with both feet on the ground. The feet don't have to be flat; the player may even squat on the balls of the feet, but both feet must stay in contact with the ground until the thrown boule hits the terrain.

The Target Jack: Pétanque's bull's-eye is initially tossed six to ten meters from the throwing circle

Holding the Point: The team with the boule closest to the jack is "holding the point". The other team must throw until they are holding the point or have run out of boules.

Four Ways to Hold the Point: Throw a boule that:
1. Stops closer to the target jack than the opponent's best boule
2. Strikes the opponent's best boule driving it away; leaving one of your boules closest to the jack
3. Strikes a teammate's boule, moving it closest to the jack
4. Hits and moves the target jack to a new location where one of your boules is closest

Number of Boules and Throwing Order: In doubles each player throws three boules; in triples each player throws two boules. Any member of the team <u>which is not holding the point</u> may throw next, but each player must only throw their allocated number of boules.

Winning the Game: The first team to accumulate 13 points or play a fixed number of ends.

Scoring: Only one team scores each end. <u>The team with the closest boule to the jack</u> is awarded <u>one point for every boule</u> which is <u>closer than the opponent's best boule</u>. One to six points are allocated with the exception of a rare null end (see *Chapter 2* for details.)

Three Steps to Start the Game
1. Pick teams
2. Flip a coin
3. The winning team selects the terrain and draws a 50cm (20") diameter circle in the dirt.

Six Steps Repeated Each End
1. A member of the winning team steps into the circle and throws the target jack 6m (19.5 ft) to 10m (32.8 ft) from the circle's edge. After three failures the opposition gets three tries to throw the jack. **However, the winning team always makes the first throw**.
2. A player from the winning team places both feet completely in the circle and throws a boule attempting to make it stop near the target jack. That team is now holding the point.
3. A player from the other team steps into the circle and throws attempting to accomplish one of the four ways to hold the point as specified above.
4. The team **not holding the point** throws until either they are holding or have run out of boules.
5. When all 12 boules have been played the end is complete and points are allocated.
6. If neither team has yet accumulated 13 points, a new end is started. The team which won the last end draws a circle 50cm (20") around the jack and <u>play resumes at Step 1)</u>

Chapter 2: Skills, Strategy & Etiquette

Skills Drive Strategy and Strategy Returns the Favor

Outwardly Pétanque is a simple game. The *Two-Minute Novice Quick Start Guide* shows how quickly the basic rules and game flow can be understood. The subtle layered strategies are only revealed through skill development and experience. Watching the French Pétanque Master's summer series one might see a skilled pointer make a throw that stops 1m to the left of the jack. Many fans react by thinking, "He really blew it. I can point better than that!" It's impossible to determine the success of a pointing throw without context; the "bad" throw was probably a setup, forcing the opponents to make a better point which will be immediately shot. *Skilled teams don't make individual throws; they architect a sequence of throws linked to their opponent's response.*

However, the goal of a novice pointer is simple - make the boule stop close to the jack. There's no precise objective such as, "stop the boule about 75cm in front and slightly to the left of the jack." The jack is a bull's-eye and they want to hit it. That's why novices chronically throw long. Unlike a conventional bull's-eye the jack moves when struck. Hitting the jack doesn't guarantee that the boule and jack will eventually come to rest in close

> All novices start as pointers!
> Pointing is Pétanque's essential skill.

proximity, especially if other boules are already in play. Many novices mistake Pétanque for ten-pin bowling. But striking an object (especially through the air au fer shooting) requires different skills, swing mechanics and touch than making a boule come to rest at a precise location on a sloped, inconsistent gravel spotted terrain. That's why the pointer and shooter are specialized roles.

A novice practicing pointing should emulate the golfer preparing to sink a long putt, getting on hands and knees to analyze contours, breaks and slopes. The putter walks just beyond the hole and looks back to the ball. He images the putt, aware that the ball must be struck hard enough to get to the hole, but not so hard that it hits the far lip of the cup and pops out; or if it completely misses the hole, it doesn't roll so far as to create a difficult second putt.

Before you make a pointing throw you must precisely determine where you want the boule to come to rest in reference to the jack or another boule. A teammate may point with their toe (but must not make any mark on the terrain) to indicate the desired spot. Often providing a novice with a precise target location elicits an uncomfortable reaction which is often verbalized as *"I'm not good enough to even think about throwing the boule to a specific location yet."* I've learned to use a different phrase; I point my foot and say, "pretend that the jack is here." It's easier for the novice to think in terms of a bulls-eye.

In intermediate play the majority of the boule's movement is through the air, not rolling on the terrain. For strategic reasons even pointing throws travel a significant distance

> Bocce is ground-based, Pétanque is aerial!

between the rond and jack through the air. The pointer must focus on the donnée (landing spot) where the boule impacts the terrain, not the location where it should eventually come to rest. Throwing a precise point starts with choosing the ideal donnée. The concept of the donnée, arc and rétro (backspin) is discussed in detail in the next chapter.

Refined and comprehensive skills drive ever more subtle and precise strategy, which forces the development of more comprehensive and precise skills. *Skill is driven by intent.* Casual players may feel that imposing structure or expectations strips the game of joy and spontaneity. When novice and accomplished player are teamed-up they inhabit separate dimensions and have different expectations. It's important to remember the multilevel, game-within-a-game nature of Pétanque; transcending simple to complex is only accomplished after many hours of play and focused skills development.

Allocating Points

Only one team is awarded points at the completion of an end. In doublettes and triplettes one to six points may be scored. The exception is when the jack is declared dead because it is knocked O.B. (Out-of-Bounds) or is otherwise unplayable as addressed in *FIPJP Rules Articles 9 & 13*. We examine dead jack point allocation later in this chapter.

> **Skills and strategy are harmonious**
> **Never "just throw!"**
>
> **Commit to a strategy (*however simple*) and then make it happen.**

Each end starts by throwing the jack and concludes when all boules have been thrown or the jack is declared dead. *One point is awarded for each boule which is closer to the jack than the opponent's best boule.* A few examples are illustrative and provide insight into basic strategies. To improve diagram readability, the Black Team has black boules and the Silver Team silver boules. In normal club play boules may look so similar that it often takes close inspection to determine the boule's owner. The final arbitrator is that all three boules in a competition certified set are stamped with the same unique serial number.

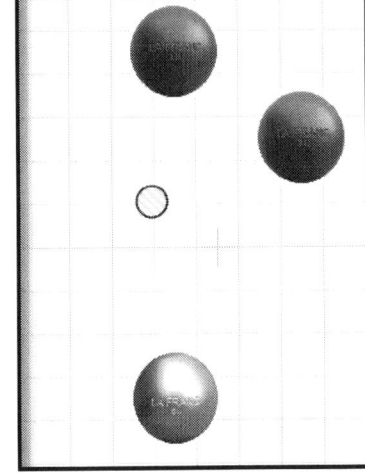

Two Points for Black: In the diagram on the right the two closest boules to the jack are Black. Silver's best boule is third closest. Black gets two points. *For scoring purposes boules beyond the opponent's best boule are irrelevant.*

One Point for Silver: This illustrates the heartbreak of Pétanque. Although Black has four boules very close to the jack, Silver has the best boule. Silver gets one point and Black gets nothing. *It doesn't seem fair, does it?*

If Black had shot Silver's boule away from the jack, instead of Silver getting one point, Black would have gotten four points. *That represents a five point swing!* You can see how quickly fortunes can flip-flop. It takes just one great boule to neutralize an opponent. That's why defensive, blocking boules well in front of the jack are as important as boules lying within centimeters of the jack.

<u>Three Points for Silver</u>: Black has one point on the ground and one boule in hand. The Black pointer gets greedy (or reckless) and tries for one more point by rolling his boule between Silver's boule on the left and his own best boule on the right. But he throws a little right and long, strikes his own team's boule and both boules roll far beyond the jack. *Pétanque punishes greed*. Black had one point and ended up giving Silver three points.

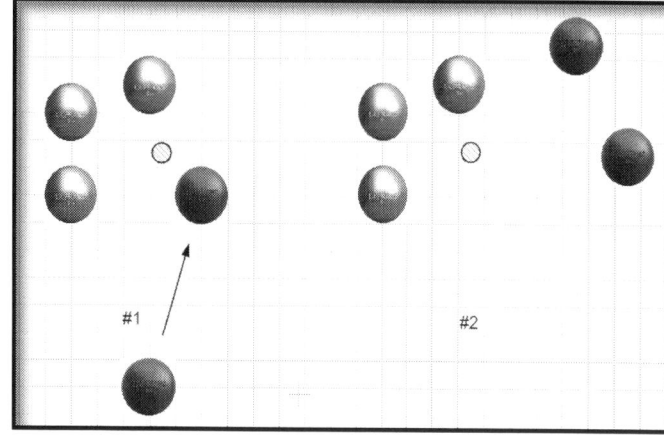

You must consider the potential benefit and possible downside before attempting any throw into a congested area. In this example the pointer should have overcompensated a bit to the left. Not only is that the safe throw but the Silver boule would act as a backstop to improve the Black boule's chance of scoring a second point.

The absolute distance from the jack doesn't matter; the issue is how many of your team's boules are closer than your opponent's best boule. Depending on the distance and terrain often the most effective strategy is to shoot opponent's boules away from the jack's vicinity rather than throwing your boules close to it. *The pointer scores points by placing boules into a strategically precise location. The shooter scores points by ensuring that his team's boules are closer to the jack by removing the opponent's best boules from play.* The pointer/shooter synergy is the Yin/Yang which makes Pétanque unique among bowls games.

> The goal of Petanque *isn't* to throw a boule as close as possible to the jack.
>
> It is to complete the end with the maximum number of *your team's boules lying closer to the jack than your opponent's best boule.*

As a novice your focus is precise pointing. But during a game never miss the opportunity to ask, "If I were a reliable shooter how would our strategy change?" That may inspire you to commit the time and effort to develop new skills to embrace ever more subtle and effective strategies.

Freeform and Constrained Terrains

By nature Pétanque is freeform, play radiates outward in any direction. O.B. (Out-of-Bounds) starts 1m from a tree, planter, bench, fence or any other disruption in the continuous terrain. Any boule passing into O.B. is dead and not considered when allocating points. To support the maximum number of simultaneous games while minimizing interference, large open terrains are subdivided into individual pistes - in French "piste" means a track or runway, Americans think of them as lanes as in a "bowling lane". Pistes can be defined with chalk, string, webbing or any material which is visible, not a trip hazard and has minimal rolling resistance to boules. *The IFPJP specifies 12m by 3m pistes for club and regional-level championships and 15m by 4m pistes for national and international-competitions.*

I find individual pistes monotonous. Every end is repeated on the same pitch (to use the English term) of dirt and gravel. One quickly memorizes every contour, slope and obstacle. This one-dimensional experience is often preferred by skilled players because it less vulnerable to random bounces and rolls produced by complex freeform terrains. (Which always seem to always favor the novice!)

Playing the First End

Let's examine game flow, rules, etiquette and strategy within the context of a triplettes game.

Selecting Teams and Preparing to Play

A common method of team selection is the "simultaneous throw-out" which is a physical version of a mêlée tournament in which teams are selected by drawing random lots.

1. The jack is tossed to a legal distance (6m to 10m)
2. Players stand side-by-side equal distance from the jack
3. At the count of three everyone simultaneously makes their best pointing throw
4. The chaos of flying boules produces random collisions and the jack might be struck and moved.
5. Teams are selected by every-other position: Odd boules from the jack (1st, 3rd and 5th) are Team One and even boules (2nd, 4th and 6th) Team Two.

Members of the two teams assemble and:

✓ *Select a captain* to participate in the coin toss, lead strategy sessions, take measurements, keep score and oversee point allocation
✓ *Specify player roles*: pointer, shooter and milieu.
  ▪ When there's a mixture of player experiences a novice is assigned pointer.
  ▪ If no team member is comfortable shooting, someone will begrudgingly take the role and shoot when there's no alternative
  ▪ The milieu assumes a specialty role when the pointer or shooter is out of boules
  ▪ Even when three novices are teamed together selecting roles is important because it forces strategic thinking and pushes players out of their comfort zone. Many a pointer forced into shooting has been transformed by the experience of smacking an opponent's boule O.B.

Jack Control and First Throw

One of the team captains tosses a coin and the other captain calls it. (The French call before tossing the coin.) *FIPJP Rules Article 6* specifies that the coin-toss winner:

1. *Selects the terrain*: On freeform terrains anything goes, pick a smooth section or a stony gully – whatever your team prefers or the opponents' disdain. On subdivided terrains a specific piste may be chosen; in tournaments pistes are pre-assigned.

2. *Draws or places a prefabbed rond and erases any existing ronds in the vicinity*: A drawn rond have a 35cm to 50cm diameter. A prefabricated rond must be rigid and have an inside diameter of 50cm.

> Make a rond from ¼" tubing or metal cable with a crimped sleeve. It's not certified for tournaments, but sufficient for club play.

All edges of the rond must be at least 1m from any obstacle or O.B. Play fair, if one of your opponents is Bigfoot and wears size 16 sneakers don't draw a tiny 35cm rond just to stub his toes. The team drawing the rond must erase existing ronds in the area to ensure that a player walking back from the jack uses the correct rond. Most club players don't bother erasing ronds, which is another compelling reason to use prefabricated ronds.

3. *Throws the jack (cochonnet)*: A valid jack is 6m to 10m from the inner edge of the rond and at least 1m from any obstacle or O.B., no portion of an O.B. can be located directly between the rond and the jack –

> For a quick jack toss measurement tie knots in a thick string at 6m and 10m

such as a tree or flower bed. To avoid having to dig out the tape measure to verify jack throw distances every player should learn to accurately pace 6m to 10m. The jack should not be randomly tossed. At a minimum the team should decide the *direction and distance* that the jack should be thrown. Usually the pointer throws the jack and teammates carefully watch it roll looking for indications of contours and slope. One of the teammates may pace the desired distance and use his foot (without making a mark) as a target. Either team may call for a measurement. The *team that doesn't throw the jack may call for a measurement after the first throw and before they throw*; therefore, the team that throws the jack should always verify any questionable distance before throwing their first boule.

4. ***Throws the first boule***:
    a. After carefully walking and analyzing the terrain the pointer steps into the rond. Their feet must not touch any portion of the rond, *including the inside of a prefabbed rond*. Some part of both feet must remain on the ground until the thrown boule touches the terrain. When throwing from the squat the player is usually balanced on the balls of their feet and no part of their body, such as the non-throwing arm may touch the ground. The exception is for wheel chair players and for players with lower body disabilities. See *Appendix-A, FIPJP Rules Article 6* for details.
    b. After the first throw, that team is holding the point. Their opponents must make the second throw of the end and continue throwing until either they are holding the point or have thrown all of their boules. The players within a team may throw in any order. Every player must only throw their own boules.

> Philippe Boets of Petanque America related an alternative method to select teams. Assume there are six players. From a deck of playing cards remove the two through seven cards. Shuffle the six cards and deal one each player. Players with even numbered cards are Team One and odd numbered cards Team Two. Team One chooses the terrain and controls the jack.
> ***You can "stack the deck" to ensure a balance of experienced and novice players by shuffling the cards less randomly.***

Important Words about Etiquette and Strategy

Picture a basketball player at the free throw line, a baseball batter facing a 95mph fastball and a football kicker lining up a 50 yard field goal attempt. In all of those instances the fans, teammates and probably opponents would be screaming their heads off. Contrast that with a golfer preparing to drive or putt, or a tennis player in the middle of a service motion. In those instances all parties are dead silent and perfectly still. It's not that golf and tennis require more concentration; rather it's a function of that sport's etiquette. Every sport prescribes player and spectator conduct, explicitly recorded in written rules or established through long tradition. Sports that allow (or encourage) taunting, in-your-face player interaction attract a different breed of participants than those that are highly competitive, yet demand mutual respect and consideration.

Pétanque is played in a small area and it is extremely social. It's tough to walk that fine line between socializing with fellow players and still extending reasonable courtesy to the player attempting to throw. Because many people join a club as much for socialization as playing Pétanque, it's reasonable to expect that casual club play shouldn't be held to the same standard as formal competition. The problem comes down to the fact that to some people Pétanque's social aspects are as important as the competition. Other people throw Pétanque exclusively for the competition; the social aspects are a minor and often annoying consideration. If Pétanque was popular with multiple clubs in every large city then you could choose to play only with those of whom you are simpatico. But given its current state, well as they say, beggars can't be choosers.

Imagine how difficult it is for a thrower who is distracted (by players talking directly to him or to each other, or walking around and gesticulating) to communicate his frustration without being perceived as a spoilsport. If you are one of the 1%ers who live within driving distance of an existing club, then you'll have to live with that club's entrenched etiquette and attitudes. If you are one of the 90%ers or simply choose to start you own club, then it's up to you to mandate baseline etiquette.

Although Pétanque has well-established player behavior rules they are rarely enforced in any meaningful way at the club-level, even during tournaments. My experience is that clubs selectively and half-heartedly enforce any basic etiquette rules. When challenged they simply shrug it off as trivial and invasive. It's the good ol' boys, love it or leave and don't let the door hit you on the way out attitude.

> A bonus of observing behavior rules is that players become more engaged in the game. That improves quality of play and enjoyment for everyone.

The following are my interpretations of the most important aspects of the *FIPJP Rules Article 16* which specify player game play behavior. I enforce all of the rules in my organization, even during casual club play. Why only extend courtesy in formal tournaments? Do you feel that your fellow club players deserve less consideration?

Where to Stand During Play
Players naturally congregate near the rond which is absolutely, positively the worst place to socialize, discuss strategy or effectively observe play.

- The preferred location for all players (regardless of which team is currently throwing) is to stand beside (or behind) the jack and at least 1.5m to the side.
- Standing near the jack allows players to communicate in whispers
- The jack area is ideal to gather valuable information about the terrain by observing boule impact and rollout.

> If your shadow falls between the rond and jack be courteous and move to the other side!

- The view of the boules and their spatial relationship to each other and the jack is distorted from the rond. It's common that a player throws and is convinced that he is holding the point. Only to walk up to the jack and discover that another boule is 25cm closer! *You can't interpret boule position details from the rond.*
- Everything interesting happens near the jack. Other than walking the line to find the perfect donnée, the jack area is the only place to formulate strategy.
- Those with ambulatory limitations may elect to stand behind the rond and at least 2m to the side. You must be outside of the thrower's peripheral vision and remain completely still and silent.
- Opponents must not walk, gesticulate or disturb the thrower.
- Club play and friendly competition often involves a little teasing and trash talk; although you may not care if people are talking when you're throwing, don't assume everyone has your temperament.
- When you play with new people or visit a different club, observe standard etiquette and adjust your behavior as the situation dictates.
- A teammate may stand between the rond and the jack to provide guidance to the thrower. Because it is forbidden to mark the terrain in any way a teammate may use a foot to specify a possible donnee (landing spot) or where the boule should come to rest.

- A teammate (but never an opponent) may stand directly behind the jack which provides an excellent view to judge the quality of the donée and boule rollout.

Get Lazy and You'll Make Bad Throws

Although (or because) Pétanque requires minimal physical effort players get lazy. Contrary to good strategy and etiquette many club players hang out next to the rond. When it's their turn to throw with minimal thought or preparation they step into the rond, take a backswing and let it fly. Then they're surprised and upset when they make a terrible throw. ***Proper etiquette supports optimum performance.*** *When it's a player's turn to throw "walking the line" (the slow strategic walk between the jack and rond) is the ideal time to determine what type of throw to attempt and to identify the ideal donée.*

Take Your Time

Pétanque games proceed at a leisurely rate. Many Americans feel compelled to move things along by jumping into the rond and firing off a quick throw. No matter how fast players throw, Pétanque will never be an action sport. *If that's what you're looking for, then look elsewhere.* Pétanque demands time to form strategy and intent, and to savor that moment in the rond.

- *FIPJP Rules Article 20, Time Allowed for Play* specifies that the next throw must be made within 60 seconds of the previous throw or after a measurement is complete.
- *Use that minute.* Deliberately walk the line and choose your donnee. Enter the rond, visualize the throw, take a few deep breaths, and throw with confidence and joy.

Score Keeping

Team captains are responsible for score keeping. Most players claim that they have no problem keeping the current score in their heads. Don't believe it. I always bring two marqueur de poches (pocket scorekeepers) to the game. As illustrated in *Chapter One*, they are low-tech devices with numbered wheels marked Nous (Us) and Eux (Them). When points are allocated the captain whose team won the end announces the current score in the Nous and Eux format (his team's score first and the opponent's score second) and the opposition captain must concur before a new end commences.

Beware of the scorekeeper's brass thumb screws and threaded posts; too tight and the score wheel won't turn, too loose and it spins too freely or the brass thumb screw falls out and gets lost. Instead of brass replacements I buy 3/8" <u>aluminum threaded post with screw</u> for about $1.00 at my local hardware store. I always keep a few on hand in my accessories bag.

When the score wheels bind even when the screws are loose, remove both screws to take the scorekeeper apart. Clean the residue and torn fabric from the front and back surfaces of both score wheels. Reassembly it and it will work better than new!

The other scorekeeper issue is leaving it in the pocket and putting it through the wash. I suggest that you pay a couple of dollars extra and purchase the style in the photo with a belt loop clip. Keep it out of your pocket and it will stay out of the washing machine.

Let's Get Started

Silver wins the toss; they pick a terrain, erase existing ronds, draw a rond at least 1m from O.B., toss the jack (in this case, 8.5m) and their pointer makes the first throw. With the exception of the first diagram only the immediate area surrounding the jack is depicted. That is the perspective enjoyed by players standing by the jack instead of loitering at the rond.

Novice Strategy: Boule-Devant (Blocking Boule)

Boule-devant signifies a "boule in front" of the jack, which is both a physical and visual deterrent, thus the common description of "blocking boule."

The drawing labeled **After Throw #1** depicts a fine novice throw to start the end. Silver-1 is a bit right of center and about 80-cm from the jack; the ideal distance in front of the jack is dependent on the speed of the terrain and the rond-to-jack distance. The boule-devant is a visual distraction and a physical barrier to boules rolling directly to the jack.

It may be purposefully promoted by a teammate or accidently struck by an opponent. In either case it will probably be pushed closer to the jack. On the other hand, a blocking boule may be a double-edged sword; a boule too far out in front of the jack is a hindrance to everyone; it blocks direct pointing throws from both teams and is too far from the jack to be easily promoted.

O.B.

After Throw #1

Boules in Hand
Silver Black
5   6

Holding
Silver: 1

Jack

80cm

Good Blocking Boule
It could be at little to the
left and a bit closer, but
it still works!

Silver-1

8.5m to Jack

Rond

> "Boule-devant, c'est boule d'argent"
> A boule in front is valuable (it's silver)!

To a skilled shooter a short boule is an easy target. Shooting effectiveness decreases quickly with distance. A standard tactic to neutralize shooters is to toss the jack beyond 9m. Unless the opposition has a reliable and aggressive shooter, even at shorter jack distances a great strategy is to make the initial pointing throw 30cm to 60cm short; even consider building a wall with side-by-side boules. A wall of boule-devants (boules in front of the jack) is difficult for the opposition to point through without accidently nudging one of them even closer to the jack. The boule-devant strategy is a reoccurring theme throughout the book. It's the first and best strategy for novice through intermediate levels.

As the diagram specifies, after the first throw Silver is holding with one point on ground and five boules in hand. Black hasn't thrown yet so they still have six boules in hand.

Before we examine Black's first throw of the end let's take a moment to examine an important safety and strategy consideration.

Safety and Strategy Issues

Tracking the number of boules that each team has left to play (i.e. boules in hand) is an important habit to cultivate. Almost as important as the total number of the opponent's boules in hand is which players are holding boules: the pointer, shooter or milieu. *FIPJP Rules Article 15* which speaks to player behavior and boules is pathetically incomplete, incoherent and ineffective.

In my experience the majority of club players don't physically hold their boules in hand; they haphazardly leave boules lying all around the vicinity of the rond. It's no joke that boules are a dangerous trip hazard. I've spoken with several players who have taken nasty falls by stepping on unattended boules. Most times the fall results in nothing but embarrassment, but a sprained ankle or wrist or even something as serious a broken hip is possible, especially when one considers Pétanque's elderly demographics.

A second consideration is that not holding one's boules is contrary to good sportsmanship because it makes it extremely difficult to determine the number of boules each opposition player has yet to throw. It can be argued if you are engaged in the game, then you'll always know the "how many and who" of your opponent's boules. But even when you're tracking the "boules in hand" in your head, it's important to be able to visually verify the count before committing to a strategy.

The following are suggestions of how boules should be handled during play. These are not official rules, but I consider it to be an issue of safety and sportsmanship. In international and professional competitions boules are never left on the terrain. Each player holds their remaining boules in plain sight making it easy for everyone to determine who has boules left to throw. My inclination is to always fault to the safest and most sporting behavior.

1. Every player should hold their remaining boules.
   - ***If a strength issue or hand condition makes it uncomfortable to hold multiple boules, then the boules should be laid directly behind the rond, which is a location where no player should ever stand***.
2. A player must never hold another's boules or a boule that is not part of the current game.
3. When asked to announce the number of boules in hand all opposition players should hold their remaining boules in plain sight and verbally specify the number
4. The player who is currently throwing may lay additional boules on the ground on either side of the rond.
   - When finished, the remaining boules must be immediately picked up

Now returning to our game, Silver has thrown one boule; they are holding the point with one point on the ground and have five boules in hand. Black is yet to throw so they have six boules in hand.

Black's First Throw

The Black team can hold the point in three ways:

1. The pointer throws a boule that stops closer to the jack than Silver-1.
2. The shooter shoots Silver-1 and when both boules come to rest Black-1 is closest to the jack.
    - As described in *Chapter One*, the carreau is one of petanque's most celebrated events. A carreau is a shot in which the shooter's boule strikes the target boule and occupies its original position. It is both a shooting throw and a pointing throw.
3. Striking the jack and when the dust has settled, Black-1 is closer to the jack's new location.
    - If the jack rolls O.B., further than 20m from the rond or several other conditions occur then the jack is declared dead and the end is null. *Near the end of this chapter we examine the definition of a dead jack condition and how points are allocated.*

FIPJP Rules Article 20 specifies that a team has 60 seconds to throw after the previous throw comes to rest or a measurement is complete. The Black team huddles for 10 to 20 seconds to discuss strategy. Black considers standard novice to intermediate level strategies (listed in order of difficulty):

1. The pointer attempts to outpoint Silver-1
2. The shooter shoots Silver-1 and drives it well beyond the jack (in best case into the O.B.)
3. The pointer may point a *setup throw*, typically about 50cm to the side of the jack. Although Black won't immediately hold the point, it sets up a second Black throw in which the shooter shoots Silver-1 resulting in Black holding with one or two points on the ground.

> A setup pointing throw is usually thrown to the opposite side of the jack so it doesn't screen the opponent's boule from being shot.

This is Black's first throw and the second throw of the end. Refer to the diagram, **After Throw #2**. Black decides to be conservative and attempts to outpoint Silver-1.

Unfortunately Black's pointing throw hits the Silver-1 blocking boule, pushing it to within 15cm of the jack. *Never underestimate the value of blocking boules in novice to intermediate play.* Silver is still holding and has one point on the ground, so the Black team must throw again.

As mentioned earlier "points on the ground" specifies how many points would be awarded if the end was complete. It's a key strategic consideration. The team holding always has one or more points on the ground.

Each diagram in this series indicates the number of boules in hand for each team, which team is holding and with how many points on the ground. Also remember that O.B. stands for Out-of-Bounds. Boules in the O.B. are dead – i.e. no longer in play.

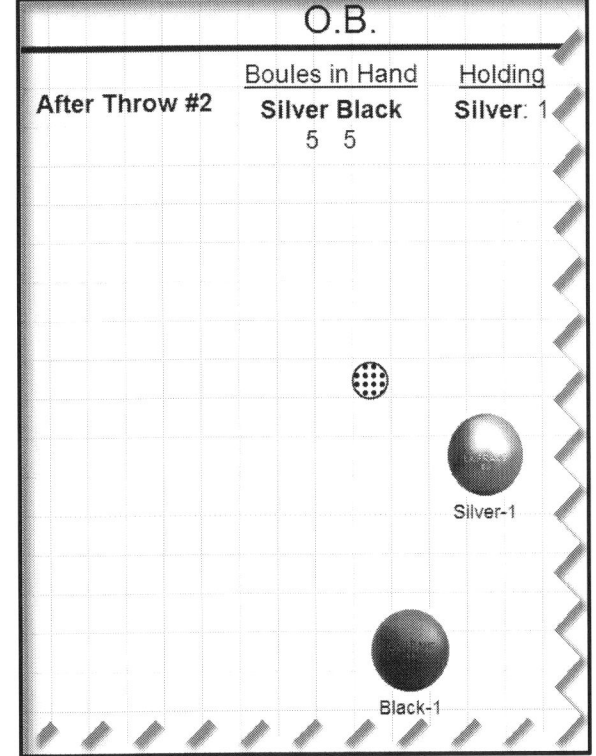

After Throw #2	Boules in Hand		Holding
	Silver	Black	Silver: 1
	5	5	

O.B.

Silver-1

Black-1

Black's Second Throw

This is the third throw of the end. Americans are reluctant shooters. If there's a good chance of outpointing an opponent they will forego the shot. On the contrary, the advice of hardcore shooters is, *"take the shot when you've got a shot."* i.e. shoot first, point second.

An example of the "shoot first" wisdom is that Black's first throw didn't just promote Silver-1, but it is also partially blocking Silver-1 from being shot. The shooter has to make a precise au fer shot that barely clears the top right side of Black-1 to strike Silver-1. If the shot is a wee bit short or to the left, Black-1 is accidently shot. That would put the Black team two boules down and still not holding the point.

The Black team decides that discretion is the better part of valor and sends the pointer back into the rond. As illustrated in *After Throw #3* the pointer's throw, Black-2 comes to rest a few centimeters to the left and slightly behind the center of the jack. Black is holding with one point on the ground and four boules in hand. But, Black's pointer is out of boules, the rest of the end is in the hands of the shooter and milieu.

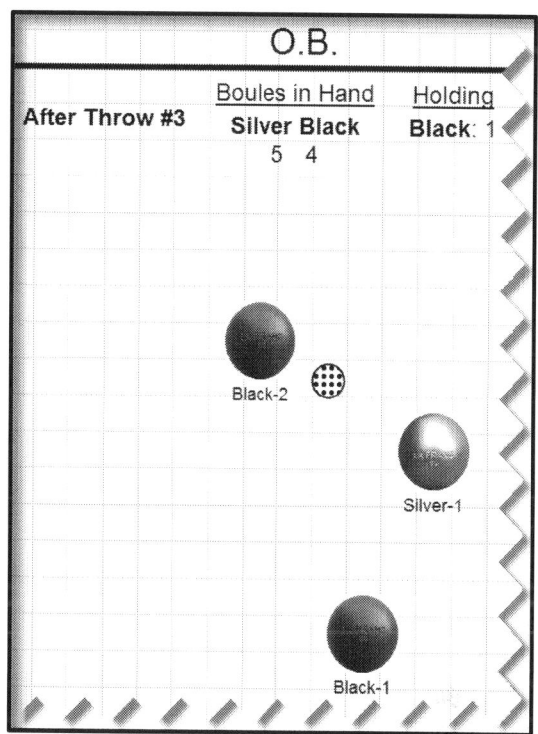

Silver's Second Throw

This is the fourth throw. Black-2 is too close to the jack to outpoint. Silver's shooter steps into the rond and throws Silver-2. The shot strikes Black-2 and drives it into the O.B. as illustrated in *After Throw #4*.

FIPJP Rules Article 18 specifies that a boule is dead when it completely crosses into an O.B. If a boule rolls O.B. and rebounds back onto the terrain, it is still dead and must be immediately removed.

This was a good shot, but not a carreau because after striking Black-2, the Silver-2 boule rolled about 60cm beyond and to the left of the jack.

It's obvious that Silver is holding, but the Black team calls for a measurement. They want to know whether Silver-2 or Black-1 is closer to the jack. The measurement determines that Black-1 is over 10cm closer, so Silver only has one point on the ground. The 60-second timer for Black's next throw starts at the conclusion of the measurement.

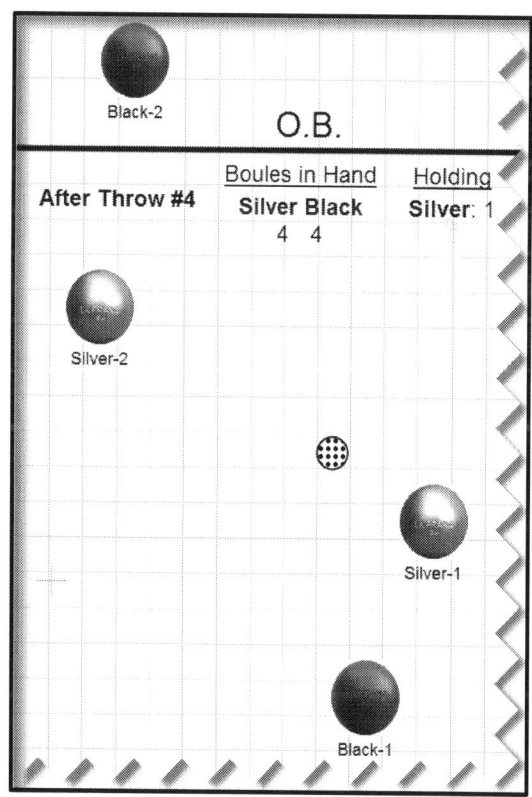

Black's Third Throw

This is the end's fifth throw. The ideal throw would be to shoot Silver-1. But the Black team's shooter isn't confident that won't shoot short and hit Black-1.

Black's pointer is out of boules, so the milieu is up. Black-1 is almost directly in-line between the rond and jack and about 75cm short. The milieu decides to promote Black-1 by tapping it just hard enough to push it closer to the jack than Silver-1.

As illustrated in **After Throw #5**, the pointer squarely kisses Black-1 with a firm, but delicate touch. Black-1 stops a few centimeters from the jack and Black-3 stops just to the right and about 50cm in front of the jack. Black is holding with one point one on the ground and three boules in hand.

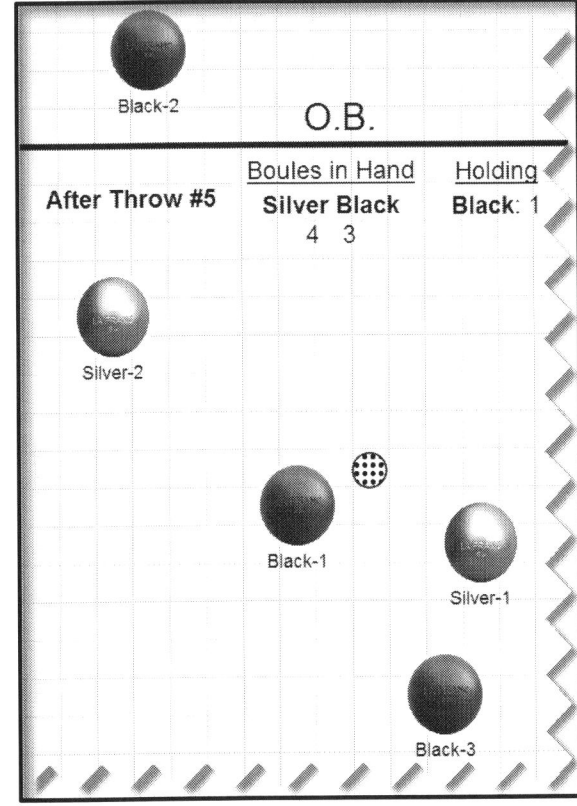

After Throw #5	Boules in Hand		Holding
	Silver	Black	Black: 1
	4	3	

Promoting Blocking Boules for Fun and Profit

Think, "Point First & Promote Second." Don't throw as if you are trying to shoot your teammate's boule. 1) If you hit your teammate's boule too hard you'll knock it long. 2) If you miss the promotion your own boule rolls well beyond the jack. Either way, your team is not holding the point.

There are many factors to consider before attempting the promotion:

1. How far the boule to be promoted is from the jack. The further it needs to be pushed, the more difficult the promotion. Especially if the boule is not directly in line with the jack.
2. How good is the opponent's best boule? The goal is push your teammate's boule close enough to hold the point; in best case your boule may also stop close enough to be a second point.
3. How fast and rocky is the terrain? Smooth terrains are great for promotions because rollout is fast and true. The smooth clay surface of a baseball infield is ideal for promotions. Rocky terrains inhibit true rollout and have much more friction. It's often very difficult to gauge how hard to push your teammate's boule.

> If your teammate's boule is close to the jack or the terrain is fast, then promote as if you are pointing just a wee bit beyond the jack. If you miss the promotion, your boule may still stop close enough to hold the point.
>
> However, if the boule is far up front or the terrain is slow, then the promotion throw needs significant momentum. Miss the promotion and your boule will roll well beyond the jack.

Silver's Third Throw

Refer to the diagram *After Throw #6*. The Silver team decides that Black-1 is too close to outpoint, it must be shot. Silver's shooter has one boule in hand and makes the slow walk back to the rond. He clears his mind, focuses on a small spot at the base of Black-1, takes a deep breath and then throws a clean miss that sails over the top of Black-1 and bounces into the O.B.

> Shooting isn't for the faint of heart, it takes guts and a bulletproof ego. When you score a hit, you're a hero - when you miss you miss big or worse, accidently shoot a teammate's boule and gift your opponents several points. Keep at it, in America reliable au fer shooters are a rare species.

The novice shooter must learn how to shake off a clean miss and wait patiently, and with great anticipation, for the next carreau. Unfortunately for the Silver team their shooter is out of boules and the Black team is still holding with one point on the ground.

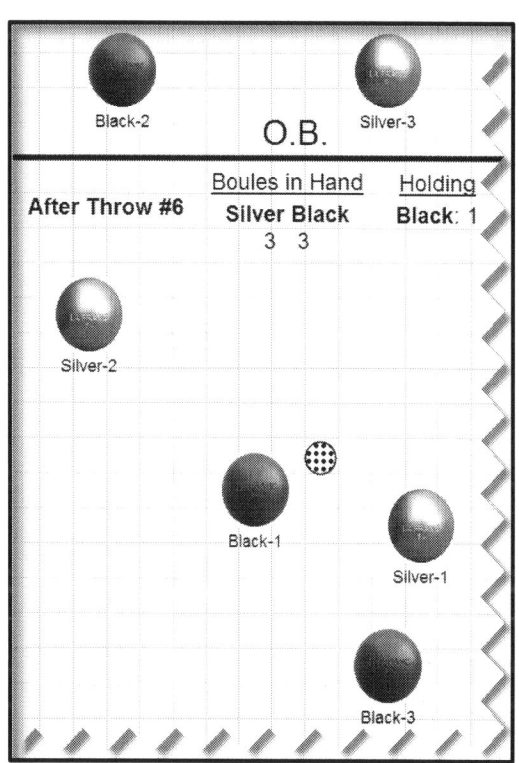

Silver's Fourth Throw

This is the seventh throw of the end. Silver's shooter had one solid shot and one clean miss. Silver's pointer has one boule in hand and the milieu has two. Instead of having the milieu shoot Black-1 the Silver team decides to point.

Earlier in the end the Black team couldn't shoot Silver-1 because it was partially screened by a Black boule. In the current situation the Silver team could promote Silver-1 by brushing it on the right side, there's a chance that it might get pushed closer to the jack than Black-1. This strategy is reinforced by the fact that the Silver pointer should stay away from the left side so he doesn't accidently nudge Black-1 even closer to the jack.

Refer to *After Point #7*. The Silver team's pointer throws the promotion wide to the right, just missing Silver-1 and stopping slightly behind the jack. Black is still holding with one point on the ground.

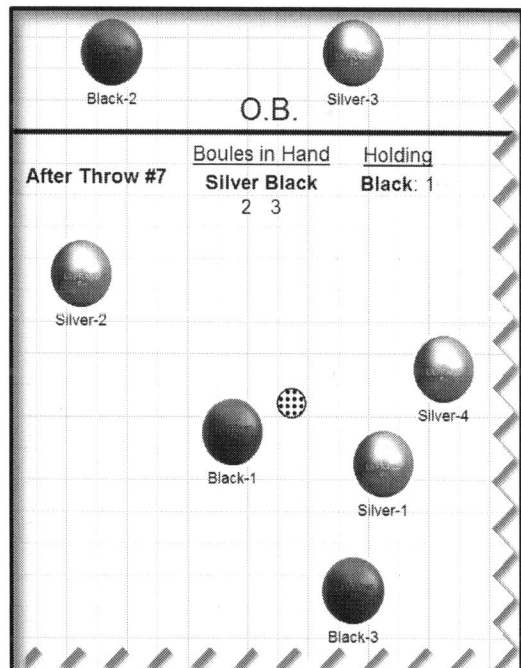

Silver's Fifth Throw

This is the eighth throw. Silver's milieu has two boules in hand. He's a strong shooter and a steady pointer. This is the first end of a new game, there's no score yet and little to lose. The Silver team feels secure with a couple of boules fairly close in, which makes it difficult for the Black team to run up a lot of easy points. So they decide to take the offensive. Instead of sliding a defensive boule to stop between Black-3 and Black-1 they decide to shoot Black-1. If successful, Silver will be holding the point with at least two points on the ground.

Silver's milieu shoots and hits Black-1 just slightly on the right side. *Refer to* **After Throw #8**. Both Black-1 (the target) and Silver-5 (the shooter's boule) are driven to the left. Black-1 stops well behind the jack and Silver-5 is in-line with the jack. *Silver is holding with at least two points on the ground.*

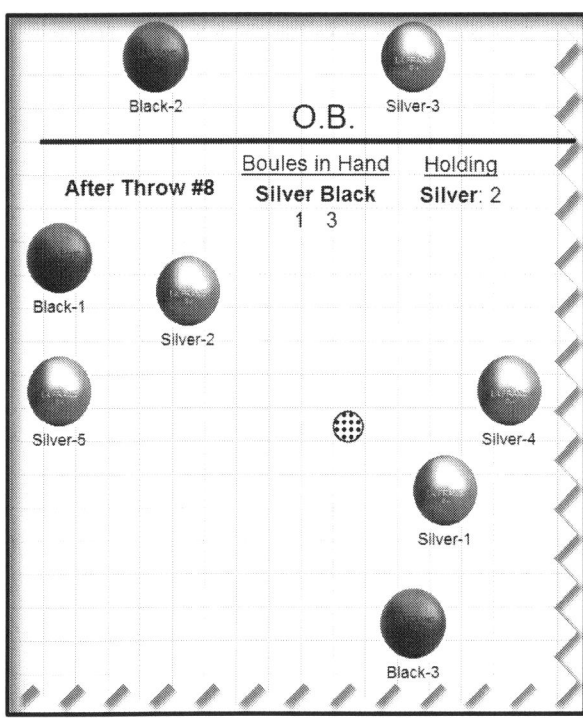

The Black team calls for a measurement to determine whether Black-3 or Silver-2 is closer to the jack. The measurement verifies that Black-3 is a few centimeters closer. Silver may have two points on the ground, but they are down to one boule in hand.

Take a moment to examine the diagram **After Throw #8**. The Black team has three boules in hand what do you think they should do?

- Should they point first, and if so where?
- Is it feasible to shoot over Black-3 and hit Silver-1 or Silver-4?
- But if both boules aren't cleared out, Silver is still holding.
- Is any kind of shot a viable in this situation?

Pétanque strategy is based on the skill of your teammates and the weaknesses of your opponents. Pointers dominate novice to intermediate level play, and shooters dominate advanced and professional play. Even if your team doesn't currently have a reliable shooter it's still important to go through the "what if" scenarios.

Take one last look at the diagram, and ask yourself, what is the weakness of Silver's current position?

> Now and then, **when the score and situation justify**, take a gamble and try a difficult but potentially rewarding shot. There's nothing like shooting in game conditions to motivate practice sessions.
>
> Attempting to win today's game with proven skills, while simultaneously perfecting advanced skills for future competitions is a fine line to walk.

Black's Fourth Throw

This is the ninth throw. Black's milieu has one boule in hand and Black's shooter is yet to throw. **The previous successful shot opened up the left side of the jack for a direct pointing throw**. Refer to **After Throw #9**. Black's milieu makes a solid pointing throw with Black-4 coming to rest in nearly the same position from which Black-1 was shot by the previous throw.

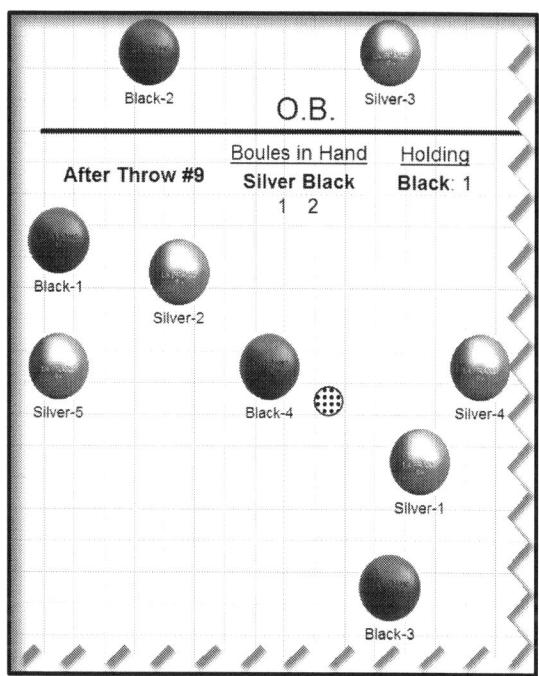

That's a common Pétanque theme. *The first team points then their opponent shoots the boule. The first team points again to the same location and the opponent shoots again.* The pointing team hopes that the shooter throws a clean miss, putting the shooting team one boule down. The shooting team hopes for a carreau putting them one boule up, because a carreau is really two throws in one. *It removes the opponent's boule and also holds the point!* That's why the carreau is such a celebrated event. The potential of a carreau sustains shooters through the frustration of the "faire un trou", or a clean miss that accomplishes nothing but to make a hole in the air!

Silver's Last Boule

This is Silver's last throw. Black has one point on the ground with two boules in hand. It's a tough spot that elicits a couple of basic strategies. The first is to relinquish the end to Black, but mitigate the damages by holding them to a single point. That could be accomplished by throwing a blocking boule just short of the jack, directly in front of Black-4. Black won't shoot the blocking boule for fear of also hitting Black-4. This strategy puts two Silver boules up front making it difficult for Black to accumulate additional points with their last two boules.

Pétanque common wisdom says, *"don't shoot with your last boule because a miss enables the opponents to rollup uncontested points"*. This case may be an exception:

✓ Silver has the second, third and perhaps fourth closest boules to the jack
✓ The Silver milieu is a clutch shooter who feeds on pressure
✓ Since the game score is 0 to 0 a missed shot won't create an unrecoverable disaster

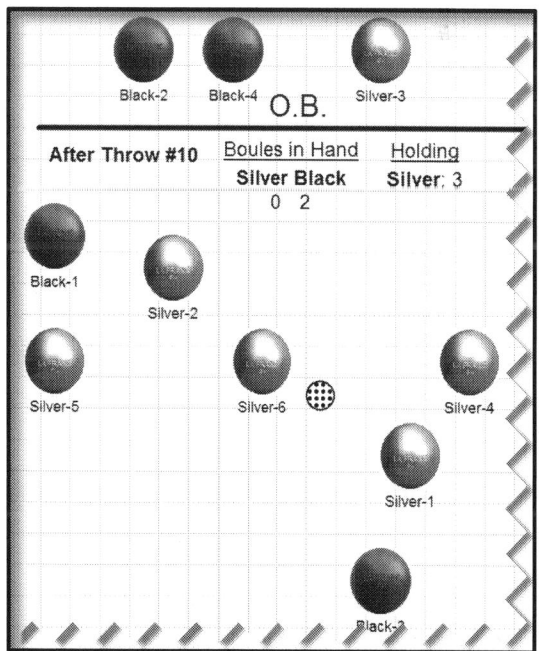

The upside potential is too great to resist and the milieu throws the shot and delivers a carreau! See **After Throw #10**. The carreau produced a four point turn-around; Black had one point on the ground now Silver has three points on the ground but is out of boules.

Black's Fifth Throw

This is the eleventh throw of the end. Silver has three points on the ground, but Black's shooter has two boules in hand. If Black shoots Silver-6 the entire left side of the jack will be open for a last pointing throw. This is a situation which calls for the shoot first, point second philosophy:

✓ Only the shooter has boules in hand
✓ A short point may screen Silver-6 from being shot with the last boule

If it was a pointer with the last two boules, then they might elect to point hard directly toward the jack using Silver-6 as a backstop. But the boules are in the hands of a shooter; when the pressure is on, the player should always go to their strength.

The shooter steps in and successfully shoots Silver-6. But there's an unintended, though not necessarily bad, side-effect. The shooter's boule, rebounding from the collision with Silver-6, clips the left side of the jack which bounces about 50cm to the right. See **After Throw #11**. The shot and unintended jack displacement reduces Silver to one point on the ground.

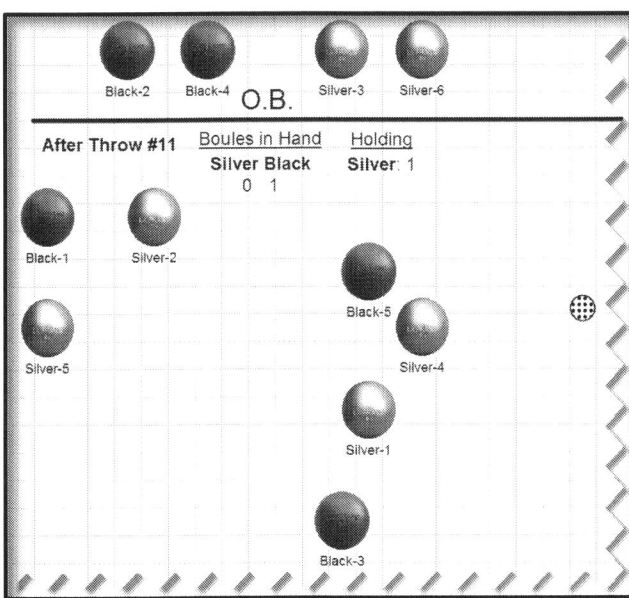

Shooting or even gently pushing the jack is a legitimate strategy used to move the jack away from the opponent's boules toward teammate's boules, or to create a dead jack condition by shooting it into the O.B. Accidently striking the jack produces random chaos.

The Last Throw of the End

Black's shooter has one boule in hand and Silver has one point on the ground. The boules in play are bunched up on the left side of the jack. Even if Silver-4 wasn't screened by Silver-1 there's no reason to shoot because the jack is a wide open and begging for an easy pointing throw.

Pétanque's fundamental skill is pointing; all shooters are also capable pointers. Black's shooter is happy to point to a wide open jack.

FIPJP Rules Article 15 clearly states that it is forbidden to draw a line or mark the terrain as a throwing aid. Since Silver-4 is the best boule, Black's shooter carefully examines how far it is

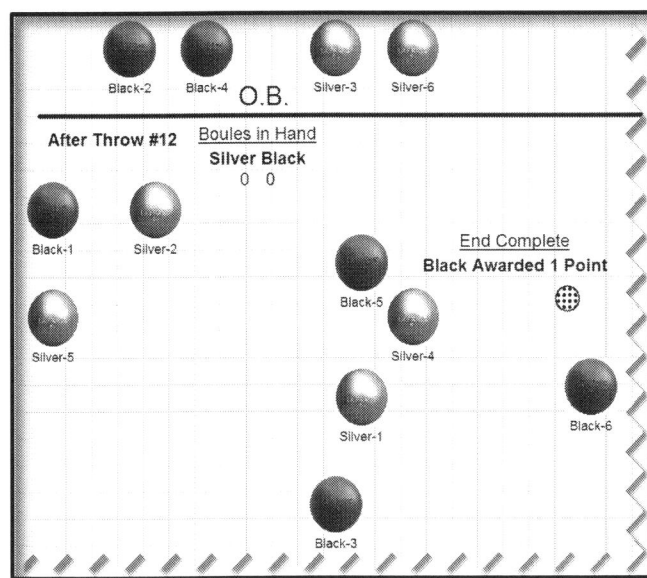

from the jack and notes exactly where he wants his boule to come to rest. His pointing throw is dead-on and it stops about 10cm from the jack. See **After Throw #12**. The end is complete.

The Black team is awarded one point and starts the next end by dropping the rond over the jack, then tossing the jack and making the first throw.

When to Pick Up Your Boules

Nothing puts a damper on a well thrown end more than when one of the players picks up his boules before the point allocation has been agreed upon. *FIPJP Rules, Article 26* state that it is forbidden to pickup any boule in play (regardless how far it is from the jack) until:

- the end is complete
- points are allocated
- and most important, both team captains are in agreement

> 💣💣 If a boule is picked up prior to point agreement, that boule is *declared dead* and is not included in the point allocation. 💣💣

As mentioned earlier, the captain of the team that won the end announces the updated score and the opposition captain concurs, before any boule is picked up.

Dead Boules

The chapter ends with an examination of several important and misunderstood rules that are critical to point allocation and game flow. In the previous example four boules crossed into the O.B. and were declared dead. *FIPJP Rules, Article 18* defines dead boules.

- A boule is dead when it <u>completely crosses</u> into any portion of the O.B. even if it subsequently rolls or rebounds back onto the terrain.
- When playing on marked terrains a boule is dead when it crosses <u>more than one</u> piste (lane) or the end line.
- A dead boule must be immediately removed from the active terrain.

In the rare occurrence that a boule crosses into the O.B., rebounds onto the terrain and strikes a live boule or the jack, the live boules and jack affected should be returned to their original positions, by best estimate, and the dead boule removed from the terrain.

Dead Jack and Point Allocation

The jack may be purposefully shot or accidently hit. When displaced from its original location (6m to 10m from the rond and at least 1m from O.B.) it may be ruled dead. *FIPJP Rules, Article 9* defines dead jack conditions:

- It is driven O.B., even if it rebounds back onto the terrain
- It comes to rest further than 20m from the rond
- There is an O.B. area directly between the rond and the jack, even though the jack may be positioned on a legal portion of the terrain
- It isn't visible to <u>every player</u>, such as when it slips into a gopher hole or deep rut
- It is freely floating in water because it's no longer a stationary target
- It is lost and can't be found within 5 minutes
- While playing on marked-out terrains, it is knocked <u>more than one</u> piste to the side

When the jack is declared dead the end is ruled null; play stops because there's no longer a legal jack to point against. *FIPJP Rules, Article 13* specifies point allocation after a dead jack incident:

- If <u>both or neither team</u> has boules in hand, the end is void and no points are allocated
- If <u>only one</u> team has boules in hand, they are awarded one point for each boule they are holding

Example1: Silver is holding the point with 3 boules in hand. Black has one boule in hand. Black throws their last boule which strikes the jack and knocks it O.B. Since only the Silver team has boules in hand, they are awarded one point for each of the three boules that they are holding.

Example 2: The Silver and Black teams are playing in a tournament on a terrain which is subdivided into pistes. Black is holding the point with four boules in hand. Silver has two boules in hand. A Silver team member strikes the jack and it bounces <u>two pistes</u> to the left. *FIPJP Rules, Article 9* specifies that the jack is dead. **Since both teams have boules in hand the end is null and no points are awarded.** The team that won the previous end:

- places the rond in a location of their choice
- tosses the jack
- throws the first boule of the new end

Promoting the Jack

Refer to Promoting the Jack on the right. The Black team only has one boule in hand. Silver has three boules in hand and three points on the ground. Silver's pointing boules nearly surround the jack; whereas Black's best boules are 15cm to 25cm behind the jack. What are some strategies that Black may consider for their last boule?

Try shooting Silver-3, also hoping to remove Silver-2. But the Black boules behind the jack may act as backstops and Silver still has three boules in hand. There are too many random possibilities for that strategy to be viable.

A conservative approach would be to throw a blocking boule that stops just in front of the jack. If thrown accurately Black's last boule would be very difficult to shoot without displacing the jack.

The best tactical approach is dependent on a smooth terrain in which the boules are tracking well and the player to throw is a steady pointer with a good touch.

Promoting the Jack

Boules in Hand
Black Silver
1   3

Silver is holding with three points on the ground

Black could promote the jack, gently pushing it straight back about 15-cm so it comes to rest between Black-5 and Black-2. If successful Black would have four points on the ground representing a seven point turnaround. Quite an enticing risk-to-reward ratio!

However, if the jack is struck too hard and rolls into O.B. it is ruled dead. Black would be out of boules and Silver would still have three boules in hand. So Silver would be awarded 3 points as explained in the previous section. In this example the goal is to gently push the jack to a specific location, rather than to brutally shoot it! A typical boule weighs sixty times

Practice Tip: Place a jack between two boules with a third boule 15cm to 25cm directly behind it. Practice gently pushing the jack back to the boule.

more than a jack. The best approach is to throw the boule with the intent that it comes to rest between Black-1 and Black-2. The fact that the boule is pushing a little wooden jack the last 15cm has a nominal effect on its momentum and rollout.

The "Year in Provence" Gambit

Peter Mayle's book (and miniseries) A Year in Provence chronicles the first year of a British couple's move to a small village in Provence. Describing Pétanque as "a simple game that any child can understand" the British couple challenges the village champion to a match of doublettes. In the later part of the game the local team apparently makes several bad throws that overrun the jack by about a meter. The smug British couple thinks that they are going to score several points and continue to roll their boules close to the jack. On the last throw of the end the local French champion reveals his strategy by expertly pushing the jack back into the middle

When your opponents have several boules behind the jack consider placing a blocking boule that shields the jack from being pushed or shot.

of the group of "overthrown" boules to score five points – thus revealing the Brits shallow grasp of Pétanque strategy and French life in general for which Pétanque serves as a metaphor.

Equidistant Best Boules

Measuring Boule Distance

Before addressing the issue of equidistant boules let's take a moment to see the most reliable way to measure the distance between the jack and the boule, being extremely careful not to move either one of them. With a steady hand and a rigid metric tape measure the distance can be determined within a few millimeters.

- Place the end of the tape gently touching the boule at its equator
- Keep the tape level and measure to the center of the jack (its highest point)
- Look directly down onto the tape and announce the distance before proceeding to the next measurement

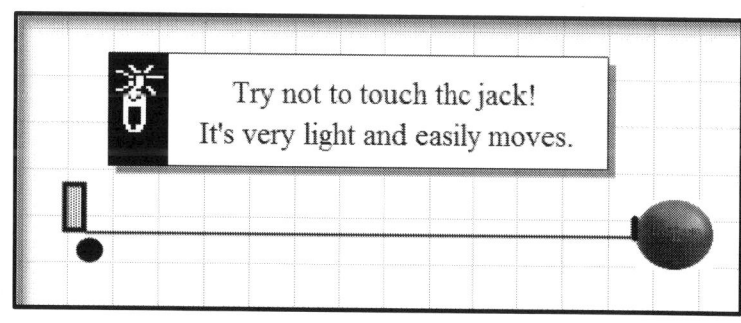

Try not to touch the jack!
It's very light and easily moves.

- For longer distances use a second person to hold the end of the tape against the boule and keep the tape under tension to keep it from drooping.
- It's easier and more accurate to measure in centimeters (cm) rather than inches

A variety of caliper-style devices provide 1-mm tournament level precision. For club play an inexpensive mini-metric tape measure is fine. **Regardless of your measurement device, understanding *FIPJP Rules, Article 28* is important**. Two questions that must be addressed are:

- Who holds the point when each team's best boules are equidistant from the jack?
- How is point allocation affected by equidistant boules?

Using the most precise measurement device on hand, when it is impossible to reasonably determine which team has the closest boule to the jack the following rules are applied:

1. *No Boules in Hand*: <u>If both teams are out of boules</u> the end is declared dead and no points are awarded. The team that scored on the previous end retains jack control and makes the first throw in the next end.

2. *One Team Has Boules in Hand*: <u>If only one team has boules in hand</u>, they play their remaining boules. The end is scored as normal where the team with the closest boule is awarded one point for each boule <u>that it closer than the opponent's best boule</u>.

Example: If Black has the best boule and the next closer boules are equidistant Black and Silver boules, then Black is awarded one point because they only have one boule closer to the jack than Silver.

3. *Both Teams Have Boules in Hand*: <u>If both teams have boules in hand</u>, the team that threw the last boule throws again. If the two closest boules are still equidistant, then the opposing team throws. They alternate throws until one team is holding the point or neither team has boules (see #1) or only one team has boules (see #2.)

Example: It's the middle of an end and Silver is holding. Black throws and it's determined that Silver and Black's best boules are equidistant from the jack. Since Black threw last, they throw again. If they don't throw a better boule, then the Silver team must throw. They alternate until one team has a better boule or the situations #1 or #2 occur.

4. If, after completion of the end, all boules are O.B. (Out-of-Bounds) the end is void and no points are awarded.
   - This may happen when the jack is very close to the O.B. and all of the boules are overthrown or shot. This is an extremely rare (and embarrassing) circumstance.

Chapter 3: Throwing Techniques

Pétanque Pointing Throws: Variations on a Theme

The fact that with a few minutes of instruction a person can be playing an actual game of Pétanque is both the game's greatest attraction and ultimately its biggest limitation. Within a couple of weeks the novice blends into the club mainstream and often their learning curve immediately plateaus. Every club has an upper echelon – especially among the shooters. But I think it's nearly impossible to walk into a *FPUSA* member club and without knowing a soul, after watching a few hours of games sort the members according to how long they've played Pétanque. I believe that the problem lies in the *FPUSA* attitude that refuses to treat Pétanque as a competitive sport that demands structured development, training and strategy practice.

Giving Pétanque a Universal Appeal

Anyone can be taught basic pointing throws in a matter of minutes. The intent of this chapter is to extend Pétanque's allure to accomplished athletes seeking to complement physically demanding sports with a less physical game, not just as a change of pace but also as a vehicle in which less athletic friends and family members can participate on an equal footing.

> **Who cares if Pétanque is portrayed as a competitive sport?**
>
> Many veteran club players say, *"Keep it simple – don't burden the novice with details or expectations."* But that's the mindset that deters competitive athletes from embracing Pétanque. Tell a good athlete that the majority of skills and strategies to play Pétanque can be learned in a few weeks and his response will be, *"Why bother? Where's the challenge in that?"*

"Out and Up": Horizontal and Vertical Throwing Forces

There are three characteristics that must be considered when learning throws:

- The boule is thrown from a stationary stance without the momentum of a run-up
- There is no such beast as a standard Pétanque terrain. Every surface is distinctive and profoundly influences throwing choices and strategies
- Because terrains are unmaintained (other than an occasional raking) their characteristics change based on rainfall, temperature, humidity and the season.

Rolling the boule the majority of the distance to the jack is an effective pointing technique when one has the luxury of playing on a smooth terrain such as a clay-composition baseball infield, simple hard packed dirt or a layer of packed D.G. (decomposed granite). On the other extreme, some terrains are so hard, soft, rocky, inconsistent, sloped, undulating or just plain evil, that the best strategy is to bypass the terrain and throw the boule the majority of the distance to the jack through the air.

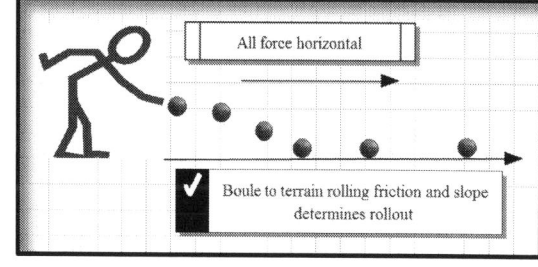

All Horizontal Force

When a player rolls the boule (like a bowler) almost the entire force of the throw is horizontal. The player uses the friction between the boule and terrain to dissipate the boule's energy and cause it to stop in the jack's vicinity.

All Vertical Force

This is obvious, but when a boule is thrown straight up it falls straight down – thank you Sir Isaac Newton. If the donnée is smooth and flat most of the energy of the descending boule is absorbed on impact and it comes to rest at the player's feet.

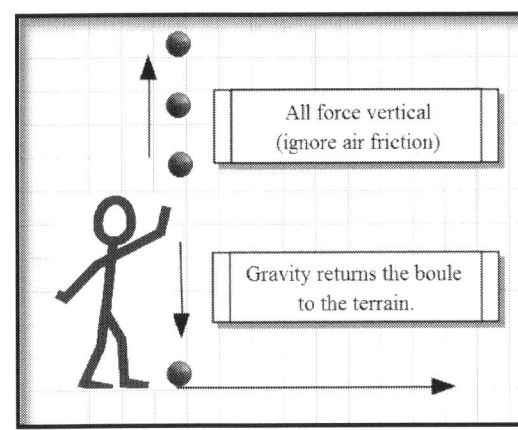

I think of all pointing throws as a combination of "horizontal and vertical" or "out and up" forces. As expertise develops pointing throws become much more aerial and boules are thrown in beautiful soaring arcs. *The most accurate path to the jack is not necessarily a straight line*.

General Pointing Throws in Four Steps:

1. Determine the appropriate type of throw and exactly where the boule should come to rest (e.g. 25cm to the right of the jack or 10cm directly in front of an opponent's boule). *Don't think: Anywhere near the jack is good enough!*
2. Carefully evaluate and choose a precise donnée, then visualize boule impact and desired rollout
3. Make the throw with a combination of "out and up" forces to land the boule on the donnée
4. After impact the horizontal (out) force completes the rollout

Pointing throws are a variation of "out and up." The position of the jack defines the horizontal distance; the variable is how high the boule is lofted. The roulette stays at ground level. The plombée, the most aerial throw often has an arc over 4m high.

Boules and Projectile Motion

Boules are heavy, dense and thrown at low speeds for short distances. Air resistance can be ignored when playing Pétanque. I've played Pétanque while hiking at over 10,000 feet in elevation. Although I moved a little slower, the boules didn't fly any differently. I've also played in 30-mph winds (one of the desert's less beguiling traits) and the boules didn't fly any differently.

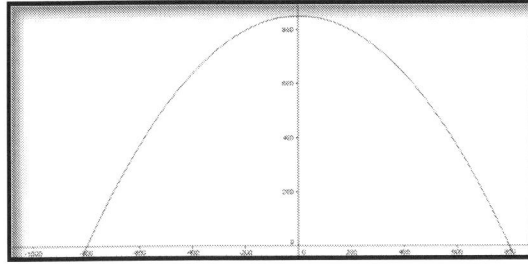

Gravity and ground friction are the only elements that affect boule flight and rollout. A boule always flies in a symmetric parabolic path as illustrated in the diagram. If a boule thrown from ground level travels 5m before reaching its apex, it travels another 5m before returning to the ground.

I mention this because a few of the boule flight diagrams in this chapter are not perfectly symmetrical. Blame it on artistic interpretation. From an instructional perspective the diagrams are sufficiently realistic to effectively illustrate the concepts. *Gravity always plays fair with slow moving, dense objects that travel short distances.*

The most important concept is that the upward and downward trajectories are identical.

And a boule's trajectory has a tremendous influence on impact, rebound and rollout as the throws in this chapter illustrate.

The Roulette (Don't Make this Your Crutch!)

On the typical fairly fast hard dirt club terrain it doesn't take much effort to roll (all out, no up) a boule 10m. The roulette is a bowler's throw minus the run-up. To compensate for lack of momentum the boule is released slightly forward and typically hits the terrain a couple of meters in front of the rond.

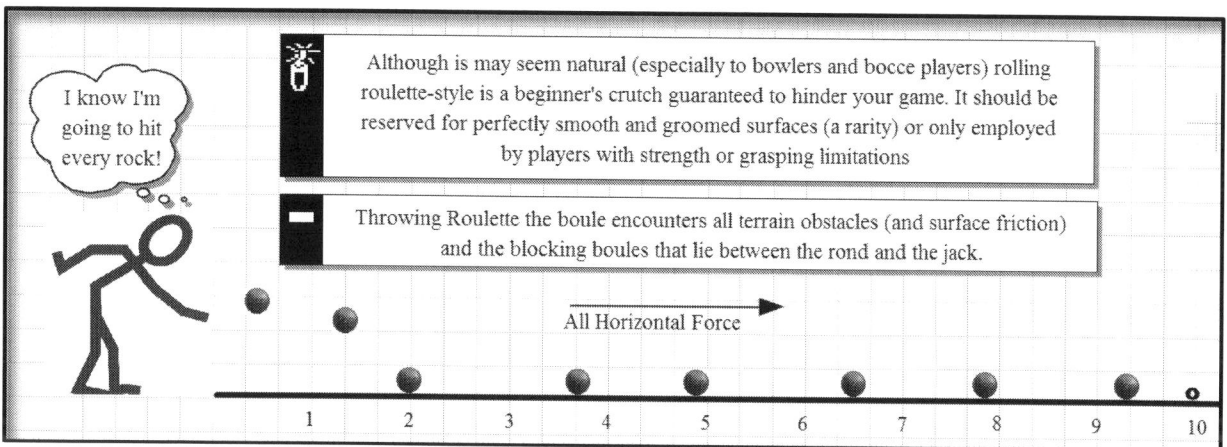

Although on the rare smooth terrain even expert pointers may roulette, overall it is a novice throw and completely *ineffective for shooting on any surface*.

- The boule encounters every obstacle between the rond and destination (usually the jack vicinity). When your competition is primarily roulette pointers throw the jack into the farthest, ugliest, rockiest, most miserable area of the terrain and then watch them weep!
- Pétanque's fundamental strategy (especially when the competition doesn't have a steady shooter) is to point blocking boules 50cm to 75cm directly in front of the jack. Odds are good, especially by rolling pointers, that one of the blocking boules will be struck and pushed closer to the jack. Blocking boules as far out front as 1.5m are still visual and psychological distractions for roulette pointers.

The Demi-Portée (Half-Lob)

This is where Pétanque throwing technique gets interesting. The demi-portée (half-lob) is the throw of choice for novice through intermediate pointers. It's a great compromise between simple roulette and the physically challenging plombée (full-lob).

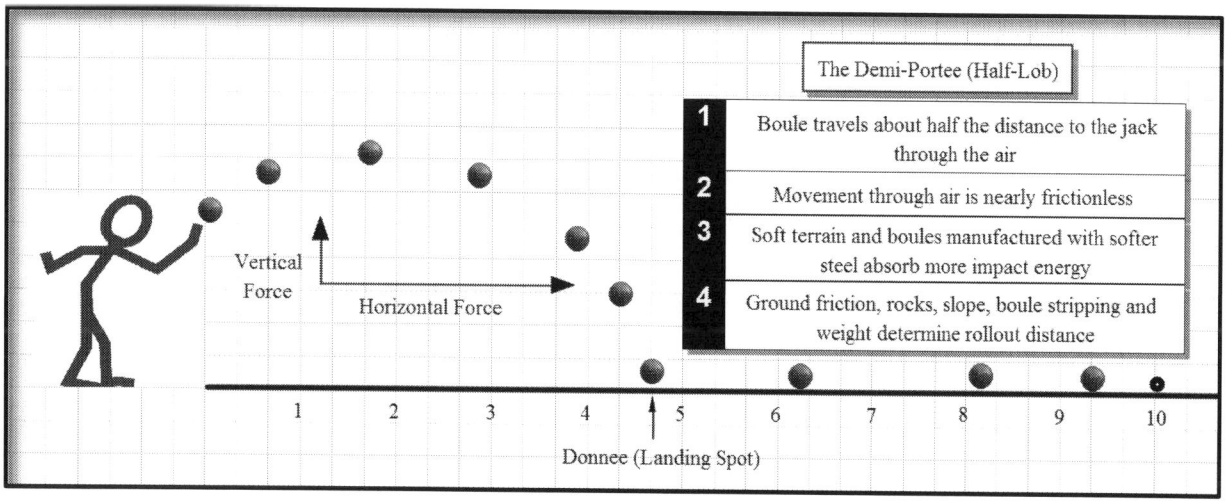

Six Steps to Pointing Demi-Portée:

1. **IFPJP rules prohibit grooming the terrain**: that includes flatting and smoothing the area with the sole of your foot. However because quality données can be rare *FIPJP Rules Article 10 — Removal of Obstacles* allows the thrower or a teammate to *fill in one (and only one) depression created by a previous boule's impact.* Filling a donnée divot is a slippery slope to terrain grooming. Watching international competition it appears that this rule is so liberally interpreted that players appear to create flat données with the bottom of their shoe.

2. **Carefully Pick Your Donnée**: Slowly walk the line between the jack and rond observing the terrain. Select a donnée approximately halfway to the jack. The ideal donnée is smooth and level, not cement hard or with loose larger rocks or other debris to deflect the boule offline.

3. **Stand in the rond and visualize**: Form an image of the boule soaring with a perfect symmetric arc and after hitting the donnée has just enough horizontal energy to complete the rollout.

4. **Gaze intently at the donnée**: The donnée is the immediate bull's-eye; don't obsess on the ultimate spot where you want the boule to come to rest!

5. **Visually follow the boule from donnée to completion**: Especially important is how the boule responds after impact: Does the rollout start true or did the boule lurch to either side? Does boule rollout trace a straight line or curve, due to slope or contours? Does the boule suddenly jump as if it ran into a larger rock or other obstacle?

6. **Evaluate the throw**. Even if you are going to immediately throw again, step out and take a few seconds for review and reflection. To modify (or duplicate) subsequent throws *you must know exactly* where the boule landed and the quality of the rollout. How close to the intended donnée did the boule land? How close to the jack (or desired location) did it stop? If the throw wasn't acceptable, should you choose a different donnée or modify the demi-portée arc?

> ### Boule-Devant, Boule-Devant!
> - A boule in front is an asset to your team
> - A boule just behind the jack is a backstop that can be employed by either team
> - A boule derrière (way behind the jack) is only useful if the jack is shot and pushed back.

Bad Landings and Lazy Habits

Engaged players stand near the jack. Before throwing they deliberately walk the line evaluating données. Before a critical throw a pointer may make the walk several times. Most recreational club players hang out at the rond and rarely bother walking the line. Inevitably they make poor donnée choices or, even more likely, no conscious donnée choice at all. With no preparation and little thought they jump into the rond, wind up and let it rip, leaving fate and the whims of gravity to determine the donnée. If you don't take the time to find the best donnée, you haven't earned the right to be upset by inconsistent throws or bad landings.

> ### Sixty Seconds
> You have sixty seconds. Don't succumb to peer-pressure and rapid fire just to make less engaged players feel better about their torpid habits. As a friend from Provence once told me, "Neither the art of French cooking nor the throwing of the boule can be made in haste." Take the time to clear your head, steel your resolve and reinforce the vision of a perfect throw that you are about to make!

Adjusting the Arc of the Demi-Portée

Since a demi-portée is a combination of "out-and-up" energies, depending on the complexity of the terrain, it may take several throws to calibrate the "out" power and "up" trajectory required to make an accurate pointing throw. It's not uncommon to see an end played in which every boule is a significant distance to the right side of the jack and you wonder why the pointers aren't compensating by throwing to the left. It's the craziest thing, but pointers get stuck in a groove and even though they consciously know that they should modify their throw, at the physical level they are stuck in "machine mode" and continue to duplicate the previous unsuccessful attempt. This is especially chronic when it comes to pointing long; i.e. boules that stop well beyond the jack. We know that a boule-devant 50cm to 75cm in front of the jack is a great novice to intermediate pointing throw because it obscures direct access to the jack and can be promoted. In novice to intermediate club play I often see pointers throw well beyond the jack three times in a row as if the previous overthrows had never happened.

> Your pointing mantra should be:
> ***Analyze, Adapt and Apply!***
>
> Pétanque demands the impossible - i.e. making consistently accurate pointing throws on an ungroomed, inconsistent terrain.

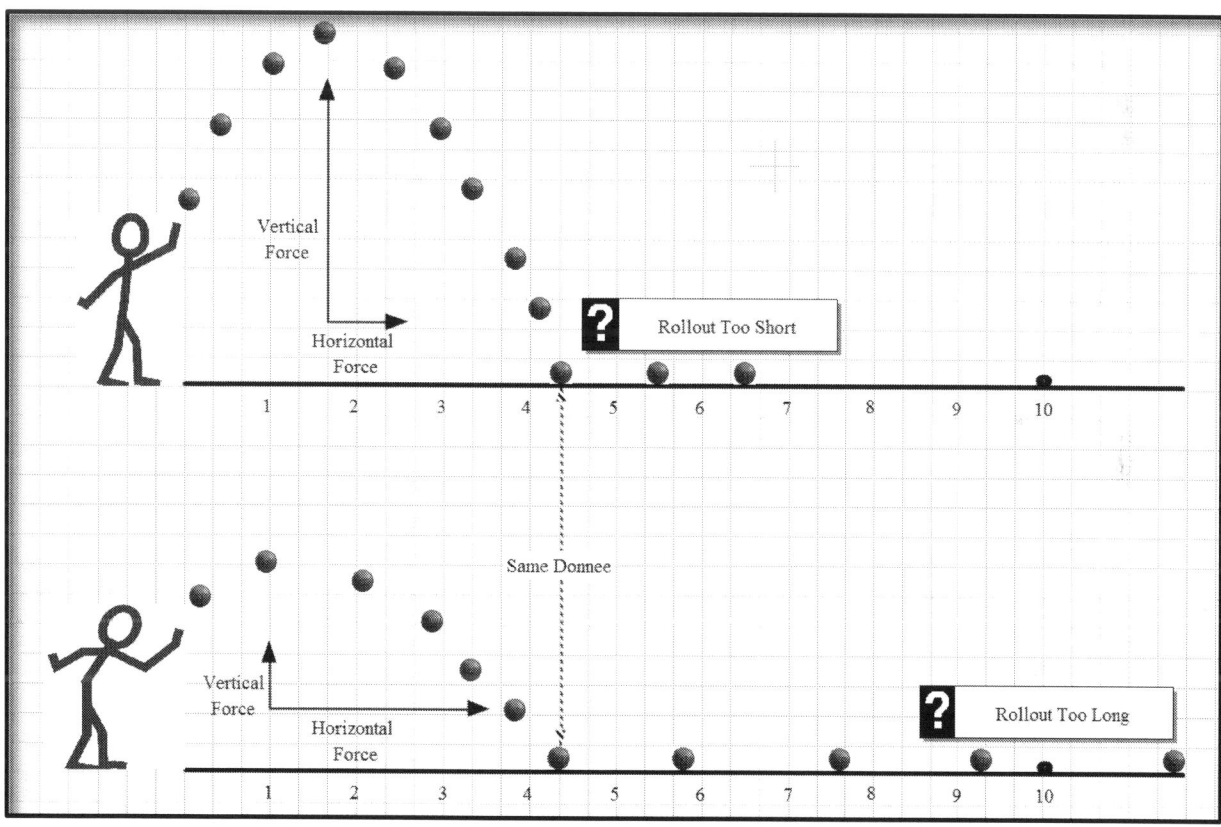

In the two examples above the jack is at 10m and both throws use the same donnée at 4.5m.

- The first throw has too much "up" and not enough "out" force. The apex of the arc is almost twice the thrower's height! Consequently the boule descends steeply, an indication that most of the force acting on the boule is vertical. On impact the vertical force is absorbed by the terrain and the boule itself. The small horizontal component of force only produces a 2m rollout and the boule stops 3.5m short of the jack.

- In the second throw the player transforms some of the "up" energy into "out" energy producing a much flatter arc indicating that the boule has much more horizontal force. Although the boule hits the same donnée the additional horizontal force produces almost a 7.5m rollout and it stops almost 2m beyond the jack.

It appears that the player over compensated just a bit. Here are three possible modifications for the next throw:

✓ *More Up Energy*: Transform a bit of the "out" energy into "up" energy which will increase the arc and shorten rollout
✓ *Less Out Energy*: Duplicate the arc of the previous throw, but with a bit less "out" energy
✓ *Try a Closer Donnée*: Duplicate the previous throw with a donnée at about 3m. This is a viable strategy only if the new donnée has similar characteristics to the original donnée.

Adjusting the Demi-Portée for Downhill Terrain

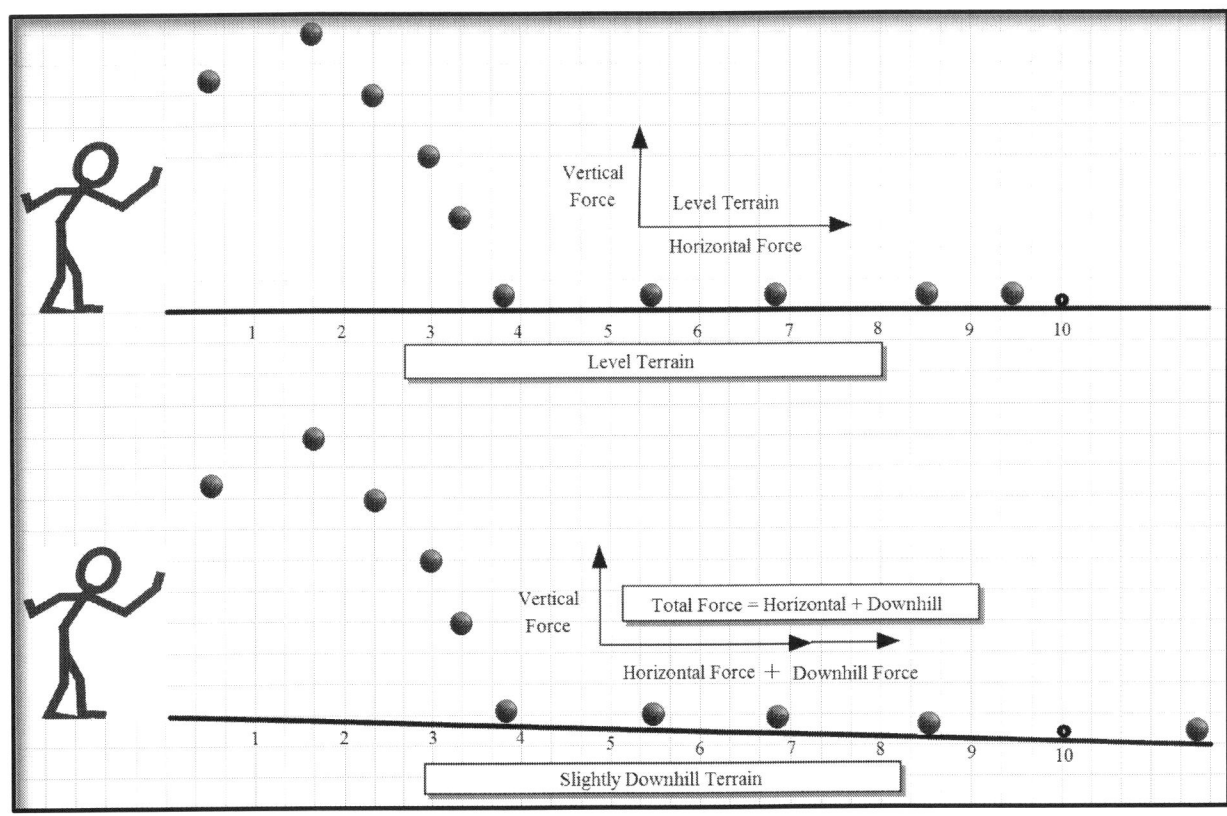

The first throw in the diagram is ideal demi-portée with a donnée at 4m and a rollout that stops 50cm short of the jack – well done. Now imagine the identical terrain, but instead it runs slightly downhill toward the jack providing an unsolicited gravity assist! The boule's equivalent "out" energy is the sum of the horizontal force in the player's throw plus gravity's downhill pull. Of course the overall slope effect is a function of the terrain-to-boule friction.

In the second illustration the pointer makes an identical throw but gravity assist produces an additional 1.5m rollout. Some downhill slopes are so subtle they are only indirectly detected by observing longer than expected rollout.

Not illustrated is the complementary situation in which the terrain is uphill and gravity opposes rollout. The total horizontal force driving the boule is the thrower's horizontal force *minus* gravity's uphill force. You've got to love

> If you are pointing long even if you can't see the slope, assume that it's there. Compensate with a little additional arc or reduce your "out" energy just a bit.

Pétanque, as if your opponents and rough terrain aren't enough challenge, gravity also gangs up on you. The toughest terrains roll or undulate, having closely spaced short uphill and downhill sections. Your boule gets alternately helped and hindered during a single rollout. *Terrain is the great equalizer it enhances lucky throws and undermines technique. If your group has a diverse mixture of Pétanque talent and experience, play on the ugliest terrain available.*

Rétro – Pétanque's Braking System

To understand rétro braking affect we must agree on what it means to roll. Take a boule (or any ball) and roll it slowly on a flat, smooth surface and carefully observe its motion. A rolling ball rotates in its direction of travel; formally stated "a rolling ball moves in a specific direction by turning over-and-over on a center axis".

Unlike a tennis ball whose trajectory is radically affected by spin, we've agreed that boule movement is not affected by air resistance. Although rétro has no effect when the boule is in flight, it doesn't have such a benign relationship with course dirt and gravel. When a rétro imparted boule slams into the terrain its rotation is opposite of the direction of travel. So by definition the boule isn't rolling - it is skidding, sliding, bouncing and biting into the terrain like a slick tire, all the while dissipating the boule's forward momentum. When the rétro is finally expelled, boule rotation reverses and it rolls forward in the conventional sense just described.

> Rétro means backwards, the opposite of rolling rotation. Enough rétro can be imparted on a tennis ball that when flipped forward rétro causes it to jump backwards and roll back toward the thrower.
>
> By virtue of greater mass and momentum, rétro can't make a boule roll backwards (except an au fer shot!) But it provides a fine braking and control mechanism.

Braking force is proportional to rotational velocity. Higher RPMs (rotations per minute) correspond to greater braking force and rollout control. You don't always have to throw with maximum rétro; sometimes a modest braking force is sufficient. *Overall rétro effectiveness is dependent on several factors which are beyond the player's control.*

- *Terrain Hardness*: Hard terrains cause boule rebound. During each bounce the boule's momentum carries it forward without effects of rétro braking. All the while rétro is dissipating, futilely spinning through the air instead of digging into the terrain. In addition to softer données, softer boules (see *Chapter 5*) reduce rebound and increase rétro effectiveness.
- *Terrain Composition*: loose crushed rock, D.G. and sand/grit provide maximum friction. *Maximum friction with minimum rebound is the ideal rétro braking formula.*
- *Boule to Terrain Friction*: Once again, see *Chapter 5* for details.
  - Boule weight
  - Number, depth and patterns of boule striations (*mostly urban myth*)

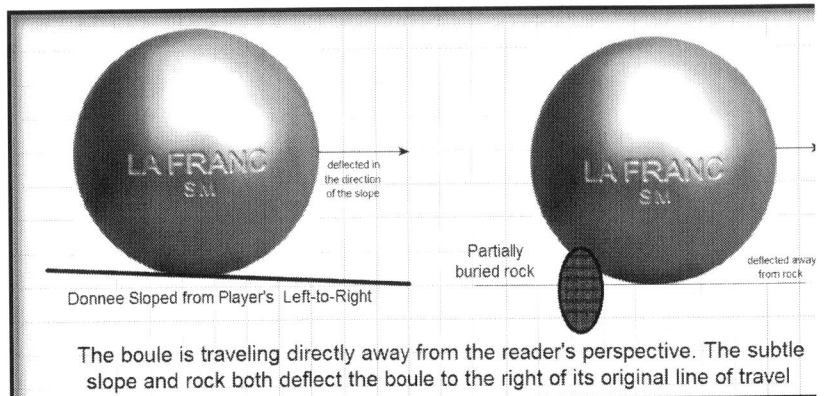

Donnee Sloped from Player's Left-to-Right

deflected in the direction of the slope

Partially buried rock

deflected away from rock

The boule is traveling directly away from the reader's perspective. The subtle slope and rock both deflect the boule to the right of its original line of travel

Lurching Boules
When a boule hits a donnée which is even just slightly slanted perpendicular to the line of travel, it may leap sideways toward the downhill slope.

In the second illustration the boule lands on a partially buried rock on the left side of a <u>flat donnée</u> and is deflected right of its line of travel.

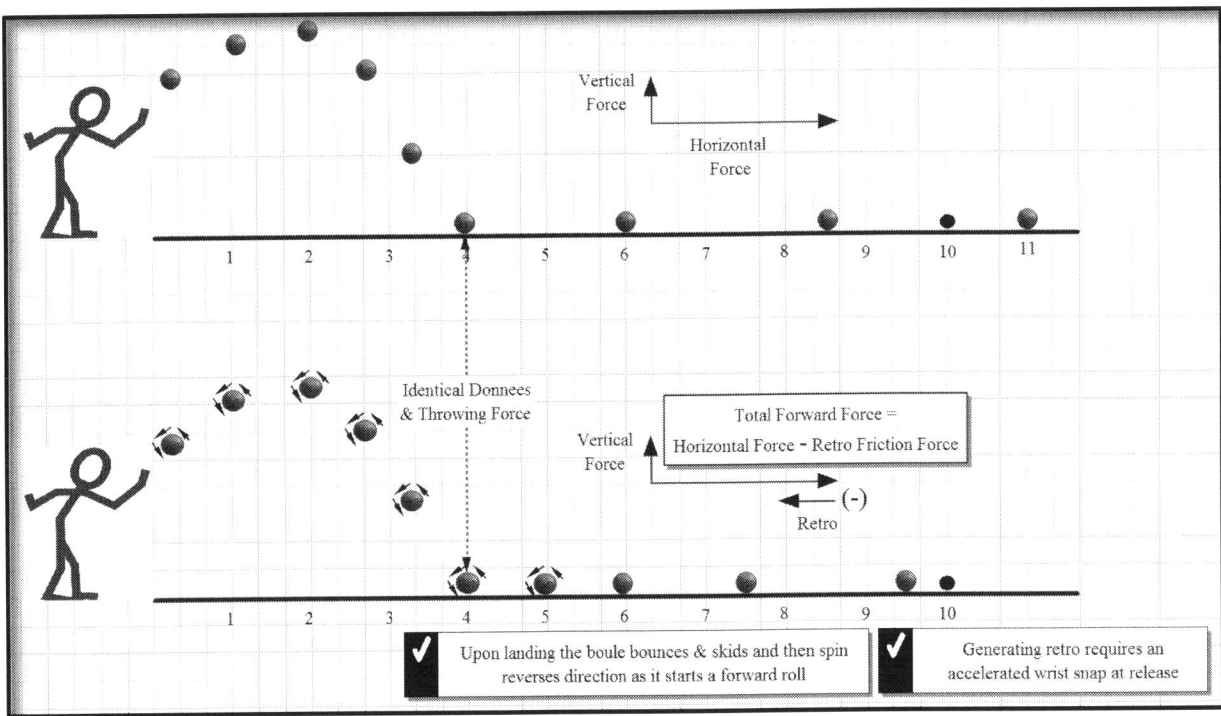

Vertical Force

Horizontal Force

Identical Donnees & Throwing Force

Vertical Force

Total Forward Force = Horizontal Force - Retro Friction Force

(-)

Retro

✔ Upon landing the boule bounces & skids and then spin reverses direction as it starts a forward roll

✔ Generating retro requires an accelerated wrist snap at release

In the first figure the demi-portée lands at 4m and rollout stops 1m beyond the jack. In the second figure an identical demi-portée is thrown with a smart wrist snap to generate rétro. Rétro braking induced friction reduces boule momentum and shortens rollout by 1.5m. The simple force diagram indicates that the equivalent force propelling the boule is the throw's horizontal (out) force minus the rétro braking force.

All advanced pointers, especially plombée pointers as illustrated in the next section, rely on rétro to reduce rollout. Rétro is generated by wrist snap, which increases the throw's biomechanical complexity. Players with wrist limitations may not be able to execute a fast snap with a heavy boule. Others may feel that imposing another component on the throwing motion isn't worth the braking effect.

The Portée or Plombée (Full Lob)

Although the full lob is formally known as a portée I prefer its other common name, the plombée. The Latin root "plumb" indirectly refers to the concept of vertical. When a wall is properly constructed it's said to be plumb, meaning that it is vertical or straight up-and-down.

A plombée is thrown with significant of "up" force with the goal of achieving a very steep (plumb) trajectory. The combination of steep descent and rétro radically reduces rollout. When a plombée lands on a relatively soft, high friction donnée and the rétro digs in, the boule may stop nearly dead with little rollout. The reduced rebound of softer boules enhances the plombée; in concert with the terrain the boule absorbs a portion of the tremendous energy generated by the long, steep descent.

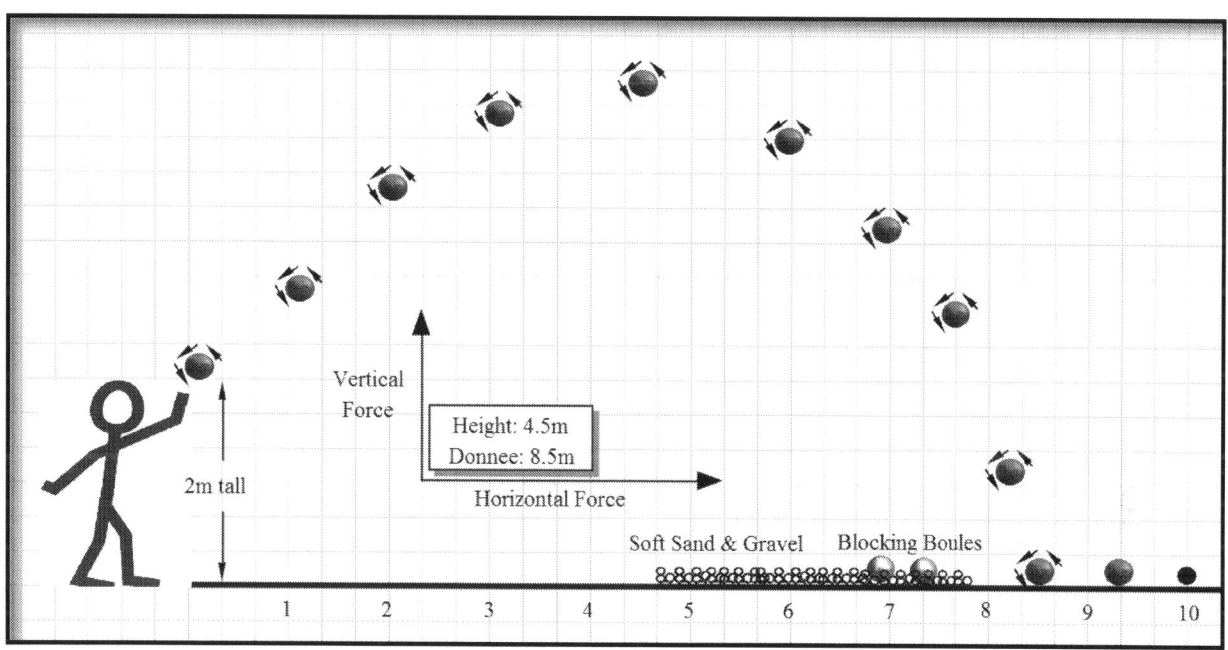

In the illustration the jack is at 10m, there is soft sand and deep gravel between 4.5m to 8m and two blocking boules reside at about 7m. The pointer has two options:

- Point to either side of the jack by throwing a demi-portée with a donnée short of 4.5m and rolling the reminder of the distance through the sand and gravel.
- Throw a plombée with a donnée just over 8m from the rond. The boule bypasses the difficult terrain and boule-devants, and is *thrown with a high arc and sufficient rétro to come to rest in front of the jack.*

The plombée demands the contradictory characteristics of power and touch. *Hitting your donnée is important for all pointing throws, for the plombée it is mandatory.* A 720g boule dropped from a height of 3m to 5m has tremendous impact energy. If the donnée is hard, slopped to the side or contains rock chunks, then boule rebound may be violent and unpredictable. The ideal plombée donnée:

- Is relatively smooth to ensure controlled rebound and true rollout
- Is soft to medium hard to minimize rebound and maximize rétro braking
- May be uphill or downhill but not sloped to the side. If the donnée is on a downhill slope a closer donnée may be required.

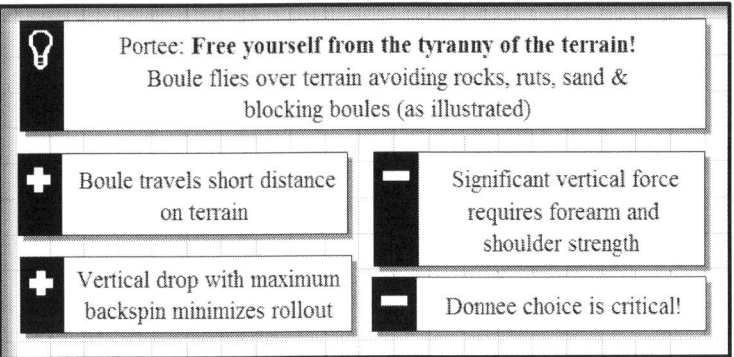

The plombée is thrown high with a steep arc. If the donnée is beyond the player's strength, the throw isn't as high and the flatter trajectory produces a proportionally longer rollout.

The Plombée and the Myth of Bad Terrains

All of the west coast *FPUSA* clubs that I've played have fairly level, packed-dirt consistent terrains. I understand that clubs want attractive, approachable terrains that minimize random luck. But there's no doubt that unchallenging terrains encourage lackluster technique. If person plays on a flat, smooth terrain they will develop the habit of only throwing simple roulette or low arced demi-portée. Why bother perfecting difficult throws when you can get by with novice technique? The issue is compounded when a person plays one terrain exclusively. After a few sessions every rock, contour and decent donnée is memorized. In this well-known and controlled environment club players may throw very well and build an unwarranted confidence. American's call it the "home field advantage" and it comes at the cost of minimal skills development and lazy habits.

> **Tip from the Pros**
> Unless the terrain is very smooth, the majority of professional pointing throws are plombées with a donnée which is typically ¾ of the way to the jack.

A troubling example of this was a spring 2011 mixed-doublettes championship for a major west-coast *FPUSA* member club which was billed as the state championships. I attended the tournament to casually interview players and observe the quality of play and strategies. The terrain was fairly level, hard-packed dirt with a few patches of smooth crushed rock and only small amounts of leaves of twigs. After a wet winter the boules still rolled quickly and easily over the surface, but underlying moisture provided the ideal soft donnée. To test the terrain I threw several plombées at an 8m donnée with an easy 4m arc, which produces a rollout of less than a 1.25m. The terrain was ideal for an aerial-oriented game.

Several times I witnessed the sound strategy of building a wall of boule-devants (blocking boules) at just over 1m in front of the jack. Much to my bewilderment instead of taking to the air and throwing a plombée over the wall, the opposition attempted to roll through it, promoting the opponent's blocking boules and rolling up many points for the competition.

During breaks I respectfully approached players and inquired why they had attempted to roll through the wall instead of throwing over it. I received mumbled rationalities, harsh stares and more than one invitation to leave the premises. (I never get that response when I interrogate tennis players or disc golfers about their strategies or techniques!)

> When someone *sincerely* inquires about your technique or strategies don't get defensive; it's an opportunity for introspection - you might get surprising insight into your own game.

It appeared to me that their simple, non-challenging terrains had lulled the players into a complacency in which they never felt compelled to develop the strength and skills to point plombée. This is interesting because even when your home terrain is not especially challenging without plombée or consistent shooting skills you are vulnerable to the boule-devant blocking tactic.

Plombée Donnée Choices

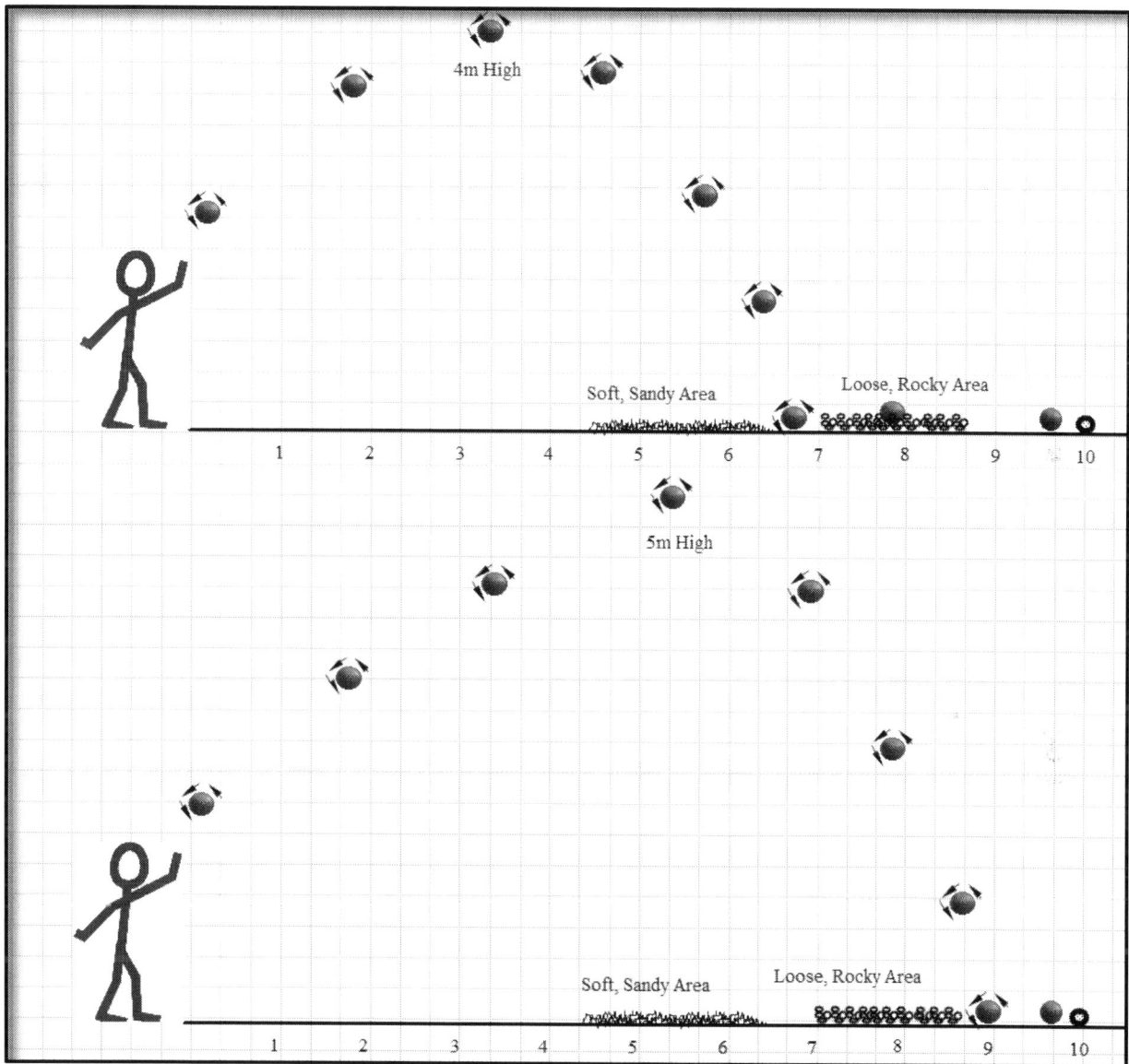

Once again the jack is at 10m. A soft, sandy area is between 4.5 and 6.5m, and a loose rocky area between 7m to 8.5m. For the pointer with plombée skills there are three obvious données:

- The smooth section between 6.25m and 7m from rond
- After the loose, rocky area 9m from the rond
- Somewhere in the loose, rocky area

The first donnée is close enough that it is reachable by most squat pointers and doesn't require an extremely steep descent. The downside is that the boule rolls out through a loose, rocky area. If this is not the first throw of the end, then the pointer has observed rollout from the previous throws and should have a good idea how much force is required to plow through the loose rocky area.

The second donnée requires skill and power. Even advanced pointers might get out of the squat and stand on their hind legs for this one. Since the donnée is only 1m from the jack, a steep trajectory and maximum rétro to slam on the brakes are required.

> There is no such thing as the "best" donnée. Examine the possibilities and evaluate them against your pointing skills and the current tactical situation.

There's no pointing throw with greater crowd appeal than a 4.5m high plombée crashing to the terrain, rétro throwing gravel like a crazed ground squirrel, terminated by the crowd's collective gasp as the boule comes to rest 15cm from the jack. Work on your plombée, Pétanque's version of performance art!

The third donnée represents the happy medium. Plombée pointers need not fear loose, rocky areas they often make fine données just as long as the underlying surface is not cement hard. A donnée in the range of 7m to 8m is reachable by most strong pointers. In this case the shorter the donnée the more gravel that the boule will plow through on rollout. A donnée just over 7m won't require a steep trajectory or excessive rétro. After watching several boules impact the gravel and rollout, the pointer will know if that area provides a viable donnée for a mid-level plombée. Of course if there were blocking boules closer to the jack, then the pointer may be required to throw to a longer donnée. That's why a donnée can only be judged within the context of the current play.

💡	The only way to choose a consistent donnee is to walk the terrain closely inspecting the area of interest
💡	The pros agree that picking the donnee and hitting it spot on is the single most important skill for consistent pointing
💡	**Be observant**: watching teammate's and opponent's boules landing and rollout is the best way to learn about a donnee's characteristics.
💡	*FIPJP Rules Article 10* state that one (and only one) boule divot from a previous throw may be filled in by foot before each throw.
☠	It is illegal pack, flatten or even test drop a boule on a potential donnee!

Plombées and the Soft Landing

We love playing Pétanque in non-dedicated, public spaces. Walk-by traffic engenders community goodwill, exposure for potential converts and public spaces provide diverse, challenging and especially perplexing terrains. But when challenging degrades to random, we sometimes hate non-dedicated terrains. At first glance many public spaces don't appear a whole lot different than dedicated club terrains. Although Pétanque revolves around the concept of ungroomed terrains club pistes are like tabby cats compared to the mountain lions of public spaces.

- Public spaces are shaped and contoured by pedestrian and bicycle traffic. Often the terrain is part of the actual walkway!
- They may abound with human and canine artifacts. Or in France, cigarette butts.
- Gravel and crushed rock ground covering is often patchy and unequally distributed, resulting in alternating fast and slow stretches.
- Water flow and sprinkler drainage cuts grooves and barely detectable channels into the terrain which tend to funnel boule rollout into a common line

Accomplished players get extremely frustrated playing in public spaces where hard, rocky erratic terrains produce random bounces and rollouts that neutralize skill and maximize luck. My groups play in many types of shared public spaces. We have a particularly exasperating terrain which is a walking trail that parallels a snow-fed spring time desert creek. At first glance it looks ideal: 4m to 6m wide, relatively flat with a hard-packed surface with an abundance of small to medium sized gravel. But the underlying layer is nearly cement hard and it abounds with softball sized buried rocks and nearly impossible to read contours. Low-arced demi-portées inexplicability leap sideways on impact and stop meters from the jack. On some ends all the boules roll long, and on other ends (even throwing in the same direction) all the boules stop well short of the jack. Beginners love it; players with craft, experience and skill hate it.

After playing there several times (and getting thrashed by a novice team) I decided to crack its evil secrets. A slow walk and careful examination (and a few dozen test boules) revealed a strategy by which skilled players could exploit the terrain. During the rare desert rains, tiny rivulets flow along and across the terrain depositing random patches of fine sand. The patches of sand are just deep enough to provide moderately soft and stable données, especially for precise plombées.

The plombée pointer is always on the lookout for a donnée to absorb vertical impact energy and provide a short and true rollout. That's why the lead pointer should throw the jack. Most players randomly toss the jack with little thought as to distance or strategy – to them any jack placement from 6m to 10m is good enough. See *Appendix C: The Art of Jack Placement* for more than you ever really need to know about tossing the jack.

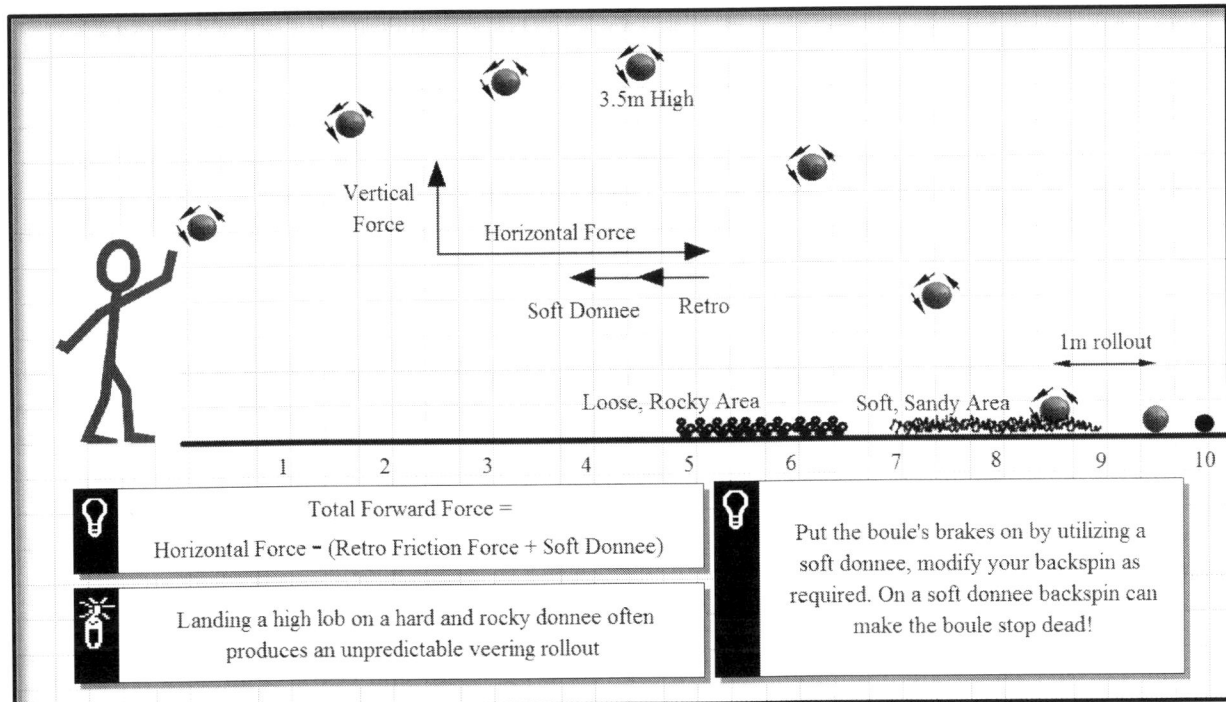

The illustration depicts a section of the terrain along the creek that was just described. From the rond the pointer controlling the jack placement walked the terrain to find a nice flat soft sandy patch about 7m from the jack. He threw the jack into the middle of the soft sand and it stopped at 10m from the rond - we like long jack placements to hobble short distance shooters.

The sandy area is just short of 9m and provides an ideal donnée because it:

- Cushions the underlying hard rocky surface
- Helps absorb the vertical impact energy, minimizing boule rebound (hop or bounce)
- Is an ideal surface to maximize rétro braking effectiveness

The jack placement is nearly perfect for our team because none of the opposition pointers are skilled plombée throwers; they are forced to throw demi-portées with données in the loose, rocky area which produce random lurching bounces and inconsistent rollout.

Enter the Shooter

Pointing skills are fundamental; everybody is initiated as a pointer. After you master the demi-portée and have promoted teammate's blocking boules or gently nudged opponent's boules away from the jack with well-directed pointing throws the desire to become a shooter may start to take root. For many the experience of having perfect pointing throws repeatedly blasted into the O.B. by a smug, cold-blooded shooter provides the motivation to transform from prey to hunter!

✍ Like the unofficial U.S. Marine slogan, a pointer must "improvise, adapt and overcome." The pointers throw selection and specific delivery style is based on many variables: terrain conditions, jack distance, blocking boules, big picture strategy and current tactical requirements. Pointing relies on a deft and delicate touch, picking and hitting the best donnée and generating precise rétro braking.

⚓ The shooter's world is black-and-white; their primary goal is to smack a specified boule with sufficient accuracy and force to remove it from play. Shooting relies on the precise machine-like execution of a single style of throw. Overlay a video of the last ten shots of an advanced shooter and the stance, preparation, backswing, delivery and release will be nearly identical. The majority of targets are unobstructed boules, making distance the key variable. *For most practical purposes au fer shooters need not even consider terrain conditions*. The shooter's job is as unambiguous as it is challenging; to step into the rond and time-after-time deliver a knock-out blow!

With due respect to well-developed pointing skills, any novice can stumble into the rond and make a few lucky pointing throws. Shooting is a different animal. To become proficient a shooter must emulate a machine in body and mind. It may take several hundred practice shots before you become comfortable enough to shoot in games. When a shooter makes the shot, he is a hero – but when he misses, he misses big. And accidently shooting a teammate's boule or the jack can be disastrous.

> Watching your shot accomplishing nothing but "making a hole in the air" (faire un trou) and wind up sitting all by its lonesome 10m from the nearest boule is a sobering and soul searching experience; a challenge to the ego that few can repeatedly endure.

Why Shoot?

In *Chapter 2* we saw several circumstances where the situation suggested shooting as an alternative to outpointing the opponent's best boule.

- A steady shooter demoralizes the opposition by removing any and all boules near the jack from play. This makes the implicit statement that the shooter's team owns the jack and the competition should keep clear! Many pointers believe that they only have a few great pointing throws each game.
- The occasional carreau is also devastating because it sends the message that not only can I remove your best boules, but I'll also replace them with my shots; a 2-for-1 deal.
- When your opponents are out of boules and your team has several boules in hand, shooting boule-devant blocking boules opens the jack making it easy to pile up uncontested points.

Example 1:

Often a single shot turns around the entire end. In the diagram the Black team has one point on the ground and is out of boules. The Silver player with one boule in hand is both a pointer and a steady shooter. *For sake of argument, the score is Silver 10 and Black 7*; Silver is only three points from victory so they "jouer pour la gagne" (play for the win)!

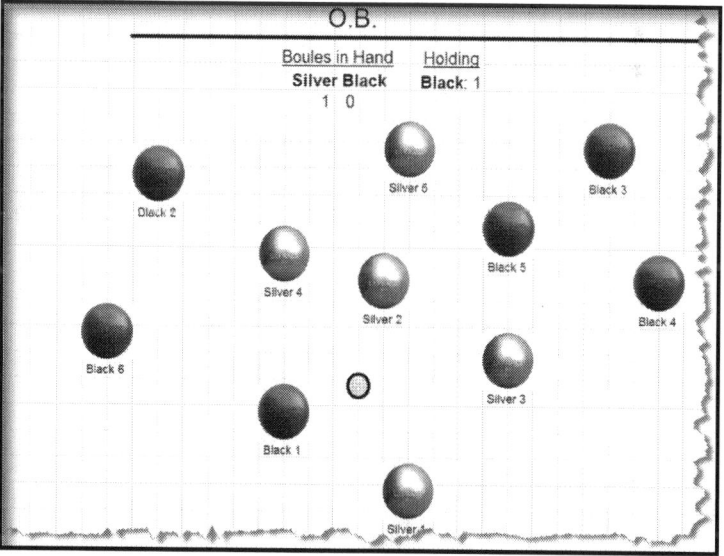

Instead of outpointing Black-1 with their last boule, they can shoot it. If they miss, the Black team only gets one point and the game score will be *Silver 10 and Black 8*. If Black-1 is successfully shot, the Silver team scores a minimum of three points and wins the game!

Example 2:

The Black team has three points on the ground and is out of boules. The Silver team has three boules in hand: the shooter has one and the pointer has two. Black-6 is the only boule within 25cm of the jack. It's an effective blocking boule that could be accidently promoted by one of Silver's remaining pointing

throws. *If it weren't for Black-6, the Silver team's pointer is confident that he could easily outpoint Black-4 and Black-5 and score two uncontested points.*

The Silver team determines (by consensus, not an individual player) that they should first take a shot at Black-6; if successful, the jack will be wide open. There's little downside because if the shooter misses, then Silver's pointer has two boules in which to minimize damage and ensure that the Black team only scores a single point.

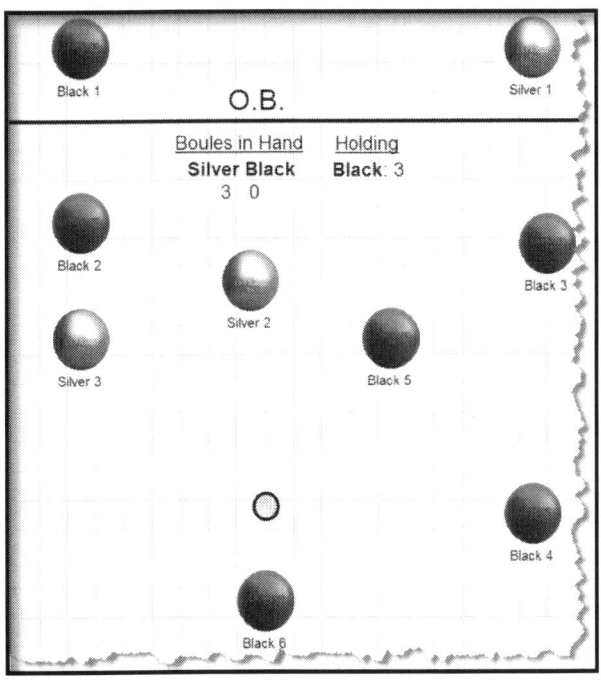

One last consideration, what happens if the shooter overthrows Black-6 and shoots the jack? When a jack is accidently shot and there are several boules behind it, no one can predict its final location. The Silver team's best case scenario is that the jack is shot O.B. The Black team is out of boules and the Silver team would have two boules

in hand. According to *FIPJP Rules, Article 13* that we examined in *Chapter 2*, the Silver team is awarded one point for each boule in hand. Even is the jack isn't shot O.B., the Silver team still has two boules to mitigate the damage regardless of where the jack eventually stops. **In this case shoot away, and don't worry about the jack!**

When Not to Shoot

Americans tend to be timid shooters. Even when the current tactic suggests shooting, they'll take the "safe choice" and point rather than suffer the humiliation of throwing up a clean miss. It's all about saving face. At the other extreme are fearless, hyper-aggressive shooters (typified by Southeast Asians) who impose their will by shooting everything in sight.

Each shot typically has three potential outcomes, with many of variations of the third possibility:

👍The shot succeeds in removing the opponent's boule without adversely displacing teammate's boules or the jack.

☞ The shot is a clean miss and doesn't displace any important boule or move the jack.

💣 The shot directly strikes a teammate's boule, the jack or after striking the opponent's boule the chain reaction adversely displaces an important teammate's boule or the jack.

An old Pétanque bit of wisdom is when your opponents have a few boules in hand and your team is down to its last boule, don't shoot if a miss will leave a wide open jack and allow them to run-up multiple uncontested points.

When in doubt restrain the shooting impulse and throw a blocking boule to limit your liability.

See the diagram on the right. Black has two points on the ground and no boules in hand. Silver has one boule in hand. Black-3 is within centimeters of the jack and would be difficult to outpoint.

Should the Silver team point or shoot?

- If they successfully shoot Black-3 , but don't get a rare carreau, Black-4 holds scores one point for the Black team.
- If the shooter overthrows and accidently hits it own boule, Silver-1, there's no harm done, but the Black team still gets two points.

Consider the possibilities if the Silver team makes a pointing throw with their last boule:

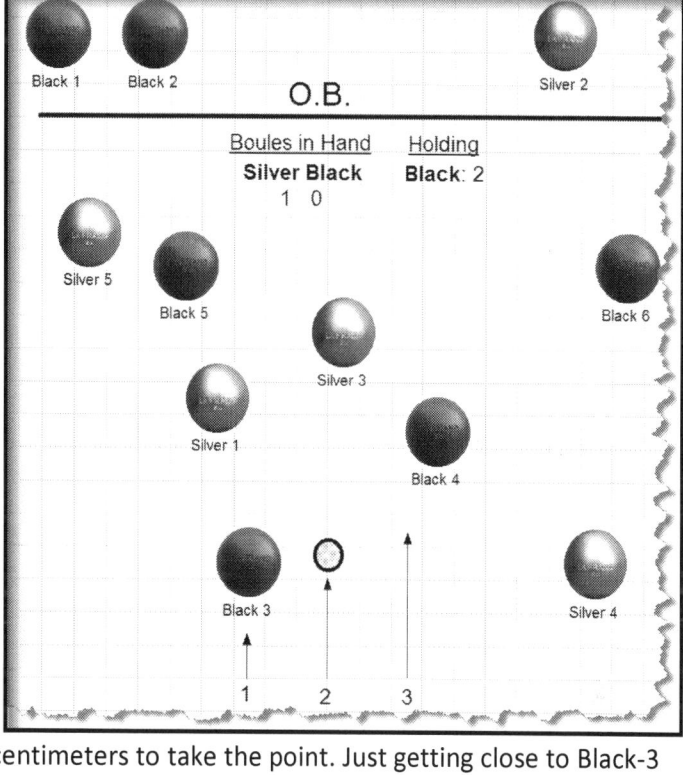

1. Point directly at Black-3. Use it as a backstop, perhaps pushing it back a few centimeters to take the point. Just getting close to Black-3 removes Black-4 as a second point.
2. If the pointer accidently threw a little right and pushed the jack back, the Silver team would benefit by reducing the Black team to one point or, just as likely, score a point or two for themselves.
3. If the right-side was more accommodating, the pointer could throw a boule between the jack and Black-4; but if the boule rolls long the Black team still scores two points.

The Silver team determines that they will make a pointing throw in the gap between Black-3 and the jack. This provides the benefit of using Black-3 as a backstop with the bonus that if they nudge it on the right side, their boule may slide between Black-3 and the jack to steal the point – in worst case they'll still reduce the Black team to one point.

Is it foolish for a novice pointer to have the audacity to believe that he can precisely point a boule between Black-3 and the jack?

Absolutely not! Without a precise intent how does one differentiate a great throw from a lucky throw? Novice pointers should always know exactly where they want their boule to land, roll and stop. Without a goal to provide a benchmark, how will you know if you're getting better?

Consider the following scenario: The Black team has one point on the ground and three boules in hand. The Silver team has two boules in hand and the next three closest boules to the jack. **With their last two boules should the Silver team point or shoot and in what order?**

The Silver shooter, holding one boule, wants to shoot Black-3. If successful the Silver team holds with three points on the ground. At first that sounds good, but without a carreau the three Silver boules would be easily outpointed by Black's next pointing throw.

Nonetheless, Silver's shooter's argument is convincing so he takes the shot and throws a clean miss! Now the Silver team is in real trouble. They have one boule in hand compared to Black's three. How can the last Silver boule be thrown to keep the Black team from running up several points?

Devant-de-Boule: A (Practically) Bulletproof Vest
A conventional boule-devant (blocking boule) directly in front of the jack would be immediately shot. A blocking boule variation is called a devant-de-boule, meaning a "boule in front of an opponent's boule." The devant-de-boule should stop just in front of (or even touching) the opponent's best boule. **It's as if you are pointing to the opponent's best boule instead of the jack.**

In the diagram Silver-6 was pointed directly in front of Black-3, devant-de-boule style. The Silver team is out of boules. Silver-6 is using its position directly in front of Black-3 to become bulletproof. If Silver-6 is shot, most likely the force striking it will be directly transferred to Black-3, and Black-3 will be driven well beyond the jack. Silver-6 would be vulnerable to be shot, but the dynamics of the game have changed:

- the Black team now only has two boules in hand
- the Silver team is holding with Silver-6 in close
- counting the three boules behind the jack, Silver has four points on the ground

That's not a bad result considering that Silver-6 was just brutally shot! How should the Black team use its last two boules?

- They will take one more shot at Silver-6. If the shot is successful, but not a carreau, the Black team will

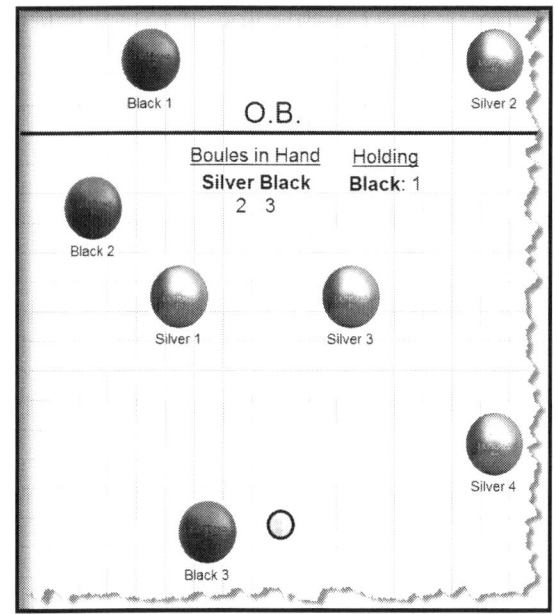

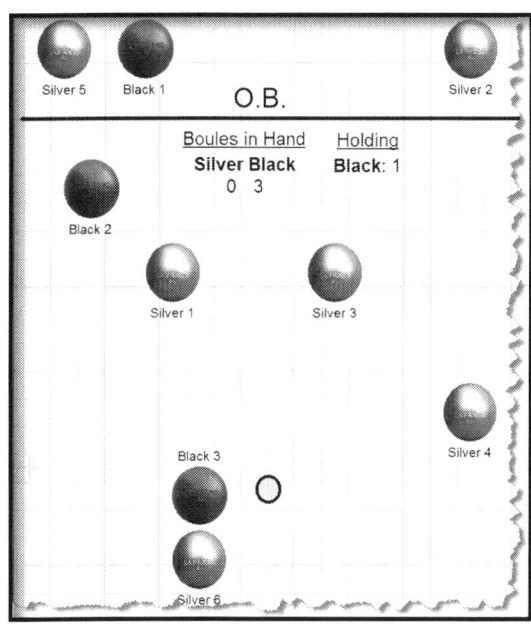

When the opposition is holding and your team concedes the end by making defensive throws to limit damage the strategy is called Serrer le Jeu or "tightening the game." When your opponent is knocking at victory's door there's no shame in hunkering down and surviving to fight one more end.

point their last boule and be award one point for the end.

- Even if the shot is missed the Black team has to do damage control and point its last boule. In the absence of a perfect pointing throw, the best outcome would be to reduce the Silver team's point total from four to one.

Depending on the terrain and distance to the jack, the devant-de-boule is a difficult defensive throw. Keep in mind that the jack has a 30mm diameter and the typical boule has a 73mm diameter. Pointing directly to another boule is not as difficult as pointing directly to the jack. On medium to slow terrains you may even gently bump the opponent's boule and its inertia should hold both boules together in the embrace of Pétanque's bulletproof vest.

The Tadpole

A tadpole (tétard) is a pointing throw that stops very close to or actually leaning against the jack. This configuration represents a challenging shot. Unlike the devant-de-boule the tadpole consists of a heavy boule kissing a light jack. If the boule is shot, the jack takes random flight – it can even rebound off of boules-derrière (behind it) and come to rest forward of its original position. I once shot a tadpole and the jack bounced off a boule-derrière and came to rest between my feet in the middle of the rond!

By definition a tadpole is impossible to outpoint, so it must be broken up. That's accomplished with a gentle pointing throw that taps the boule just hard enough to separate it from the jack by 15cm to 30cm. If the boule is bumped too hard, the jack flies and nobody can predict where it will stop.

Jack Congestion Means Danger is Lurking

In novice games, especially when neither team has an aggressive shooter, the jack area gets congested. This dense, target rich environment demands pinpoint pointing and shooting. **On the right Silver is holding with one point on the ground and two boules in hand.** They also have two other boules in advantageous positions. The Black team also has two boules in hand. Black-3 is the second best boule and Black-4 is just slightly farther out than Silver-1 and Silver-4. Without playing out the remainder of the end, what should the Black team consider before making the next throw?

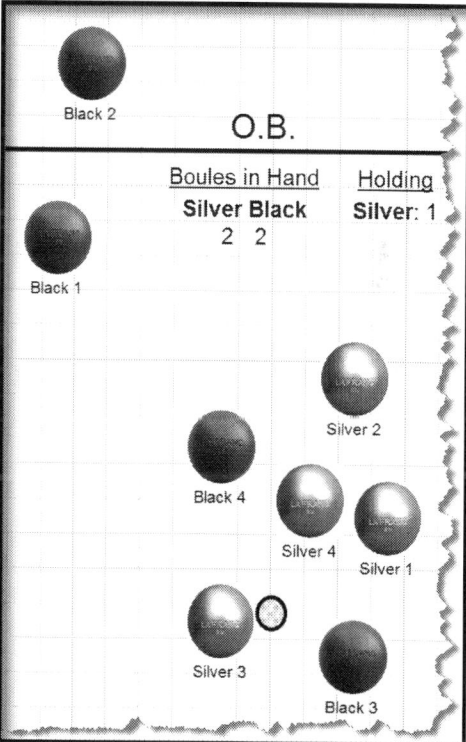

- Silver-3 is forming the most accessible type of tadpole. A precise shot could conceivably remove it from play without sending the jack flying.
- However, if the Black team's shooter overthrows Silver-3 he could accidently shoot Black-4 and remove it from play.
- If the shot strays slightly right of Silver-3 it might strike the jack which could bounce anywhere.
- If the shot is even further to the right, then the Black team's best boule (Black-3) could be shot, which would give the Silver team additional points on the ground.
- The Black team could concede one point to the Silver team and point two boule-devant blocking boules. But striking either Silver-3 or the jack could give the Silver team additional points.

Outside of novice play it's rare when the jack area gets that congested. Even just a few close boules create dangerous pointing and shooting possibilities. That's why the team should walk the line several times and discuss the best case and worse case consequences of each type of throw and weigh those possibilities against the current game score and the capabilities of the players with boules in hand.

The Big Three Shooting Throws

Like pointing, shooting has three standard throws which are variations of "out" and "up" forces and the application of rétro.

- As pointers become more proficient their throws become more aerial with an increasing emphasis on the "up" force culminating in the soaring beauty of the plombée.
- Shooting is the opposite. Novice shooters start with arced shots that are demi-portée variations with moderate "up" force. As their expertise improves shots become flatter, culminating in the nearly line-drive missiles thrown by top echelon shooters.

Palet Roulant, the Rolling Puck

The first step to shooting is to start by "pointing through the target boule" – in essence a modified demi-portée aimed at the target boule. Unlike a pointing throw which is thrown with the intent to stop in proximity to the target, (i.e. the jack) the pointing throw style shot is intended to hit the target with sufficient force to move it some distance from its current position; thus the description to "point through the target boule."

Books, articles and self-esteem intoxicated Pétanque gurus love to chant that anyone can learn to shoot, that it isn't really any different than pointing. *Let's put that feel good sentiment into context.* Points are scored by getting your boules closer to the jack than your opponent's boules. If your opponent's best boule is 75cm from the jack, any boule closer to the jack than 74.9cm only scores a single point. You point against your opponent's boules; the jack is only the reference from which points are allocated.

You point against the quality of your opponent's throws, but shooting is absolute – it's a hit or miss proposition.

In its purest form shooting exists without context. Pétanque shooters are like American football field goal kickers. They are called into the game to do a simple, well-defined job and everyone in the stadium immediately knows whether they were successful. The hardest part of shooting is the mindset and most recreational players don't want that kind of pressure or stress. Thus steady, recreational-level American shooters are a rare breed.

> You haven't done the job unless the target boule is driven out of scoring position. It doesn't matter whether you miss by a micron or 25cm or even hit the target, but with insufficient force to drive it from the jack area.

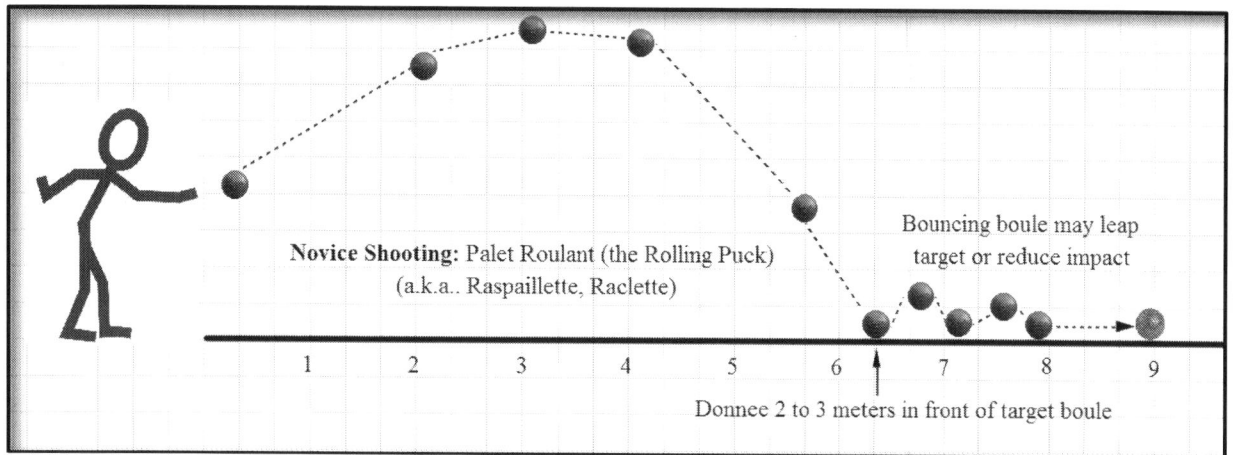

Novice Shooting: Palet Roulant (the Rolling Puck)
(a.k.a.. Raspaillette, Raclette)

Bouncing boule may leap
target or reduce impact

Donnee 2 to 3 meters in front of target boule

The horizontal (out) energy that a player puts into the throw is only diminished by ground friction, i.e. after the boule hits the terrain and starts to rollout. The palet roulant shot is a modified demi-portée with a donnée within 2m to 3m of the target boule. Although it's quite satisfying, you don't need to drive the target into the O.B., a meter or more beyond the jack is usually sufficient.

- A direct path between shooter and target is required. No blocking boules may reside between the donnée and target boule.
- The rolling puck shot uses a donnée which is 2m to 3m in front of the target boule.
- The closer the donnée to the target boule, the more knockout power the shot delivers.
- Rollout must be straight. The condition of the terrain between the donnée and target boule is critical. A slanting or loose donnée makes a difficult rolling puck shot.
- The further the boule travels through the air, the shorter the rollout. Even on smooth terrains like clay composition baseball infields, longer rollouts tend to eventually veer offline.
- To ensure sufficient knockout power on a slow or rocky terrain, the palet roulant has to be thrown with a flatter trajectory and a donnée which is closer to the target boule – too close and the shot leapfrogs the target.

The force required to generate shot momentum is a function of the distance between the donnée and target, and the terrain's speed. On a fast smooth terrain little momentum is required to drive the target boule; on a slow terrain with heavy gravel or on an uphill slope the shooter's boule must have significant momentum to displace the target.

> Common sense says that a flatter, low trajectory shot has less chance to bounce over the target boule.
>
> Think again! A fast, flat trajectory shot may only jump 8cm into the air, but during the jump it may cover enough distance to clear the target. A high, lazy arced shot might rebound 12cm on initial impact, but its velocity is slower so it doesn't travel as far during the hop. If reasonable données still leave you leapfrogging the target, try a bit more "up" and a less "out.
>
> **But remember, whatever the arc, shot velocity delivers the knockout blow.**

Many traditionalists consider the palet roulant to be a coward's throw. The French have several vulgar terms that malign the rolling shot and any player so ethically challenged as to employ it. On smooth fast terrains the only technical reasons not to throw palet roulant are the presence of blocking boules and the fact that they produce fewer carreaus than au fer shots. Palet roulant techniques and skills are useful in the following situations:

> **Throw it without shame or apology!**
>
> Don't dismiss the palet roulant just because it's considered a novice shooting style. Let the purists be enslaved to shooting au fer. In the appropriate situation the rolling puck is the highest percentage shot and gets the job done.

- Delivering a light, but smart tap to break up a tadpole or to remove the bulletproof vest of devant-de-boule
- Promoting a teammate's boule-devant while also controlling the rollout of your own boule to score two points; another 2-for-1 throw
- When the line between the rond and jack is partially blocked one may point into the congested area by delicately careening off other boules like bumpers in a pinball machine

All the situations described above use the same touch and delivery of the palet roulant shot. The only difference is the amount of force that's applied to the target or banking boules.

Shooting Au Fer: Intensity and Commitment

Challenging terrains, blocking boules, the desire for carreaus and the yearning to deliver Pétanque's equivalent of shock-and-awe inspires shooters to take to the air and shoot au fer. High-level Pétanque strategy is predicated on high percentage, unrelenting au fer shooting.

- The au fer shot strikes the target boule before touching the terrain. A well-thrown au fer shot is independent of terrain conditions. However, the effectiveness of a glancing blow au fer shot is dependent on the shot's rebound and how much energy is absorbed by the terrain.
- Striking the target square, at 45° with maximum rétro provides the greatest carreau possibility.
- Blocking boules stifle palet roulant shooting; typically they only hinder au fer shooters when they are closer than 15cm to 20cm from the target.
- Since the kinetic energy of an au fer shot is not dissipated by terrain impact and rollout, they deliver the maximum knockout punch.
- Au fer shooters often miss long. If they tighten up and come in short, dependent on terrain hardness, their shot may hop clean over the target. Au fer shooters are tightrope walkers that work incredibly narrow margins. Too long and too short produce misses; au fer shooting success demands precision and consistency.
- Great au fer shooters have "the eyes"; I call it the "feral stare." Like a cat preparing to pounce on a beautiful little song bird for several seconds they lock their gaze laser-like on the target boule as if it were the only object in the universe.
- All the other boules in play must be ignored; especially any boule within the vicinity of the target. The old saying is, "You hit what you look at." If you're worried about pulling right and accidently hitting your teammate's boule that's exactly what's going to happen!
- For some shooters locking their vision on the target boule is not enough. They create a more precise bull's-eye by staring at a single point on the target.

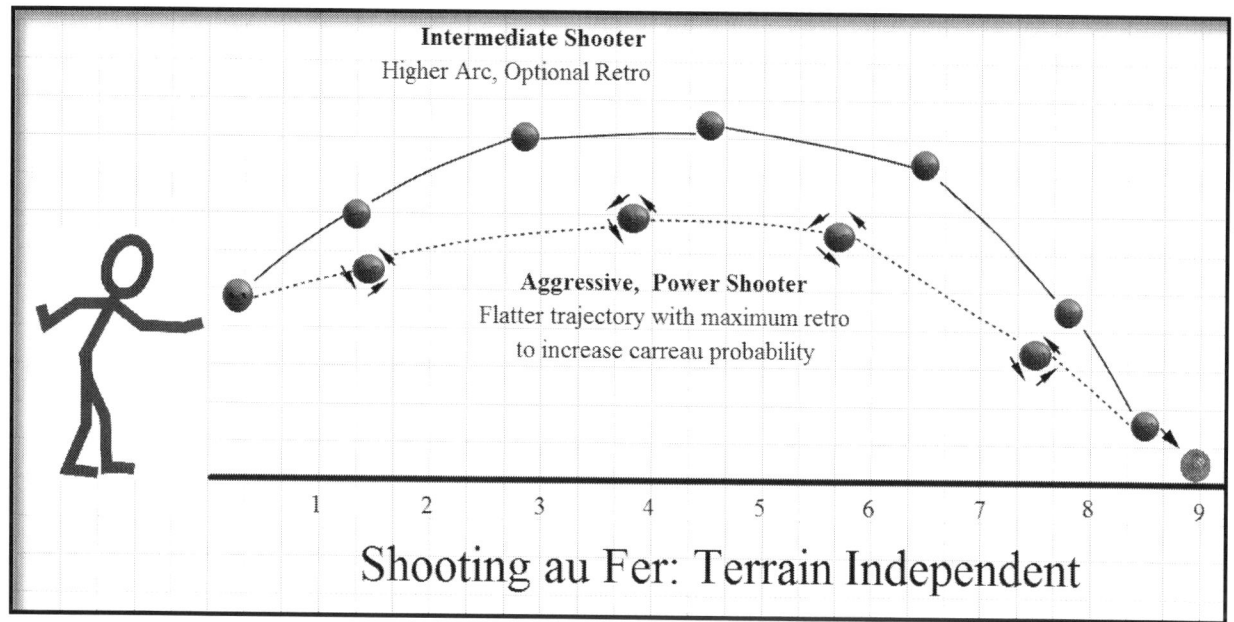

Intermediate Shooter
Higher Arc, Optional Retro

Aggressive, Power Shooter
Flatter trajectory with maximum retro
to increase carreau probability

1   2   3   4   5   6   7   8   9

Shooting au Fer: Terrain Independent

The Moderate Trajectory Au Fer Shooter

Generally speaking a demi-portée pointing throw and the intermediate au fer shot have a similar arc. The huge difference is the donnée. The demi-portée donnée is typically halfway to the jack and the au fer shot donnée is the target boule! The shot travels twice as far through the air which requires greater strength and endurance than demi-portée pointing. Since the target boule is usually near the jack the typical au fer range is the same as the jack distance. If the au fer shot is thrown with the same velocity, then height of the arc is proportional to the distance to the target. Longer shots require higher arcs because gravity is a constant force which accelerates all objects downward at the same rate.

Consider the tennis serve, one of the most biomechanically complex motions in sports. It has at least nine specific components that must be linked with impeccable timing into a single flowing kinetic chain. A player starts serving by employing a basic functional subset of components. When the current components are successfully integrated, then additional components are added. After several thousand practice serves the complete motion may be mastered. The goal is to start shooting with a functional subset of components and eventually evolve it into a complete motion.

> **The Kinetic Chain** is a sport performance term that describes the combination of nerves, muscles, soft tissue and skeleton that must be integrated to produce a complex motion.
>
> In the next chapter we'll learn about torso-torque, shoulder drop and release/follow-through biomechanics that dramatically increase the complexity of the ideal shooter's kinetic chain.

As presented in this chapter, the standard au fer shooting motion doesn't have the biomechanical complexity of the tennis serve. In fact it is considered a relatively simple motion. It's conceivable that a gifted athlete accomplished in another precision throwing sport (baseball pitcher, football quarterback or a disc golfer) could learn au fer shoot in a matter of hours. But for most of us it requires the process of starting simple and eventually evolving into the complete motion.

Pendulum: Putting the Boule's Mass to Work

The Pétanque throwing swing is a pendulum motion with the shoulder as the pivot point. As a heavy boule is elevated it gains substantial potential energy; the higher the backswing, the greater the potential energy that is released in the down and forward portion of the swing.

The boule position in the diagram indicates the release point of flat, aggressive shooters – slightly forward of the hip just as the swing starts to rise. The pendulum backswing has many variations:

Common Pendulum Modifications

- *The air rifle pump-up:* You may remember the old air rifle BB and pellet guns that were manually pumped multiple times to accumulate sufficient pressure for firing. Pointers with marginal hand or arm strength may make several consecutive back-and-forth pendulum swing motions. Each subsequent backswing achieves greater height until the boule has gained sufficient energy to supplement the power-challenged thrower. The energy accumulated from those multiple preparatory swings is released in the last down and forward motion as the boule is thrown.

- *Lock-and-Load:* At the other extreme, the backswing of many intermediate shooters is paused at apex. This provides a moment to control boule momentum before commencing the down and forward swing and release.

- *"Preloading" the backswing*: Aggressive shooters may preload the backswing. The photo shows the great left-handed shooter Pascal Milei of Equipe de France with his distinctive preloading motion. As a prelude to the backswing he raises the boule high above his head. The additional momentum gained allows his backswing to reach well above his shoulder, providing the forward swing with amazing fluid power as attested by his nearly flat and devastating au fer shots.

As the pendulum swings down and forward the boule's potential energy is transformed into kinetic energy which accelerates the swing with minimum muscle assist from the player. The downside to using the backswing to create easily accessible power is that the subsequent forward acceleration places tight timing constraints at the release point. Just a fraction of a second mistiming the release produces a clean miss. On the other hand, although low backswings don't create much energy, the lack of acceleration provides a much wider window in which to time the release.

- ✓ Higher backswings make the hand feel as if it is being "pushed" by heavy boule momentum all the way through the release
  - **The "pushing" sensation is smooth and nearly effortless**
- ✓ Lower backswings give the sensation that the player's hand must "pull" the heavy boule through the release
  - **Lack of momentum makes "pulling" the boule feels sluggish and jerky**
  - When someone remarks that you are "pulling" the boule they are indirectly suggesting that you take a higher backswing to gain momentum.

A fully laid-back (cocked) wrist with a brisk snapping release imparts rétro to increase carreau potential. There are four basic ways to simplify the critical timing components of au fer shooting:

1. *Make an abbreviated backswing*: this simplifies timing, but demands a higher arc
2. *Ground the lower body*: Simplify the motion by freezing body movement from the hips down. When your backswing height increases you will tend to fold forward at the waist, but you must strive to continue to minimize lower body movement – don't use your legs to power the shot!
3. *Forego Rétro*: To simplify the motion and timing requirements throw with flat, locked wrist.
4. *Don't try to shoot with power*: A 720g boule dropped from 2m has significant kinetic energy. (If you doubt that, drop a boule on your foot from head height!) Shoot with a lazy arc and let gravity deliver the *coup de grace*.

The Low-Trajectory Au Fer Shooter

If the high arced au fer shot is a mortar, then the aggressive, flat au fer shot is an RPG (rocket-propelled grenade). The boule is released at hip level, as specified in the pendulum diagram, with an arc that is often below head height. The low release flattens the arc and ensures maximum rétro. Because the trajectory is flat and low, the boule must be thrown with greater velocity. Although it doesn't take the raw physical strength of a high plombée, the extremely small tolerances require that a flat au fer shooter must have strong hands and forearms, and great shoulder health and flexibility to accommodate high backswings. This is especially important when playing all-day tournaments.

An important observation from the au fer shooting diagram is the shot's length of travel to the target boule. High arced shots follow a long, lazy trajectory. Since the shortest distance between two points is a straight line, the flat aggressive shot travels a much shorter distance. Somewhere between the high arc and the flat shot is your optimum path.

> **Au Fer Rules of Thumb:**
>
> 1. Higher backswings enable lower arcs
> 2. Lower arcs require a lower release point
> 3. A lower release point provides maximum rétro and transformation of swing momentum into boule velocity

Why Shoot Low-Trajectory Instead of a Gentle Arc?

Players often talk about the optimum impact angle to produce a carreau. It's true that throwing a carreau is great, (it's the home run of Pétanque) but you must master effective shooting before getting carreau obsessed. That means at least 2-out-3 shots at 8m should displace the target boule far enough that it is no longer a scoring threat or strategic consideration.

Shooting Arcs: Think Extremes

One of my favorite engineering professors started every analysis by saying, "Think Extremes!" He would consider the two most extreme possibilities and use those results to derive optimum system state. (It's a lot simpler than it sounds.) *In the following diagram, just like the Goldilocks saga, the first two examples depict extreme impact angles, while the third case is "just right."*

Case 1: The Ultimate Arc: What happens when a shot is thrown with such extreme arc that it descends vertically and strikes the very top of the target boule? Granted, it delivers quite a punch, but it's ineffective because the impact energy is directed straight down and absorbed mostly by the terrain. The target boule may end up with a flat spot (or at least quite a headache) but when the dust clears it will not have been displaced very far from its original position!

Case 2: The Flattest Shot: When a target boule is shot, it is displaced from its original position by rolling over the terrain. The ideal angle of impact for maximum horizontal displacement is 0°. Simply put, the greater the shot's horizontal force, the greater the target boule's displacement. That's one of the standard arguments in favor of palet roulant shooting. A rolling shot (that isn't bouncing along rough terrain) delivers its entire payload horizontally or at 0°. To put in contemporary terms, the palet roulant delivers "the most bang for the buck". But on the other hand, it rarely produces a carreau.

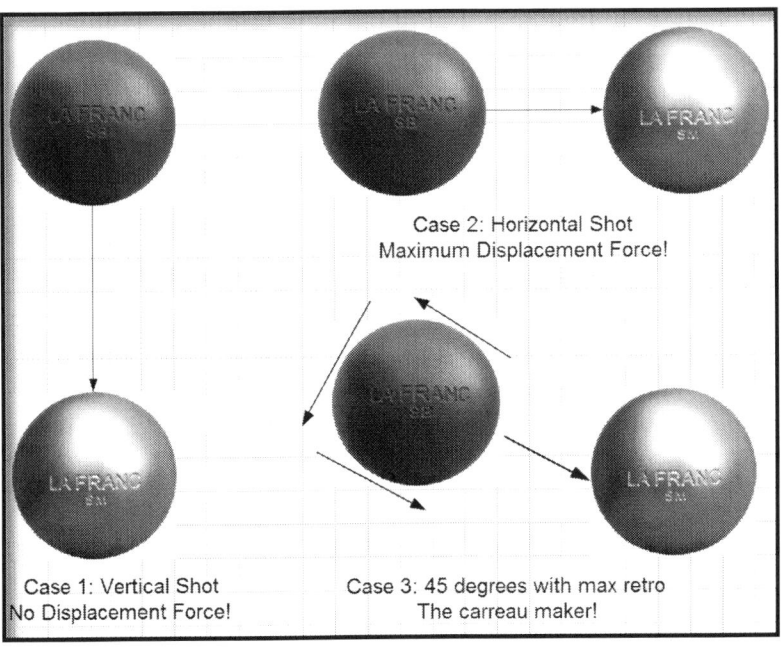

Case 2: Horizontal Shot
Maximum Displacement Force!

Case 1: Vertical Shot
No Displacement Force!

Case 3: 45 degrees with max retro
The carreau maker!

Case 3: The Carreau Maker: In Case-3 the shot is thrown with maximum rétro and strikes the target at 45°. Unlike the palet roulant, an au fer shot's impact is not diminished by rollout friction. It's no coincidence that 45° is halfway between the two extreme cases. This compromise produces the greatest number of carreaus because it leverages the target boule's mass (inertia of rest) and the terrain impact to arrest the forward momentum of the shooter's boule, while rétro wildly burrows into the terrain.

- A fairly soft surface with an accommodating layer of rock chips enables the shooter's boule to transfer the maximum amount of energy to the target boule and terrain, while rétro is digging a snug nest in which to settle.
- Top tier shooters throw with such extreme rétro that on hard terrains the shooter's boule may reverse directions and roll backwards! *I've seen a Pascal Milei shot which after striking the target boule rolled 3m backward toward the rond.*
- Shooters prefer softer boules because, in addition to the target boule and terrain, a soft shooter's boule also absorbs impact energy to arrest forward momentum and produce more carreaus. This concept is fully explored in *Chapter 5* on technical boule selection.

Practical Shooting Practice

The "Rolling Nudge"
When there's no strategic reason to shoot, a shooter points. It's axiomatic that pointing skills are a prerequisite to shooting. The rolling puck technique isn't constrained to smacking opponent's boules into the O.B. What I call the "rolling nudge" is invaluable in many situations:

- *Promoting Teammates*: depending on the target boule's distance to the jack and speed of the terrain, the impact of the rolling nudge ranges from gentle tap to a smart slap.
- *Pinball Pointing*: pointing to a congressed jack may require gently careening off teammate's and opponent's boule-devants.
- *Tadpole and Devant-de-Boule*: the distance that the pair must be separated and will scale the magnitude of the bump
- *Pushing the Jack*: Sometimes the jack is shot violently with the intention of bringing the end to an abrupt conclusion. Other times it is gently pushed backwards into the warm embrace of teammate's boules-derrière.

Learning Rolling Puck Shooting Technique
Begin rolling shot training on a flat smooth terrain with a true rollout. A baseball infield is great for rolling puck shooting pactice. Areas beyond the basepaths or outside of the foul lines tend to be smoother. Beware of subtle contours and breaks. Perform test throws to find a area with a reasonably straight rollout. As your expertise increases you can practice shooting on contoured and sloping areas. Finally, tackle a rougher gravel terrain and learn to shoot palet roulant while minimizing rollout bouncing.

Unlike a pointing throw the shooter's boule doesn't stop near the target, it blasts right through it. The rules of thumb for palet roulant shooting are:

> ### The Donnée is Critical!
>
> Ensure that the donnée lies directly between the rond and target. A shot landing to either side of the centerline will miss; landing in front or in back of the donnée should only affect impact force. A donnée which is too far from the target may not have knockout power; a shot whose donnée is too close to the target may bounce and only deliver a glancing blow, or even hop right over the target.
>
> **Farther données are more difficult to hit** – that's the difference between shooting palet roulant and au fer.

- Pick a donnée which is:
    1. Directly between the rond and target boule
    2. Smooth, flat and not too hard (to minimize rebound)
    3. Two to three meters from the target; adjusted for rollout friction and bounce
- If the rolling puck is thrown too fast, a small rock or other surface imperfection will propel it offline; thrown too slowly the rollout friction reduces knockout power to a love tap.
- Displacing the target boule by one or two meters is usually just as effective (although not as satisfying) as knocking it O.B.

Starting Au Fer shooting: The target is the donnée

Let's start from a pointer's perspective. Cardboard beer mats and disc golf marker mini-discs make great training données. Slip a few beer mats into your pocket during your next pub session. Disc golf marker mini-discs cost less than $2.00. They both have a diameter which is about 25% larger than a boule. Think of this as donnée practice. The fact that a boule is three-dimensional and the practice targets are flat isn't a concern. It's really an advantage because when you hit a flat donnée target it doesn't roll away and need to be repositioned. And you need not be concerned with angle of impact.

The position of the practice target represents the target boule. Standard practice and competition distances are 6.5m, 7.5m, 8.5m and 9.5m.

1. Place a target at 6.5m and prepare to throw a demi-portée with the target as a donnée.
2. Visualize the arc of the throw, the height of the apex and the descending flight as it lands on the target.
3. *Don't think Power!* Unlike the palet roulant, the force of an au fer shot is not diminished by rollout.
4. In this simple drill don't be concerned with the shot's angle of descent. You'll shoot target boules to fine tune impact angle and that's many hundred practice throws down the road.
5. *The target is the donnée*. Stare it, imagine that your eyes are lasers and burn a hole through it! Block everything else from your vision. For this moment the universe is you, your boule and the target.
6. Athletes usually exhale during the most exerting part of a motion. Tune into the rhythm of your breathing. *Holding your breath is a sure way to create tension*.
   - When you are ready to throw, exhale and blow the air from your lungs.
   - Inhale as you start a smooth controlled backswing.
   - When the backswing is at apex, pause for a fraction of a second, and then as you start to exhale initiate the forward pendulum and release.
7. Only watch the boule's flight through your peripheral vision. You vision should continue to be locked on the target until impact. Since you are au fer shooting the rollout can be ignored.

Carreau Impact Angle Practice

There are many props which can be used to hone the au fer shooting impact angle. Pétanque New Zealand has a tutorial called *"Shooting for Dummies"* which can be downloaded from http://www.petanquenz.com.

Among several props they employ is an old car tire (tyre in British spelling). They contend that shooting with the ideal trajectory allows the boule to just clear the front of the tire and then strike the inside back of the tire with the boule coming to rest inside the bead; if the shot is too flat, it hits the front of tire and bounces back at the shooter; too arced and it hits inside of the tire, but doesn't come to rest inside the bead.

> *Yes, Pétanque Federations in other English speaking countries provide and encourage training – imagine that!* In fact the U.K., Australia and New Zealand all stress training as a critical component of Pétanque success and enjoyment.
>
> **The U.S. Pétanque Federation (FPUSA) is the only slacker amongst English speaking countries.**

I used a tire for a couple of weeks and it was interesting. An immediate aggravation was that the tire left ugly black scuff marks on my silver shooting boules. But the biggest problem is that a car tire is not portable. Playing Pétanque in non-dedicated, public spaces requires simplicity. We encourage players to walk, bike or take mass transit. Our philosophy is that everything you need for a couple hours of play should fit into a daypack or a set of bicycle panniers.

Soft plastic disc cones typically used in tennis and soccer are as effective as a tire for au fer shooting practice and may also be used for other pointing and donnée drills. They are cheap, light, portable and indestructible. A set of 25 cones is less than $15 at Amazon.com. The typical sport disc cone has an 18cm wide base and 5cm height. ***Also see the end of Chapter 4 for a drill that uses the disc cone to simulate a bull's-eye for another au fer shooting drill***. In this example disc cones are used in two modes:

Mini-Tire Mode: As illustrated in the photo on the right, the cone's narrow end is on the terrain and the target boule is set inside. The shot's trajectory must arc over the lip and strike the target at approximately 45°. Short shots hit the base of the cone; the shot's energy is dispersed and the target boule doesn't wallow very far.

Golf Tee Mode: When an au fer shooter shoots short, whether just to be safe or because he's tightened-up, it's called "tirer a cinquante devant" or to shoot 50cm in front of the target to "slide" into it. The rationalization is that at least a short shot has a chance of rolling into the target, but an overthrow is always a miss. Depending on the terrain and the shooter's boules, (covered in *Chapter 5*) a short shot is just as likely to rebound and leap over the target or to just nip it on the top with a glancing blow known as a casquette or "capping the target."

As pictured on the left, use the disc cone like a golf tee to help a shooter overcome the fear of overthrowing the target. Place the cone with the large end down and set the target boule on top. It's now teed up 5cm above the terrain and ready to be driven. A low shot strikes the cone's base and the target boule is not displaced very far; when the target is struck au fer, it is driven far away and the cone barely moves.

Chapter 4: Throwing Mechanics

Deconstructing Complex Motions

Major league baseball pitchers have complex motions. But most fast ball pitchers employ the same general delivery, differing only in details which exploit their specific body proportions and capabilities. There's no denying the significant difference in capabilities between amateur and professional athletes. As was described in the last chapter, few amateur tennis players can emulate the entire complex kinetic chain of the professional service motion.

> Deconstructing a complex motion into essential components enables one to start simple and evolve to complex. But if you're having a great time, you can keep it simple!
>
> *Pétanque can be all things to all people.* It's up to you to determine the time and effort you're willing to invest.

When an opponent is serving well an old tennis strategy is to complement him during a break and ask if he would describe his motion. Conceivably once he describes the individual service motion components his serve will fall apart, because he's thinking about serving instead of just serving. *As O.J. Simpson said (in pre-felony days) when asked what he thought about after he had broken free and was running for a touchdown, "Thinking is what gets you caught from behind."*

Many Pétanque players feel that analyzing throwing motions is too much thinking and not enough doing. I contend that understanding the underlying process shortcuts hundreds of hours of ineffective trial-and-error practice. When you know the individual components integrating them into an immutable kinetic chain is a matter of starting simple and evolving to complex. During shooting practice the other day someone said to me, *"Practice makes perfect"* and I responded, *"No, perfect practice, makes perfect."* Repetition doesn't discriminate. Bad technique is just as easily programmed into muscle memory. *With the exception of aggressive low trajectory shooters employing complex torso torque, Pétanque's modest demands allow the enthusiastic physically-fit amateur to emulate professional style and techniques*.

I learned more about Pétanque mechanics one Sunday afternoon in Paris watching a sectional-level competition than I had watching several days of regional and national-level U.S. tournaments. *Most American club play is social; less attention is devoted to technique and strategy than the potluck dinner and trophy presentation.* The majority of U.S. players pursue Pétanque as a leisure time, social activity rather than a skills based sport. If your goal is to become an accomplished player, forget about the après tournament barbeque and dedicate yourself to quality, repetitive practice and emulating the style and intensity of the pros.

> A novice with competitive ambitions impairs his development by imitating the mediocre techniques displayed on most U.S. terrains.

YouTube has hundreds of short, low-resolution Pétanque videos. Although not ideal you will see a variety of techniques, from casual club play to masters' level. To prepare for this chapter I analyzed dozens of hours of high-resolution world class play from the past ten years. *Pétanque America* stocks the annual *Masters of Pétanque* series DVDs. The commentary is in French and the DVDs require a Region 2, PAL-capable DVD player (although they do play on all computers). I suggest that you purchase at least one set of DVDs and watch them many, many times. Be fully engaged. Use slow motion and freeze frame. Draw general conclusions about pointing and shooting motions and compare your observations to what's presented in this chapter. Learn the pro's strategy and then scale it to your current capabilities. Discover how shooters dominate high-level play; how pointers often purposefully throw mediocre points to lay the groundwork for a follow-up shot that results in multiple points on the ground. ***Pétanque strategy is based on a complete end, not just a myopic craving to hold the point!*** Like chess players, a Pétanque team thinks several throws ahead.

There are four major exceptions why physically fit amateurs may have a difficult time emulating professional techniques.

- *Pointing from the squat*: Knee, hip, back or balance issues may make squat pointing impractical.
- *Plombées*: Limited hand, wrist or forearm strength, range of motion limitations or rotator cuff injuries make extreme trajectory plombée pointing difficult.
- *Pelvis/hip clearance*: People with a low shoulder to hip-width proportions (usually women) are not able to directly face the jack or target boule. This issue is addressed in a few pages.
- *Torso torque and shoulder flexibility*: low trajectory, aggressive shooters place demands on their cores and rotator cuffs that may exceed the capabilities of most middle-aged athletes.

> **For the serious athlete Pétanque is an astounding opportunity!**
>
> Measured on an International scale U.S. expertise is so low that after a couple of hundred hours on the terrain an intense athlete can compete at the regional and national level. No other sport has such a fast track to the top!

Other than dropping into the pointing squat, most Pétanque mechanics and postures are easily customized and simplified to complement the physicality of casual athletes.

Anything Goes When You Throw

FIPJP Rules don't limit the throwing motion or how a boule must be held. Other than grounded feet and not employing any other body part for support, anything goes; a boule can be thrown underhanded bocce-style, shot off the fingertips like a basketball, tossed overhand like a baseball or flipped sidearm like a flying disc. *All of these methods are perfectly legal and equally ineffective*. The aspiring pointer quickly learns that rétro is the key to controlling boule rollout. The only effective way to generate rétro is with Pétanque's distinctive backhanded, palm-down with knuckles-up grip. Several times I introduced bocce players to Pétanque and they insisted on rolling the boule with a conventional bowler's underhanded, palm-up with knuckles-down grip. After a few frustrating games they saw the light and yielded to the conventional backhand grip.

Because of run-up, ball size and weight, and the dubious extravagance of groomed courts other bowls games are ground-based. Within a meter or two of release the bowl hits the playing surface and rolls almost the entire distance to the target. As we saw in the last chapter, competitive Pétanque is aerial; skilled players free themselves of ungroomed, irregular, rocky and sloping terrains. Pointers throw plombées that travel over 80% of the distance to the jack through the air. Shooters throw au fer, striking the target boule on iron without touching the terrain. Taking to the air imposes precise technique.

Boules and Hand Size Issues

Chapter 5 is a comprehensive technical analysis of boule selection. For the sake of throwing techniques we must consider the important issue of boule size limitations. The *FIPJP* competition boules size specification (70.5mm to 80mm) is based on the average Frenchman's hand size with absolutely no consideration to women. (Are you surprised?) As a result, the majority of women throw boules which are too large. Because the palm is facing down, *Pétanque's backhanded grip makes it difficult to throw oversized boules.*

Most people start playing with 73mm, 720g generic boules. The novice assumes that only the most effete Pétanque connoisseur could detect a minuscule 2.5mm increase in diameter from the minimum size. *But you must remember that the hand wraps around the circumference of the boule not through its diameter! A 2.5mm larger diameter increases boule circumference by almost 8mm!*

I've seen many players compensate for throwing oversized boules by unconsciously pulling their fingers apart, essentially increasing their hand width. That often produces inconsistent throws because the fingers must be kept together and perfectly straight to ensure that sidespin is not accidently imparted at release. Even after you have purchased properly sized boules you'll still be introducing novices to Pétanque with loaner sets of generic 73mm boules. It's important to learn how to mitigate the problems and frustrations of throwing oversized boules by learning variations of grip, backswing and release as presented in this chapter.

> **In Tennis 1/8" is Critical!**
> Racket grip size is the circumference of the handle measured in inches. Grip sizes are available in 1/8" increments and that is significant to a serious tennis player.
>
> In terms of a boule, 1/8" of circumference is equivalent to 1mm of diameter! That means 1mm difference in boule diameter should also be significant to a serious Pétanque player.

Grip, Ready Position, Backswing, Release and Rétro

After distilling the techniques of champions, I spent several months fine-tuning the concepts by instructing over 75 novices (ranging from world-class athletes to couch potatoes) how to throw Pétanque. This section defines a good starting place. Only through hours of repetition and experimentation does a player develop the individualized mechanics to complement their physical capabilities and playing style. Consider the basic novice ready position:

> Standard techniques achieve that status because they are effective for the majority of players. If you find yourself straying far afield and developing bizarre throwing habits perhaps you are indulging your ego at the expense of pursuing effective technique.

- Player squarely faces the jack
- Feet are only just wide enough to create a stable base
- Knees are slightly flexed
- Body may be erect or bent slightly forward at the waist. *The exception is roulette pointers who often bend far enough forward to touch their toes in an attempt to reduce rebound.*
- The boule is held out in front between mid-torso and shoulder height

Sighting Methods and Focus

Although optional, some find that sighting methods encourage swing alignment and enhance intensity. Often players look over the top of the boule like a gun sight. A more arcane method crosses the non-throwing hand over the boule as triangulation device. "Doing the Lisa", a Palm Springs Pétanque original, employs the boule hand's raised thumb as a popup sight —scowling is optional.

Pointer Focus	Shooter Focus
The jack is not a bull's-eye! Focus on the intended donnée and don't let the gaze waiver until after the boule hits the terrain and starts to rollout. Knowing precisely how close the boule came to hitting the intended donnée is critical to determine how to modify the next throw.	The shooter creates a precise bull's-eye by imagining a spot in the middle of the target boule and then stares at it – blocking out all other sensory input. Focus doesn't shift until the shot is complete. This enables the shooter to modify the next shot as needed.

Ready Positions

Always take a moment in the ready position to allow the boule to settle comfortably into your hand and to visualize the throw and its desired intended results.

Another important function of the ready position is to gain potential energy for the backswing. The higher the boule is held in front, the more momentum it provides the backswing. Aggressive, low trajectory shooters use high backswings. But most pointers, even when throwing demanding plombées, employ an abbreviated backswing that doesn't require a high pendulum assist.

Palm-Up Ready Position

Many novices find palm-up to be the most comfortable and least physically demanding ready position. *It's especially appealing to players with oversized boules and those lacking in grip and forearm strength.* Its major drawback is during the backswing the boule must rotate 180° into the palm-down throwing position. The center of the boule nestles comfortably where the fingers meet the palm. Just before starting the backswing

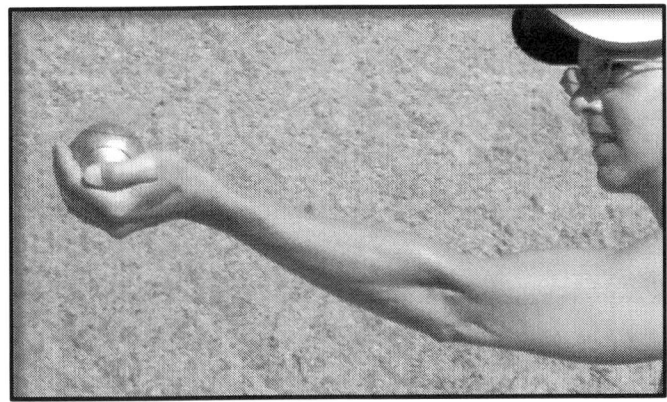

the boule is gripped only tight enough to secure it as the hand rotates. The boule then rests in the hand cradle with a minimum grip. Squeezing too hard produces forearm fatigue, release hang-ups and a curving rollout induced by sidespin.

Palm-Down Ready Position

The palm-down ready position simplifies the backswing. The arm simply pendulums straight back and need not be rotated. It is preferred by many intermediate shooters due to its simplicity and clean release. The key is to squeeze just tight enough to control the boule momentum generated during the pendulum swing.

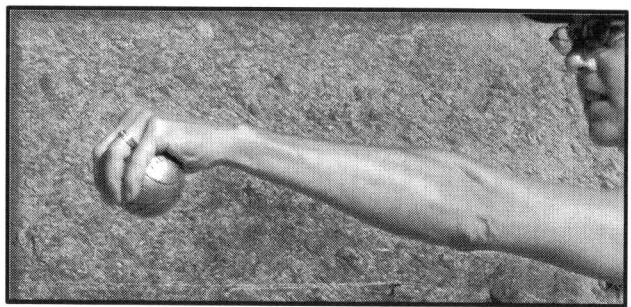

- *Beware of the thumb*: Other than advanced pointers employing it to impart sidespin to produce a curving rollout, the thumb should **only incidentally touch the boule**. To ensure a clean release and true rollout many players get the thumb out of the way by tucking it beside the second knuckle of the index finger.

- *Oversized Boules Again*: **Players throwing oversized boules often have chronic sidespin and release hang-ups due to thumb grip friction at release**. Until you acquire smaller boules, consider employing the palm up ready position which produces less thumb induced sidespin.

- In general terms the hand should wrap at least halfway around the boule. Even though she is throwing 71mm boules (only ½ mm larger than minimum) Kathi's hand barely wraps halfway around the boule. She can't grow bigger hands and the *FIPJP* won't reduce boule size specifications to accommodate women, so *she compensates with great hand strength and impeccable technique – which is a poetic metaphor for most women's issues.*

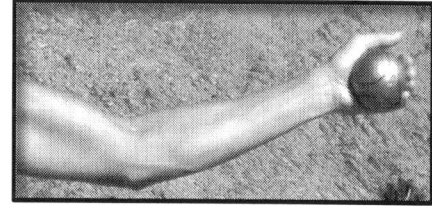

Palm-Vertical Ready Position

Holding the boule in a vertical palm with the thumb up is a favored ready position of several current great French squat

pointers. *It requires minimal effort and gravity tucks the boule into the palm safely away from the thumb.*

The transition to the backhanded grip is a simple 45° (quarter-turn) inward wrist rotation to initiate the backswing. The forearm may stay nearly parallel to the ground. Squat pointers tend to hold it close to the body with the elbow tucked near the hip. Standing pointers may extend their arm and "Do the Lisa" using the thumb as a pop-up sight.

The Crane Ready Position

The crane is a variation of the palm-vertical ready position favored by Southeast Asian players, especially the Thais. It's great for pointing, but rarely used for shooting. If flexed too tightly the crane places a significant load on the forearm flexor muscles. In the other ready positions the wrist is laid-back (cocked or flexed toward the forearm) during the backswing.

The crane ready position starts with a fully loaded wrist reminiscent of Kung Fu's Crane Beak Strike. The forearm is tilted up just high

enough so that the boule hangs vertically when the wrist is flexed.

Squat pointers may bring the top of the boule hand just underneath their chin. The crane provides simple backswing mechanics and timing, and is ideal for generating rétro.

Compensating for Wide Hips

The following procedure determines if your stance should be rotated to compensate for wide hips or for players that prefer an extra-wide stance:

1. Face the jack and stand at attention with your feet together and your chest pointing directly at the jack.
2. Move your feet just wide enough apart to create a stable throwing platform.
3. Hold a boule in the palm-down ready position.
4. Lower the boule let your throwing arm hang vertically next to your hip. Your arm must be straight and perfectly vertical.
5. Keep your arm perfectly straight. Swing the boule front-to-back with a smooth and easy pendulum motion.

> The most effective way to throw from a standing stance is to face the jack or target boule squarely.
>
> A more precise description is that your navel should be pointing at your eventual target be it the jack, a specific area on the terrain or, when shooting au fer, the target boule.

If your shoulders are significantly wider than your hips, the boule will pendulum front-to-back with a straight and vertical arm without hitting your hip.

Women tend to have wider hips in proportion to their shoulders than men. (Don't blame me, have a talk with Mr. Darwin.) Players with wider hips unconsciously move their arm out from the side of the body to create clearance. This produces a looping swing in which the throwing arm and pendulum motion are no longer perpendicular to the ground. Looping swings are much more difficult to throw with consistency.

> If you don't have wide hips, but still have a boule clearance problem, then your feet may be too far apart. A wide stance produces the same issues as wide hips. Try a more compact stance in which you still feel strong and stable.

To provide additional clearance for the boule to pass by the hip the body may be rotated slightly away from the throwing hand.

1. Squarely face the jack with your feet in a narrow, yet stable stance.
2. Imagine that you are standing on a turn-table or for the more domestic, a Lazy Susan.

> You lose power as your body rotates away from squarely facing the jack or target; rotate only the minimum distance to attain hip clearance.

3. Rotate your feet and body **slightly away from the direction of your throwing hand**. *Right-handers rotate left; left-handers rotate right.*
4. For a right-handed thrower, rotating to the left causes the left foot to fall slightly behind the right foot.
5. Repeat the hip clearance test until you have calibrated your throwing stance

Once you are convinced that this position works for you, memorize it and always try to assume an identical stance every time you throw.

Squat Point Like the Pros

A golfer preparing to putt gets down on hands-and-knees to "read the green". Getting down helps one discover the slopes and contours between the ball and cup. Depending on the terrain's complexity and the type of throw "reading the dirt and gravel" may be essential to an accurate pointing throw. Even on a relatively tame terrain, donnée selection is critical.

When you are playing on a new or challenging terrain there are two ways to discover imperfections between the rond and jack that may affect boule impact and rollout:

1. *Watch other players point*: Stand by the jack and concentrate on the boule as it is released. Follow the arc and carefully watch impact, rebound and rollout. On complex terrains the privilege of tossing the jack and throwing the first boule is not necessarily an advantage. With the exception watching jack rollout, the first pointer throws cold. The other players use the first, and subsequent throws to map the terrain. If after several boules have been thrown and every boule is away from the jack in the same direction (short, long or off to one side), then the players aren't paying attention and modifying their throws!

2. If you are the first pointer or are using a different donnée area than previous throws, you must make a **careful examination of the terrain between your intended donnée and the jack**. The length of terrain that needs to be inspected is determined by the type of throw. A plombée pointer may be looking at less than 1m of terrain, whereas a roulette pointer has a lot dirt and gravel to scrutinize.

In the beginning I asked many squat pointers to explain their choice of stance. The standard reply (after much interpretation and amplification) implied that squatting provides a more revealing view of contours, obstacles and desirable données. But that doesn't make sense because one can squat to examine the terrain and then stand to throw. In fact, even on smooth and level terrains most squat pointers continue to point from the squat!

The prerequisite to precise and consistent pointing is controlled rebound and true rollout. All things equal while in the squat the pointer's release is only about half the height of a standing release. *Thus the squat pointer's arc is lower, rebounds less and has a truer rollout.*

Although I have seen a few players shoot from the squat at short targets, my suggestion is don't bother. Shooting is predicated on ensuring that every shot, regardless of distance, uses an identical motion. It's true that some players find shooting short targets more difficult than mid-range targets, but to maintain consistency and precision you should strive to develop and employ one shooting motion for all distances and situations.

Depending on terrain speed and throw selection, pointing from a squat beyond 8m demands superior strength, balance and technique. Unlike our cousins in the Far East where sitting on one's haunches is a way of life, Americans rarely have reason to squat. Many Americans have back, knee, hamstring or blood pressure issues that make squatting uncomfortable, unstable or dangerous.

The Squat Pointer's Stance

When I started playing Pétanque I asked accomplished club-level pointers the two obvious questions: "Why squat" and "What's the most effective squatting stance." Nobody seemed to have a clue. For all I knew one should emulate an American baseball catcher sans mask and padding. How wrong I was!

 I found the answers in France where I observed and interviewed several accomplished squat pointers. Bribed and lubricated with cold Kronenbourgs (France's most popular beer, forget about Ricard pastis Pétanque's traditional beverage) I verified that their explanations were consistent with the many hours of DVD analysis that I had performed.

FIPJP rules specify that only the feet and no other part of the body (e.g. knee or hand) may be used to support the player during the throw. Instead of a hip issue, when throwing from the squat the throwing hand must clear the fully flexed thighs. Most of us can't squat like a baseball catcher and still have a free flowing pendulum swing. There are many ways to modify the basic stance, but several factors are common to all accomplished squat pointers.

Keep in mind that the Kathi (on the right) is throwing left-handed, Thai-style with the crane ready position. If you want a right-handed reference see the two photos on the previous page.

Knee and Thigh Rotation

- The knee on the throwing side points directly to the jack or is slightly rotated inward to provide thigh swing clearance
- The throwing side thigh is nearly parallel to the ground
- Although it is possible for especially lean squat players to keep their thighs parallel, most players rotate the off-knee as far as 45° away from the jack (as illustrated in all three squat pointing photos.)
- To provide stability during the moderate backswing and release, especially when throwing plombées, the off-side knee often point downward (as illustrated in two of the squat stance photos.)
- To ease the backswing and promote torso torque *the throwing side shoulder drops several inches below the non-throwing side shoulder, either before or during the backswing.*
- The shoulder is often dropped so far that the throwing hand and boule only have a few centimeters of ground clearance.
- **The key for me is hooking the heels which provide additional stability and power.**

Squat pointing requires more creative compensations than any other throwing posture.

The Backswing and the Non-Throwing Arm

One of the most important aspects of the backswing is what to do with the non-throwing arm. Unfortunately most club players let it dangle by the side of the hip, leaving the throwing arm to do all of the work. *There's no dangling with accomplished players, their non-throwing arm is equally involved.* Try this experiment to understand why pointing and shooting is easier, more accurate and more consistent when both arms are active:

1. Stand in your normal pointing or shooting stance
2. Let your non-throwing arm hang limply by the side of your hip, but don't hold it in place when you swing. Let to go wherever your body wants to take it.
3. Hold a boule in your normal ready position and perform several aggressive forward-and-backward pendulum swings.
4. Pay attention to any sensations or resistance on the non-throwing side of your body.

- ☠ Most people notice that during the backswing the throwing shoulder slightly rises and the non-throwing side shoulder dips proportionally (which is the opposite of what we want!)
- ☠ During the backswing the non-throwing shoulder and arm torques (twists) forward and toward the center of the body. During the forward swing they twist back to dangle near the hip. *The non-throwing shoulder and arm are dead weight, opposing power and fluidity!*

Power and accuracy are compromised when the non-throwing side is either passive or, even worse, actively opposing the throwing side. Try the following experiment to see what it feels like when your body works in harmony. **You'll need two boules, one for each hand**.

1. Stand in your normal throwing stance
2. Hold a boule in each hand
3. Hold both boules out in front in your preferred ready position.
4. Imagine that you are throwing both boules simultaneously.
5. **Synchronize your arms and simultaneously** perform several aggressive pendulum swings. During the backswing your body will tend to bend forward at the waist. Don't fight it, that's an important component of the swing!
6. Maintain symmetry with both shoulders facing forward.

The effort to achieve a high backswing should be significantly reduced. Your swing should have more power with less effort. Instead of opposing the throwing motion, the non-throwing side is now a partner; **it's what new-age gurus call "a mutually advantageous conjunction of distinct elements", in a word, synergy!**

There's just one more aspect to get the full benefit of firing on both cylinders (i.e. taking a two arm backswing.) *This little experiment is advanced technique and requires healthy shoulders.* **Repeat the previous sequence, but this time purposefully drop your throwing shoulder during the backswing and let your non-throwing shoulder rise and non-throwing arm loop out to the side as demonstrated by the right-handed squat pointer in the photo.** It's a lot easier to do standing than squatting.

Hopefully you experienced a sense of additional power centered in your core (abdominal muscles). Dropping the throwing shoulder, and letting the non-throwing arm loop away from the body coils your abdominals like a twisted spring in a technique called "torso torque." When the pendulum swing starts forward the uncoiling action provides an effortless and fluid power boost. Torso torque is an advanced technique of which most club players are blissfully unaware.

> For those with a fully functional rotator cuff and core, torso torque is the most subtle component to integrate into the throwing mechanics of your kinetic chain.

> **For the Novice**
> Don't be overly concerned with shoulder drop and torso toque issues. **But do synchronize the backswing motion of both arms**; always imagine that you are simultaneously throwing two boules – one from each hand. You'll gain power, consistency, and endurance and be less susceptible to injury.

In the next few pages we consider how torso torque is generated and applied to plombée squat pointing and low-trajectory shooting. You need to accumulate many hours of hard work on the dirt and gravel before harnessing this complex beast. However, you now have a glimmer that throwing a boule is a bit more subtle than *winding up and letting it rip*, which is the modus operandi of the recreation player. Layers of complexity can't be understood and integrated into your kinetic chain without dissembling the throwing motion into quantum components. Evolve your game from simple to complex; it's worked on Earth for 4.5 billion years, why stop now? (**That one was for you Professor. Dawkins!**)

As described in *Chapter 2*, for reasons of etiquette and safety players hold their unthrown boules in their off-hand. When playing doublettes your non-throwing hand may be holding two, one or no boules. Be aware of the load and modify your off-hand effort accordingly.

The stance of players that rotate to gain hip clearance (or simply as a preference) is already slightly torqued. Let your non-throwing arm find the appropriate backswing height and direction to create symmetry, stability and balance. Don't force the issue, experiment and you'll know when it's right. This is especially true for squat pointers.

Squat Bounce Power Assist

"Squat bouncing" takes strong thighs, solid knees and good balance. It may increase plombée range 1m to 1.5m. The squat bounce technique is intutive, much easier to learn than torso torque.

- Just before the start of the backswing lift a few inches out of your regular squat stance.
- At the start of the forward swing, drop down at and bounce up like a shock absorber. For maximum power the apex of the bounce should coincide with the boule's release.
- Most players drop back down into the full squat, but you may continue to rise into a standing stance.
- You can't lean on the ground for balance and the feet must stay grounded until the boule hits the terrain.

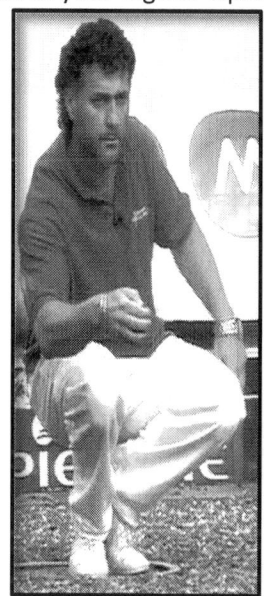

In the first photo on the right the great Zvonko Radnic is in a squat stance with a palm-vertical ready position. It's obvious that he's preparing for a long throw because he's sitting up in the squat with the thighs parallel to the ground. The photo on the far right shows as he starts his backswing he also rises several inches up to build up potential energy. **To initiate the forward swing Zvonko will drop down and bounce up, synchronizing the apex of the bounce with the boule's release.**

Torso Torque Revisited

Baseball, tennis, golf (especially disc golf) and sea kayakers employ shoulder and core rotation to generate power. Picture a baseball batter or a tennis player hitting a serve. During the backswing the shoulders rotate and the core coils. Initiating the swing the body uncoils, unleashing rotational energy from the core.

We've touched on torso torque as a function of lowering the throwing shoulder and rotating the non-throwing shoulder up and backwards. Most players drop the throwing shoulder before the backswing starts as indicated in the photo. ***During the forward swing the non-throwing shoulder continues to pull back and up, as if trying to touch the ear.*** This subtle movement is part of the follow-through and maximizes torque induced power.

Other than playing in France for a couple of weeks, this technique is best learned by watching hours of high-quality Masters level videos. Look for off-shoulder rotation during the backswing and how torque is converted to power by uncoiling the core while the off-shoulder continues up and back.

Low-Trajectory Shooting and Torque Generation

One of the goals of this book is to shed Pétanque's image as a static leisure-time activity whose exclusive domain is the aged, obese and infirm. We must encourage fit, accomplished athletes to play Pétanque as a supplement to their otherwise physically demanding sports. *It provides the elite athlete with the unique experience to be humbled by an opponent who is twice their age, half their height or maybe both.* Pétanque's readily accessible and elegant blend of strategy and teamwork is found in few sports. To that end this section analyzes the complex biomechanics of aggressive, flat-trajectory shooters as exemplified by the new generation of slim and well-conditioned European and Southeast Asian players. This section is for serious athletes who are driven to understand the biomechanics of the aggressive, low-trajectory shooter.

High backswings and torso torque challenge the balance of even the most stable squat pointer. The amazing backswings and aggressive torque employed by low-trajectory shooters are constrained only by shoulder flexibility and core strength. *The first photo on the right shows the full backswing of a right-handed shooter on the France Team.*

Throwing arm

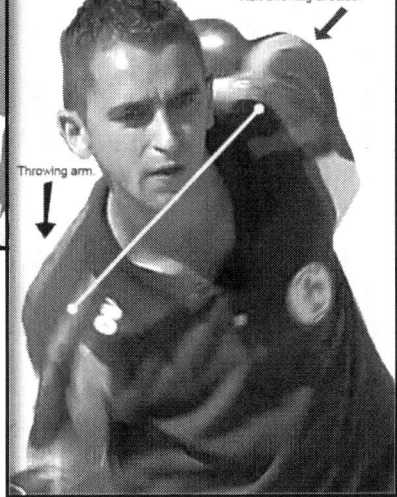

Non throwing shoulder

Throwing arm.

The backswing is so high and torque extreme that the throwing hand is hidden behind his head. As we've discussed, the non-throwing arm and shoulder almost mirror the throwing side. The major difference is that *the left arm is looped away from the body to provide balance and leverage*. It's important to note that although the shooter is bent at the waist, *at the apex of the backswing both shoulders are nearly horizontal.*

The photo on the right shows the instant that the boule is released. Aggressive, flat trajectory shooters have a hip level release. Examined without context, the second photo appears to be a left-handed shooter in full backswing! Now that you understand torso torque it's obvious that the second photo shows the release of a right-handed shooter because of the shoulder positions. The critical points to key on are: *The throwing side shoulder is low. The non-throwing side shoulder is high and pulled back, and no longer looped away from the body!*

The torque sequence starts with the high backswing coiling the body. The rotational energy is released with the synchronized movements of the throwing hand and shoulder coming forward and low, while the non-throwing shoulder continues to pull up and back; squeezing every bit of rotation energy from the player's core. It's fairly easy to explain and visualize, but extremely difficult to execute.

On the right is Pascal Milei the intense Team France *left-handed shooter* with the distinctive preloading motion. Here he is captured at the apex of the backswing. ***Notice how the non-throwing arm is in full back-swing and slightly looped from the body for balance and leverage***.

1. At full backswing both shoulders are parallel to the ground
2. As the left hand starts forward the left shoulder drops
3. The right shoulder stays high and moves backwards toward the right ear
4. The shoulder movement pulls the right arm from the looping position back in line with the body.
5. The reverse torquing action continues until the boule is released and the follow-through is complete.

In all sports torso torque is generated in the core by six sets of abdominal muscles. The arms and shoulders are simply the levers that assist the player in winding up the core. Who says it doesn't help to be in shape to play Pétanque? It's time to treat Pétanque like a sport and work on your six-pack, and I don't mean the one brewed from malts and hops.

The Standing Pointer's Backswing

With the exception of the palm-down ready position the hand must rotate into a backhand grip and the wrist flexed to provide a boule cradle. There's no need for a tight grip, lightly cupping the boule keeps it secure during the entire swing. Like the ready position, the pointer's backswing is a matter of personal preference. It's also a function of the player's strength, flexibility and whether the throw is made standing or squatting. The backswing is the most variable component of pointing throws. For most players longer throws require proportionally longer backswings. Standard considerations that affect the pointer's backswing are terrain speed, jack and donnée distance and arc height.

As described in the last chapter there are at least three major variations of the conventional single, smooth and continuous backswing.

- Some roulette pointers do an "air rifle pump-up." They pendulum swing the boule several times ratcheting up height and boule momentum.
- Intermediate shooters and pointers may "lock-and-load" pausing the backswing at its apex
- "Preloading" raises the boule high above the head before starting the backswing.

Different heights, strengths, body proportions, flexibility and throw selection produce distinctive backswings. It takes hundreds of throws and a lot of tweaking to discover the backswing that fits a specific body type and playing style.

The Moderate-Trajectory Shooter's Backswing

We have examined quite a bit about the flat trajectory shooter's extreme backswing and torque generation. But the backswings of most moderate to high-trajectory au fer shooters are barely higher than their pointing backswings. They often take the philosophy that we examined in the last chapter; they think of the target boule as the donnée of a long pointing throw.

To simplify the backswing some shooters prefer the palm-down ready position. To ensure that the entire pendulum swing stays perpendicular to the body many shooters purposefully brush their hip with the boule during the backswing as a means to keep their elbow in tight and throwing arm in a direct line with the target boule.

> Aggressive, low trajectory shots must be thrown at a high velocity. The only way to generate speed and maintain accuracy is with a high backswing and body torque.

Imagine a Masters level triplettes competition in which the shooter and milieu are out of boules, and the pointer is pressed into service to shoot. At that level, all pointers are also competent shooters, but they're not dedicated shooters. It's obvious when a pointer is called on to shoot. Their abbreviated backswing is typically half the height of the dedicated shooter. The boule travels a higher trajectory and takes quite a bit longer to reach the target.

In the photo below Kathi demonstrates the mechanics of *a moderate trajectory au fer shot, employing minimal torso torque*. The backswing is full, but not extreme; the non-throwing arm is a little lower and looped-out for stability. The throwing shoulder is just slightly higher than the non-throwing side. After release, the throwing arm points straight ahead and the non-throwing arm and shoulder stays back, but does not rotate up and toward the ear to generate counter-torque. This is the simple, clean nearly effortless motion preferred by all, but the most aggressive, flat trajectory shooters.

The extreme torque employed by aggressive shooters may cause the throwing-side shoulder and arm to follow-through and twist toward the center of the body, producing a distinctive finish in which the throwing hand points across the body, instead of straight head. This is an effect which is produced by the non-throwing shoulder counter-rotating back and up; *it should not be a conscious movement! When a player purposefully whips his hand across the center of the body, he is confusing cause-and-effect!* As depicted in the photo, the moderately aggressive shooter finishes with the fingertips of the throwing hand pointing straight ahead, either directly at the target boule or following the arc of the shot.

Pendulum Pushing and the Short Backswing

With the exception of the "air rifle pump-up" of some roulette pointers, the majority of U.S. club players employ the simplest possible short backswing that stops just behind the hip. The flexed wrist is a secure boule cradle and controlled snap generates variable rétro. Strong standing pointers may choose to use the abbreviated backswing even for long throws.

> Squat pointing high plombées beyond 8m may require a higher backswing amplified by squat bounce assist or body torque.

As described in the last chapter, the backswing should provide enough momentum for the boule to "push" the player's hand through the release. A short backswing may feel sluggish and jerky because the player "pulls" the boule, overloading his forearm flexors. ***Try this experiment to experience boule "push":***

1. Hold a boule in your throwing hand
2. Bend slightly forward at the waist and make a high backswing and hold it (lock-and-load technique)
3. Ensure that the boule is secured in the hand cradle with a minimal grip and then completely relax your shoulder and arm muscles
4. Keeping your arm passive, let the boule drop
5. It should "push" you hand through the forward pendulum swing
6. Powered only by momentum the forward swing is almost as high as the backswing.

Pulling the boule is not always bad as the next section on flick pointing demonstrates. However when your throws feel forced and you experience a jerky "pulling" sensation with a sticky release, elevate your backswing until the boule has sufficient momentum to "push" your hand through the entire swing.

"The Flick-Skim"– No Choke Pointing

I've noticed that many novices habitually throw long, well beyond the jack. No matter how much I encouragingly murmur "boule-devant, boule-devant!" they continue to chuck it long. I find this spectacularly frustrating because (as stated many times) the primary strategy of novice Pétanque is blocking boules. The best way to help the pointer stop throwing long is to stand 1.5m to 2m in front of the jack and using your foot as a target say, "Pretend the jack is here!" To provide a stable target don't move your foot until the boule is in the air.

Other than shuffleboard and arguably golf (club or disc), I can't think of any American sport where a projectile is thrown, hit or rolled with the intent of making it *stop near a target*. **Apparently, the concept of coming to rest near a target instead of blasting into to it is contradictory to the American psyche.**

Building on that concept, I want to scream when I read the typical Internet misinformed contention that the object of Pétanque is *"to throw a steel ball so it stops as close as possible to a target jack."* Put your ego on hold and repeat after me:

 "In Pétanque one point is awarded for every boule which is closer to the target jack than the opponent's best boule. If the opponent's best boule is 100cm from the jack, then any boule from 99.99cm to a tadpole scores the same, i.e. one point!"

When the following four conditions occur, it's as if you've won the lottery!
1. Your opponents are out of boules
2. Their best boule is not very good
3. Your team has several boules in hand
4. The line to the jack is wide open

To cash in the ticket you must:

👍 Close your eyes, tap your heels together three times and think to yourself, *"Close enough is Good enough, Close enough is Good enough, Close enough is Good enough"*

👍 Then reach into your bag of tricks for a clutch, never-miss pointing throw

<u>Meet the "The Flick-Skim"</u> the ultimate in simplified bio-mechanics; a moderate trajectory *semi, demi-portée* with barely a backswing and extreme *rétro*. Picture that you're skipping a flat stone over the surface of a tranquil mill pond.

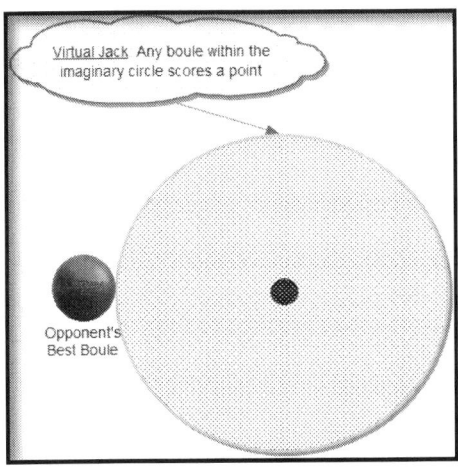

1. *The Virtual Jack*: create an **imaginary circle**, with the jack at the center and your opponent's best boule defining the radius. **Any boule inside the virtual jack is another point for your team**.
2. Pick a flat, smooth donnée one-third to two-thirds of the way to the jack.
3. Depending on your forearm power, wrist health and the terrain, take a short backswing and lock-and-load it just behind the hip, *as illustrated by Kathi.*
4. This is one throw where your off-arm may dangle harmlessly by your hip.
5. Lay-back the wrist fully flexed and get ready to transform your boule into a gyroscope.
6. With the grossly abbreviated throwing motion use a low release just in front of the hip and whip crack your wrist to generate maximum rétro
7. Hit the donnée and watch as the boule skids, plows and hopefully stops safely within the virtual jack.

The flick should be nearly effortless.

Maximum rétro and low to moderate trajectory allows the boule to *skim and skid* (remember it won't be rolling until the rétro is exhausted) over the worst of the terrain plowing a straight line to the jack. Don't expect tadpoles, but it should get you close.

The mechanics are so simple and repeatable that "the flick-skim" begs to be your go-to, no-choke pointing throw when you have a clear line and getting, "Close Enough is Good Enough."

The Follow-Through

The fingertips provide the last boule control input. ***Keep the fingers parallel and touching each other; the top of the hand must be parallel to the ground before the wrist is snapped and the boule's arc follows the outstretched fingertips.***

- Brushing the boule with the thumb or snapping the wrist non-vertically imparts sidespin which may produce bizarre, and otherwise inexplicable, twisting bounces and curving rollouts
- Players throwing boules that are too large are especially susceptible to release malfunctions because the thumb is often used to stabilize the boule. *If you must throw oversized boules, think of the hand and palm as providing a stable cradle that requires a minimal grip.*
- Plombée pointers have the highest follow-through. Standing pointers may leave their fingertips pointing toward the arc of the boule's flight.
- The high follow-through of a plombée squat pointer may cause a loss of balance. A hand cannot be placed on the ground for assistance, so most squat pointers immediately pull the throwing hand back to the chest to stabilize the squat stance.
- As an alternative, some pointers extend the follow-through by lifting completely out of the squat into a standing stance. Be Careful! A part of both feet must stay grounded until the boule hits the terrain. If you step out of the rond too quickly, then your boule is ruled dead and taken out of play as specified in *FIPJP Rules, Article 6 Start of Play and Rules Regarding the Rond.*
- Demi-portee pointers and palet roulant shooters have a similar follow-through. Wrist snap release occurs just under chest level and the fingertips point to the boule's arc.

Lower Body Assistance

Earlier we talked about simplifying the throwing motion by grounding the lower body. Aggressive shooters bend forward at the waist during the backswing. With the exception of torso torque induced thigh and knee twisting, extraneous lower body movement should be minimized.

- *In an extremely easy and simplified version of the squat bounce power assist, a standing pointer can add significant plombée power to reach distance jacks by involving their legs.* Before or during the backswing the knees flex and the player drops several inches into a mini-squat. During the forward swing the player fires-out of the mini-squat finishing with a high follow-through.
- The difference between standing and squat pointer leg assistance is that most people are strong enough to smoothly fire-out of a standing 3" to 5" mini-squat. Few athletes have the leg strength, flexibility and sturdy knees required to fire-out of a full squat. The squat pointer's practical alternative is to bounce on the haunches.

Pétanque Training Drills and Games

Most Pétanque players want to play games, not practice technique. The structure of a game is to score points, not experiment with new throws or strategies. Even if you decide to be bold and try a different pointing throw or shot, one or two attempts is not enough to program your muscle memory. Learning new technique takes repetition and that never occurs within the context of even the most casual conventional game. Yes it's possible that you might try a shot and after badly missing, someone suggests that you retrieve the boule and try it again. But that's not a substitute for structured practice.

As a compromise for players with limited time who sincerely want to develop skills but also want to play games, we developed several meta-games that integrate play and practice. Pétanque singles is rarely a preferred game because with only six boules in play it just isn't interesting. Several of our practice games can be played as singles because practice and skills are their driving motivations. When there are only two players available the pair would be much more entertained and their skills enhanced by playing one of the training meta-games rather than squandering a couple of hours on conventional singles.

Boule-Devant du Jeu: The Game of Up-Front Boules

You know the value of blocking boules and that novice pointers tend to throw long. This game reinforces the value of the boule-devant, the up-front blocking boule. Often a novice throws a boule that's perfectly in-line but stops 1.5m short of the jack. They are usually disappointed, but more likely than not during the next few pointing throws someone is going to hit that blocking boule; even if it isn't hit, it's still a visual distraction.

But there is a major problem with boule-devants that are thrown too short. They are just as likely to block teammate's pointing throws as their opponent's. They are so far in front of the jack that, whether purposefully promoted or accidently struck, it is doubtful that they will ever be pushed far enough to score a point. *Boules that are too far up-front are an equal opportunity hindrance*.

The goal of this training game is to reinforce the value of blocking boules that stop close enough in front of the jack to be converted into points.

It's played like Pétanque singles with a few twists:

> As the end plays out, a boule-devant 50cm in front of the jack will probably be more valuable than a boule-derrière which is only 25cm behind the jack.
>
> *Although this contention may be debatable, the skills developed and reinforced in this game are invaluable.*

- Any boule that is initially pointed beyond the jack is O.B. and removed from play
- Pointing throws only, no shooting is allowed.
- If a blocking boule is subsequently hit (either by the boule's owner or the opponent) and driven beyond the jack, that boule remains in play and is included when allocating points

You may designate the O.B. by drawing a line in the dirt, but I prefer to use disc golf markers placed about 1.5m apart. The line is visual - when in doubt leave close boules in play. Of course like any of the training games in this book you are free to change the rules. For example, you may choose to create the imaginary line 15cm behind the jack with the rational that someone shouldn't be punished for throwing just a bit long. It's your game, play it anyway that makes sense to you.

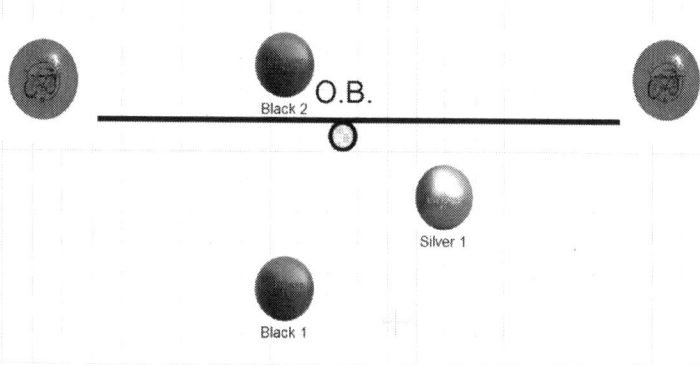

In the example Silver is holding the point. The Black team points Black-2 which stops slightly beyond the jack. Black-2 is closer to the jack than Silver-1 and would normally hold the point. But in this training game Black-2 must be picked up and removed from play because it is beyond the jack. Consequently Silver is still holding and Black must throw again.

Close Enough is Good Enough: A game for two or more

Shooting is based on hitting a precise spot on the target boule. Some instances of pointing require that the boule follows a precise path to the jack. Most pointing throws only demand that the pointer get "close enough" to the jack.

This game helps players to stop thinking about the jack as a precise bull's-eye and embrace the concept of the "virtual jack" as defined by the opponent's best boule. The concept of the "virtual jack" was introduced in the section on "The Flick." I use **three equal spaced boules** to define the virtual jack. I also like to keep the line between the rond and jack wide open as illustrated in the diagram. You can use a single boule (much more realistic to game conditions) or even disc markers to define the virtual jack. Just remember that it symbolizes the opponent's best boule which must be beat to score a point.

1. The player that wins the coin toss throws the jack.
2. That player defines the virtual jack. Typical virtual jack diameters are 25cm to 100cm, but the player can configure the end any way he pleases.
3. **The players alternate throws** because they are pointing against a virtual jack, not the opponent's best boule.
4. The end is complete when each player has thrown three boules.
5. Contrary to conventional Pétanque, each player is awarded one point for each boule that falls within the virtual jack.
6. The player that wins the end controls the jack toss and defines the virtual jack for the next end.

The obvious question is what happens if one of the boules defining the virtual jack gets struck and moved? That's up to you, but whatever you decide you must agree on before starting the game. I prefer to use three boules because it provides the best visual target, so I always replace the marker boule back to its original location; my virtual jack doesn't change during the end. One advantage of using flat disc golf markers is that they don't move when run over by a boule. If you use a single boule then you can have a "variable virtual jack." That opens up interesting strategies, such as striking the boule that defines the virtual jack and moving it to maximize point allocation. Have fun and get competent at "proximity pointing" because in Pétanque (say it with me) *"Close Enough is Good Enough."*

Eight Ball: a Game for Two

Eight Ball was originally developed to enhance singles by making it more strategically challenging and entertaining. It's like conventional singles but uses two additional boules. ***The player that wins the coin toss throws the jack and places the two extra boules. The only restrictions are that the boules must be at least 15cm apart (about two boule widths) and a minimum of 30cm from the jack.***

- At the start of the end the two extra boules are unowned
- The first player to "touch" an extra boule owns it *for the remainder of the end*. We originally called the game, "You Touch It, You Own It!"
- A "touch" is defined as directly striking an unowned extra boule. *Combinations in which a player's boule first hits another boule which, in turn, strikes an unowned boule do not count.*
- The player's original three boules and the boules for which they have ownership (if any) are included in point allocation.
- Unowned boules are not considered in point allocation.

In the diagram the player who threw the jack placed Extra-1 about 30cm in front of the jack and Extra-2 about 30cm to the left of the jack. The player who places the extra boules throws first. The strategy in this example is to "touch" Extra-1 with a soft promotion throw. The player would then be holding with two boules (his original and Extra-1 which he now owns) very close to the jack.

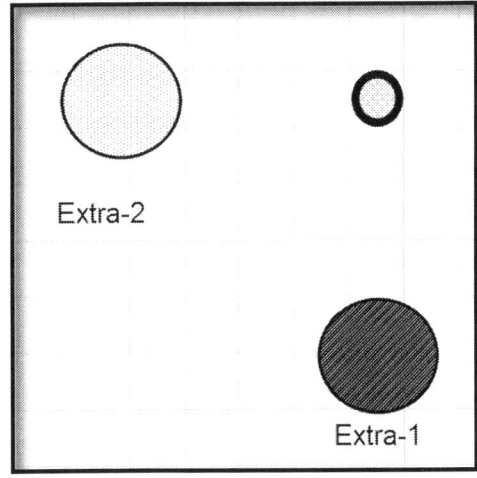

This is great training and also entertaining because it gives the player who throws the opportunity to set up a scenario in which he can immediately have two points on the ground. *However, if he misses the promotion and doesn't touch either Extra Boule, that golden opportunity passes to his opponent.*

One of the first issues we had to work through was that both of the Extra boules were identical, so it was difficult to keep track of who owned which boule(s) and which ones were still unowned. To make it easy I dedicated two cheap generic boules to the game. One boule is spray painted glossy red and the other yellow. That makes it easy for a player that "touches" an unowned boule to say, "I now own the red (or yellow) boule."

Poison Ball: A Nasty Eight Ball Variation

Promotion is an essential skill to master. An equally important skill is pointing through congestion, where accidently just nicking an opponent's (or teammate's) boule might result in an unmitigated disaster.

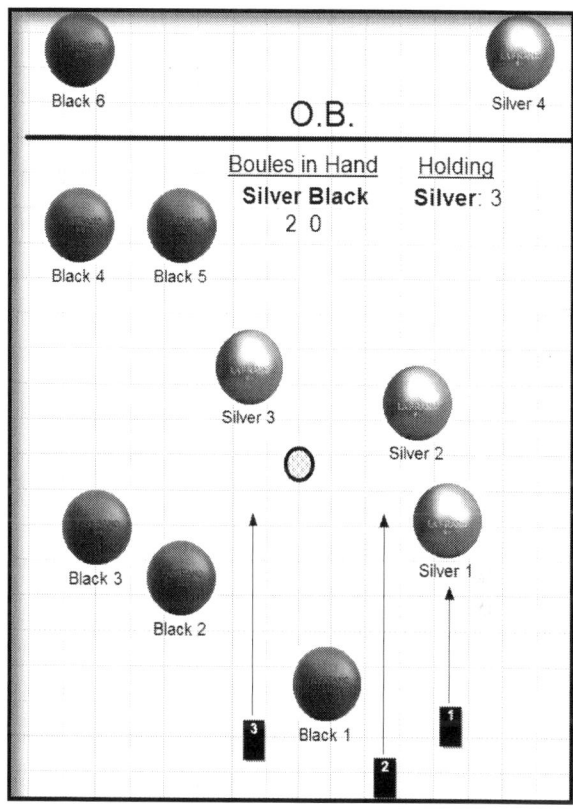

Consider the diagram. The Black team is out of boules and the Silver team has three points on the ground with two boules in hand. They are in great shape, but danger is lurking in the shadows.

If Silver gets greedy and attempts to run up more points, one of the Black boule-devants may accidently be struck. In worst case it could be pushed close enough to the jack to hold the point. From Silver's perception that represents a potential four point turnaround from Silver +3 to Black +1.

How should Silver point through the traffic?

1. *Route 1:* Point into Silver-1, use it as a backstop
2. *Route 2*: Point the Silver-1 to Black-1 gap. <u>*Danger!*</u> *Wander a bit left, strike Black-1 squarely and it may be pushed close to the jack.*
3. *Route 3*: Point the Black-1 to Black-2 gap. *Danger! Just a bit left and a minor tap may push Black-2 close enough to erase 1 to 3 points!*
4. Bird-in-the-Hand Approach: Play it safe and throw the last two boules away

It comes down to factors such as the current score, the speed and smoothness of the terrain and how comfortable the Silver team players holding boules are pointing gaps. That's the intent of Poison Ball, to develop the skills and confidence to point the gaps. ***Poison Ball is the evil twin of Eight Ball***. It's identical to Eight Ball with one ugly twist - when one of the extra boules is "touched", instead of the player that touched it, his opponent owns it! The original name of Poison Ball was "You Touch It, I Own It!

Poison Ball develops precision gap pointing skills and confidence. In the diagram the player placed the extra boules to create three paths. The most direct route is through the gap between the extra boules. But since Extra-2 is fairly close to the jack, accidently tapping it in the center or on the left side not only gives ownership to your opponent, but might push Extra-2 close to the jack.

On the other hand, if you tapped Extra-2 on the right side it would be driven to left and your boule could easily career and stop close to the jack. It's what we

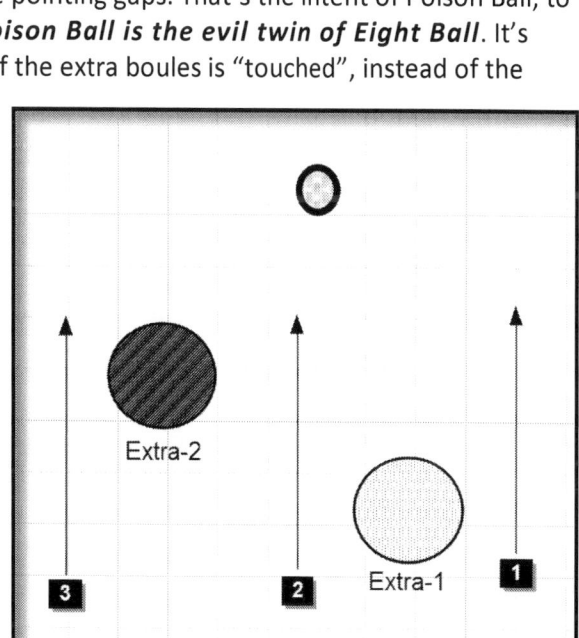

earlier called a "pinball throw." Even though your opponent would own Extra-2, you'd be holding the point with a great boule and that might be worth the compromise.

Eight Ball and Poison Ball teach different skills (promotion verses gap pointing) in a similar context. They are so complementary that we often let the player who controls the jack call the game, either Eight Ball or Poison Ball and then place the two Extra boules accordingly.

Bottle Cap Pétanque

This is not a different game but an enhancement for any Pétanque game. You carefully walk the line to determine the best donnée for the next pointing throw or palet roulant shot. Finding the donnée is one thing, but being able to pick it out

> Every interview of a world-class pointer always stresses the same issue: ***The key to accurate and consistent pointing is picking and hitting the donnée!***

when you are in the rond can be difficult. A rock, twig, leaf or a patch of discolored gravel - anything that makes it standout is helpful. But often your choice of donnée, which was so obvious when you were standing over it, disappears by the time you enter the rond.

- *FIPJP Rules, Article 15 Throwing of the First and Following Boules* states that a player must not use <u>any object</u> or draw a line on the terrain to use as a guide to play a boule or mark a donnée.
- However, a teammate may be directed to point to the donnée (usually with his foot) to help you identify its location from the rond.

In direct violation of Article 15 during practice games we optionally use bottle caps to mark the preferred donnée location. This encourages novice players to develop the habit of precisely choosing a donnée, locking into from the rond and knowing exactly where the boule lands in reference to it. Beer bottle caps are preferred for several reasons:

- They are available in a variety of colors and patterns. You are sure to find one that will stand out regardless of the color and texture of the terrain.
- They are just big enough to be seen, providing the ideal sized bull's-eye
- They have a low profile and soft metal. Unlike plastic water or soda bottle screw-off caps, if a beer bottle cap is hit dead-on (a rarity) rebound and rollout is minimally affected. Hitting a beer bottle cap with a high plombées completely flattens it.

I carry a dozen beer bottle caps with my Pétanque accoutrements. *When we play Bottle Cap Pétanque everyone picks out a cap and uses it to mark the donnée for pointing throws and palet roulant shots.*

- The player walks the line to choose a donnée and marks the spot with his bottle cap
- The player goes to the rond and ensures that he can see the bottle cap
- One of the player's teammates stands just off to the side of the bottle cap

> Taken seriously, Bottle Cap Pétanque is the fastest and most effective way to improve your pointing and palet roulant shooting accuracy and consistency.

- Carefully watching the throw, the teammate marks the true donnée with his own bottle cap and carefully observes rebound and rollout
- The player compares the actual donnée (marked by the teammate's bottle cap) to the position of the desired donnée marked with the thrower's bottle cap.
- The player considers the quality of the throw and the desired versus actual données

- The teammate picks up his bottle cap. If the player is going to immediately throw again, he may leave his bottle cap in its current location or move it to a new donnée.
- When the player has finished throwing he retrieves his bottle cap
- Lost bottle caps must be immediately replaced after play is concluded (if you get my drift.)

Although using a bottle cap to mark the desired donnée may seem trivial, players who take it seriously develop the habit of scanning the terrain for the best donnée and employing it as the legitimate bulls-eye for pointing throws and palet roulant shots. The immediate feedback provided by evaluating the quality of the throw in the context of donnée accuracy enables the player to compensate for terrain conditions. *Not deliberately choosing a donnée and using it as your bulls-eye is usually the product of lackadaisical instruction and playing on one-dimensional terrains*.

The Last Word on the Importance of the Donnée (I promise)	
On a smooth and level terrain hitting the intended donnée always increases accuracy. Choose the donnée carefully and make it your bull's-eye. You'll still make an occasional bad throw, but it will be the exception rather than the rule.	Mean and nasty terrains force a player to become a donnée devotee. Landing on a rock, soft spot, hard spot or subtle slope can produce disastrous rebounds and rollouts. I've seen Zvonko Radnic hit a bad donnée that left his boule sitting by its lonesome over 2m from the jack. Shake off that bad landing and find the ideal donnée.

Au Fer Shooting Bull's-Eye Practice

This is the third way to use a disc cone for au fer shooting practice. (See the end of *Chapter 3* for the introduction to the disc cone.) Lay a target boule on the terrain and slip the hole in the cone over it. The perfect shot occurs when the shooter's boule strikes the target boule without hitting any plastic. If the shot doesn't have the correct impact angle or it doesn't strike the target boule squarely the plastic cone is sent flying and the target boule is barely displaced.

Cutthroat: a Game for Three

It's tough when only three players are on hand. If one player has six boules, then the trio can play modified doublettes with the singles player throwing six boules and the doublettes players throwing three boules each. But I look at a gathering of three as an opportunity to force people into the secretly desired, but often uncomfortable role of shooter.

Summary

Cutthroat is Pétanque singles with a *nasty twist*. Each singles player *must employ the services of a designated shooter two times each end*. The singles players score points just like a conventional singles game; the shooter accumulates points based on the effectiveness of each shot. Roles are rotated at the completion of each end.

The Designated Shooter

The singles player *not holding the point* may order the designated shooter to shoot a boule. After the shot, the shooter <u>immediately removes</u> his boule from the terrain. After either player has thrown their last boule, if that player has not yet used the services of the designated shooter twice, he must do so before play continues with the other singles player or the end is declared complete.

The Jack as a Target
The jack may be specified as the target only if it can be directly shot (not screened by a boule.)

Scoring
The two singles players are awarded points just like a regular game. The shooter accumulates points on-the-fly based on each shot's effectiveness. To score, a shot must <u>directly strike</u> the designated target; if the shooter directly strikes any other object he is assessed <u>one penalty point</u>. Rebounding off of the target into other boules is normal play and does not result in a penalty.

Exception
If the direct line between the rond and designated target boule is obscured by other boules, the shooter may declare a "combination shot" specifying that another boule will be shot first, and that boule will rebound into the designated target. The shot is declared a hit only if the combination is successful.

Per Shot Point Allocations (disputes are settled by majority vote)

🚫	0 points	<u>Clean Miss</u> doesn't hit any boule or the jack
👍	+1 point	<u>Incidental Hit</u> (tick, nick or cap) metal-to-metal contact that moves target less than 1m
👍👍	+2 points	<u>Solid Shot</u> drives the target boule more than 1m
👍👍👍	+3 points	<u>Carreau!</u> Solid Shot and shooter's boule stops within 50cm of the original target position
👍👍👍	+3 points	<u>Shooting the Jack</u> and driving it more than 1m
☠	(-1 point)	Initially striking any object other than the designated target (except a declared combination)

Choosing the Initial Roles
Players stand side-by-side, the jack is thrown a legal distance and on command everyone tosses a boule.

The order of the boules from the jack specifies the order in which players choose their preferred role for the first end.

Role Rotation
At the completion of the end after singles points are allocated each player verbally announces their accumulated score and roles are rotated as specified in the diagram.

1. Lead Pointer becomes Second Pointer
2. Second Pointer becomes Designated Shooter
3. Designated Shooter becomes Lead Pointer

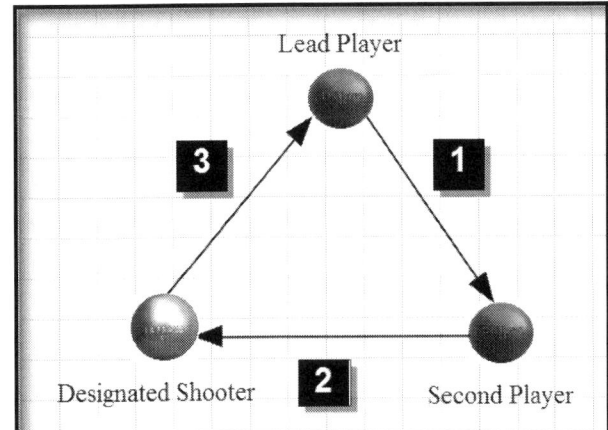

The Lead Pointer always tosses the jack and throws the first boule.

Strategy

The game is called "cutthroat" because players may form an ad hoc, untrustworthy alliance to attack the current leader. The shooter may purposefully miss a shot or even shoot the wrong boule and lose a point, if it has a greater negative impact on the current scoring leader.

The shooter can be neutralized by specifying a target boule that is far away, behind blocking boules and can only be shot au fer, or requires a difficult combination. Declaring the jack as a target is a gamble. It is a low percentage shot, but a solid hit yields three points. The two singles players are not restricted from shooting, but they don't accumulate points like the designated shooter. Alliances are temporary, fluid and dependent on each player's competence in their current role; alliances often terminate in back-stabbing and double-crosses. That's, Cutthroat!

How to Play Casual or Novice Level Pétanque

I doubt that the typical distance runner routinely spends time jogging around the block with his couch potato neighbor. Neither does a competitive tennis player choose to hit ground strokes with a week-end warrior who can't keep the ball in the court. The nature of competitive sports is exclusivity; the tendency to participate only with those who share a common skill set and commitment. When you compete with less skilled players, your quality of play will probably be dragged down to their level; focus and intensity diminish, and feelings of guilt may arise from humbling a less skilled or experienced opponent.

In most sports the frustration of playing against an unmatched opponent occurs because the quality of the experience is tied to the performance of all participants. If a runner's normal pace is 8-minute miles, unless they're wearing ankle weights or put their shoes on backwards, they won't be challenged running with someone who does 12-minute miles. The same is true in tennis; the quality of play is dependent on both players' abilities. If one player can't hit with pace, move well and constantly double-faults, that diminishes the experience for both participants. Even in golf, someone who shoots in the low-80s will be bored to tears (and their game will suffer proportionally) if they are paired up with a player who rarely breaks 100.

> Unlike runners who prefer to train at a certain pace or tennis players that must strike a ball returned by their opponent, *in Pétanque your quality of experience is not directly tied the performance of your opponents.* Playing with the novice won't provide strategic challenges, but you'll still have the opportunity to perfect your craft while having a great time.

And I repeat - one of the best aspects of Pétanque is that it can be all things to all people. Currently in the U.S. there isn't a deep pool from which to recruit partners and find competitors. Pursuing Pétanque as a grassroots, community-based activity means that you must be prepared to embrace anyone who shows up at the terrain. **I love debating politics and religion but limiting your attention on the terrain to throwing boules and talking strategy creates the most receptive and inclusive environment.**

> ***Everyone But***: I draw the line at playing with trash talking, teasing types who refuse to extend basic courtesies such as a moment of silence when a player is throwing.
>
> It's up to you to reinforce the etiquette and courtesy that defines the tone and accessibility of your grassroots organization.

Skilled players often find themselves participating with the novice or recreational players who have absolutely no competitive aspirations. *How can a competitive, serious player enjoy and benefit from playing with less skilled, less focused, less intense and less engaged players?*

Use the game structure to practice the shots that you've yet to develop well enough to confidently use in competitive games. *Experiment and have fun, but stay focused and intense.*

- ☝ If you're not a shooter, force yourself to get aggressive and shoot
- ☝ If you're a shooter don't shoot. When your opponent throws a boule-devant, then try placing a devant-de-boule. It's a tough throw which requires a lot of practice to master. Later in that end, shoot your own boule to demonstrate (and reinforce) the concept of bulletproof boules.
- ☝ If you're a palet roulant shooter, it's a good opportunity to step up and shoot au fer
- ☝ Promote teammate's boule-devants instead of pointing directly to the jack.
- ☝ If you're feeling especially cocky, precise point a few boules long and then pull off a Year in Provence throw by pushing the jack back into your nest of boule-derrières. It's a crowd pleaser.
- ☝ If your team is winning big, purposefully point away from the jack, e.g. throw a boule that stops exactly 75cm to the right of the jack. (They'll think you're having an off day. No one has to know that you're practicing precision pointing in a nonconventional manner.)
- ☝ For instructional purposes call your throws. Precisely describe to your teammate(s) what you intend to do. Such as, *"I'm going to slide my boule between those two blocking boules and stop it about 15cm to the right of the jack."* Then of course, you have to do it!
- ☝ If there is a wall of boules 1.5m in front of the jack, demonstrate the grace and effectiveness of a soaring plombée with maximum rétro.
- ☝ For every pointing throw or palet roulant shot call your donnée. Show your teammate(s) exactly where your boule will land and describe how you expect it to rollout and stop.
- ☝ Encourage great habits in the novice by demonstrating their effectiveness

Find a challenge in the most mundane game. If you can learn to concentrate and focus at this level, doing so in serious competition will be effortless.

Step Out of the Rond

When a pointer makes a particularly bad throw their first inclination is *to immediately throw again*. The desire, the need to throw again and throw quickly with no thought or consideration can be overwhelming. *Three common rationalizations are*:

1. The player learned something critical from the bad throw which can only be reinforced by immediately throwing again. If he waits, even a second, that flash of profound insight will dissolve into thin air.
2. The player missed the intended donnée and is going to try using it again, so there's no need to wait.
3. The boule slipped from the player's hand or he thumbed it during the release; it was a simple malfunction that won't happen again – why wait?

> **Tip from the Pros**:
> Masters level players <u>never rapid fire</u> consecutive throws! After one throw (assuming that they are not yet holding the point) the player always leaves the rond, walks the line and exchanges a few words with teammates.

After a particularly bad throw the player may be seized in the grip of a form of temporary insanity called *"irresistible impulse."* You must fight the irresistible impulse to immediately throw again and **step out of the rond**! When a novice pointer rapid fires, the second and often third throws are duplicates of the horrible first throw! (That's not what we mean when we urge players to learn consistency.) Use the allocated sixty seconds between throws to clarify your intent.

- Your team has one less boule and may have to reconsider strategy
- The shooter or milieu might step in and make the next throw
- If you hit the intended donnée, you must walk the line to determine what actually happened and why the rebound and/or rollout didn't occur as projected.
- If you missed the intended donnée are you going to attempt to use it again, or find an alternative donnée in a more advantageous location with a greater margin of error?
- You might radically change the type of pointing throw. After throwing a plombée that hit the intended donnée dead-on, but then rebounded like a drunken basketball, you might get conservative (read: *lose your nerve and play it safe*) and decide to toss a nice, medium arced demi-portée.

If a shooter misses a shot, especially a clean miss, the instinct is also to rapid fire. ***Step out of the rond!*** After a clean miss shooters often pace the distance to the target boule to ensure that it agrees with their visual estimate. If you're shooting palet roulant then you have the same concerns as pointers regarding donnée and rollout.

Again, give your teammates the courtesy to verify strategy. A shooter may get so caught in the impulse to quickly shoot again, that he forgets he's holding his team's last boule and should be tightening the game by throwing a defensive boule-devant instead of taking a high-risk second shot.

> On more than one occasion I've stepped into the rond holding three boules. After missing a routine shot with my first boule, in a flash - a dizzy blur, suddenly and inexplicably my hands are empty and I gaze, bewildered, as the target boule snugly sits in its original location.
>
> Make a blood pact with your teammates that no one will throw a second consecutive boule without stepping out of the rond and taking a few deep breaths.

A Quick Word about Warm-Ups

Americans rarely bother to perform proper warm-ups even for physically demanding sports. For most Pétanque players the pre-game warm-up is to toss a couple of pointing throws. I don't believe that's a sufficient warm-up even for players who only throw roulette or low-arced demi-portées. Plombée and squat pointers, and aggressive shooters put significant stress on their rotator cuff. I'm not suggesting that you have to crank off several sets of pushups, pull-ups and dips. Remember, if you are middle-aged or beyond, your hands, wrists, elbows and shoulders already have a lot of wear-and-tear and not properly warming-up accelerates the aging process and the onset of chronic overuse injuries.

I won't suggest a specific warm-up routine. Everyone has access to a variety of written and online sources that provide comprehensive leg, arm and shoulder warm-ups. The specific movements aren't nearly as important as the commitment to perform a structured warm-up every time you walk onto the terrain. A two to four minute investment is a small price to assure long-term arm and shoulder health. And, as an immediate bonus, you'll probably play better.

Hand, Wrist and Forearm Strength

Strength is no substitute for technique as demonstrated by squat bouncing, torso torque and the flick. Given the choice, I'd opt for flawless technique. Strong hands and forearms mitigate many of the limitations which confound the technically challenged player. But most important, resistance training is the most effective means to reduce soft tissue (tendon/ligament) overuse injuries. As a long time rock climber, tennis player and sea kayaker the threat of chronic wrist, elbow and shoulder injuries motivates me to perform hand and forearm strength training at least three times a week.

Why Structured American Pétanque Training Doesn't Exist

Elitist FPUSA policy has all but guaranteed that reliable, world-class instruction is not available in the U.S. When I expressed the desire to become a *FPUSA* certified trainer I was unabashedly informed that no U.S.-based trainers are authorized to train other trainers, i.e. teach certification classes. Other than a one-shot event held in May of 2010 at the Fresno Club, there are no future plans to offer Pétanque trainer certification classes in the U.S!

My only path to certification is to apply to be accepted into a four-day, French language-only class in (you guessed it) France. Welcome to Pétanque, the International Sport!

As Cole Porter said,
I love Paris in the springtime, I love Paris in the fall.
I love Paris in the winter when it drizzles, and I love Paris in the summer when it sizzles.

I prefer Paris in the fall. Perhaps I'll see you on my favorite terrain at the Jardin du Luxembourg. You'll recognize me as the obnoxious American with huge forearms and mediocre technique usually surrounded by a group of infuriated Frenchman.

Most U.S. club players only point roulette or flat demi-portées, and shoot palet roulant because of strength limitations or chronic injuries. One of the most important aspects of hand and forearm training is to work sets of the complementary antagonist muscles: flexors and extenders.

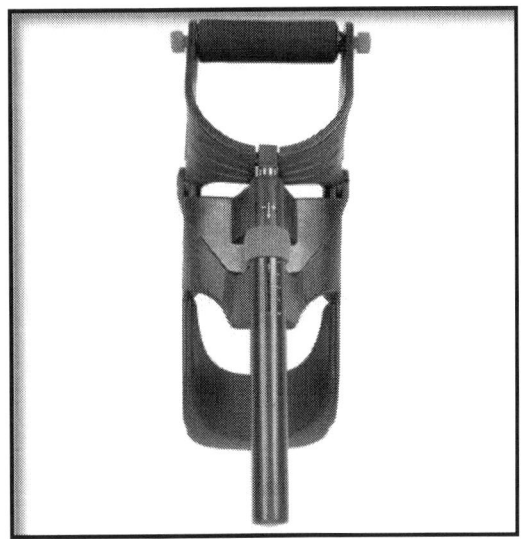

My favorite forearm exerciser is a popular style which is available from Marcy, Bollinger and several other companies. The price ranges from $20 to $32 at Amazon.com. From the orientation in the photo, the arm is inserted with the palm-down to exercise the forearm flexors and the palm-up to work the extenders. When used in a controlled, yet enthusiastic manner it feels as if you are mainlining battery acid. I have to wait about twenty minutes after doing forearms before I can work a computer keyboard. Use this device three times a week in five to eight minute sessions and within months you'll be throwing 5m high plombées with minimum leg assist.

Chapter 5: Competition Boule Selection

The Pétanque Boule

A boule is a hollow steel ball fabricated from two sections of steel bar. In this chapter we examine boule characteristics, selection criteria and go boules shopping on-line.

The Best Place to Start

If you live near a petanque club you may have access to club member's expertise and advice as well as a collection of different types, sizes and weights of boules.

Step Four) Weld two half-shells into a sphere

Step Five) Smooth the boule on a lathe

Step Three) Forge the disk into a half shell

Step Two) Shape a bar section into a disk

Step Six) Finish with optional stripes, tempering, polishing and, for carbon steel boules, zinc and chrome plating

Step One) Start with a section of steel bar

For those on a budget and without the benefit of loaner boules from a local club the best course is to start with a set of non-certified inexpensive generic boules. After a few hundred throws you'll start to settle into a comfortable motion and develop a preference as a pointer (pointeur), shooter (tireur) or all-arounder (milieu). Then you'll be ready to apply the comprehensive concepts of boule selection to your first purchase of *FIPJP* competition certified boules.

Boule Specifications

The official boule specifications are defined in the *FIPJP Rules, Article 2 — Characteristics of Approved Boules*. Boules used in sanctioned tournaments must conform to the following criteria:

1. Must be metal: typically carbon steel or stainless steel (inox)
2. Diameter: 70.5mm (2.8") to 80mm (3.15")
3. Weight: 650g (1.43 lb) to 800g (1.76-lb)
4. Minimum hardness: 110 kg /mm² or 35 HRc (explained in a later section)
5. Must have a dynamic balance which is less than 1.3% of the boule's weight
6. Must be completely hollow: generic boules have thin carbon steel skins and are filled with grit and waste material to add weight and stabilize rollout
7. Must not be post-production altered or re-tempered to modify hardness
8. Must be imprinted with:
   - *FIPJP* approved manufacturer's trademark seal of approval
   - boule model
   - weight (in grams)
   - unique identifier (serial number)
9. Optional imprints allowed are diameter, player's name, initials or other minor identification which may be cold stamped by the manufacturer

Junior Competition: For 11 years and younger competitions junior *FIPJP* approved boules weigh 600g (1.3-lb) and have a 65mm (2.55") diameter.

There's No Such Thing as Demo Boules
Professional tennis shops have a selection of "demo" racquets which customers may try prior to purchasing. High-end golf shops have computer simulated indoor driving ranges and artificial putting greens to demo clubs.

Even in France the stores that carry a large selection of petanque supplies don't provide an onsite demo facility or loaner boules. Holding a boule in hand and imaging a carreau isn't a viable substitute for making a few dozen throws. For the 90% of Americans not living near an existing club the grassroots Pétanque organization that you start will be the demo facility for future players in your area. After completing this chapter you'll know more about the technical aspects of boule selection than the great majority of experienced club players.

The Generic, One-Size-Fits-All Starter Boule
Since it's going to take dozens of hours of play and thousands of throws to find and develop your playing style, it's unlikely that your first set of boules will sustain your growth beyond the advanced-novice level of play. Until you accumulate a few weeks of play, boule selection details are academic. Like a casual tennis player who is happy to hit with any racket, the novice Pétanque player is thrilled to be out throwing with any available set of boules. I've already said it several times, but you'll always need many extra sets of generic boules for running drills, pointing scenarios, shooting practice, alternative games and for guests. It's heartbreaking to have a house full of potential Pétanque players and not have enough boules on hand to get everyone out onto the terrain.

Tennis and golf commercials on T.V. and magazines often claim that one's game will take a quantum leap with the purchase of a new high-tech racquet frame or oversized titanium driver. There's no "silver bullet syndrome" in Pétanque. We'll learn in this chapter that there are a few wonkish reasons that one might purchase different sets of boules for pointing and shooting, but most club players own one set that they throw for many years. The essence of Pétanque is the boule in hand and six to ten meters of dirt and gravel separating the pointer from the jack or the shooter from the opponent's boule – and nice shiny boules don't make that daunting task any easier.

Certified Manufacturers
The *FIPJP* has certified over a dozen boule manufacturers. As one might expect the great majority are headquartered in France, with La Boule Obut leading the pack. You can trust the quality of every *FIPJP* certified manufacturer. La Franc Boule (a subsidiary of FBT) is headquartered in Thailand, a country that supports a huge number of Pétanque players. Their boules represent the low end of the price range, but their quality and consistency is on par with the major French manufacturers. Although I own a fine, high-end set of Obut boules, my daily pointing and shooting sets are from La Franc Boule.

Boule Size and Weight Selection
We're ready to examine the five technical boule specifications: size, weight, striations, hardness, type of metal and finish. Size, weight and hardness are the primary playability factors. Metal type and finish affect hand feel, maintenance requirements and ascetics. Striations are the most controversial boule characteristic. Striations help identify boules, affect hand feel and release. Many players argue that striations enhance rétro effects by providing friction and stabilizing rollout. If that's true, then why do most competitive players throw smooth boules (boules lisses)?

Boule Size: Pointing versus Shooting

When play is dominated by pointers there are many boules close to the jack, so point allocation may come down to a few millimeters. When play is dominated by shooters the area around the jack is not nearly as congested, making close points much less common. By virtue of its greater diameter a larger boule is closer to the jack than a smaller boule centered in the same location. Many club players contend that a pointer should use the largest boule he can comfortably throw. But boule size is a double-edged-sword; a bigger pointer's boule is also a bigger shooter's target! Be skeptical of most club-level boule selection advice (especially when someone is trying to sell a set of used boules) because it is often based on urban myth and contradictory inferences.

Shooters also have similar boule size selection issues. Au fer shooting tolerances are tight. A 10m shot thrown 1° off trajectory results in a clean miss. Common wisdom says that shooters prefer bigger boules because a bigger boule is a bigger bullet and a bigger bullet produces more hits. But when the shooter throws a carreau his bigger bullet is now a bigger target for the opponent to shoot.

The boule size issue may be a zero sum game; it's dependent on whether a match is dominated by pointing or shooting. In a few pages pointer and shooter perspectives are applied to fine tune boule size, but first we must determine how to establish a base-line, role independent basic boule size.

Boule Size and Hand Strength

Hand size is the primary factor in boule size selection, but hand and forearm strength is also an extremely important criteria. As described previously, to achieve optimum touch and retro the boule should be centered where the fingers meet the palm and secured with only the lightest squeeze. Picture the apex of the backswing, palm up with the wrist laid-back at 90°and the boule lightly cradled at the base of the fingers. Now imagine the forces exerted on the fingers as gravity, the shoulder and upper-arm accelerate the boule downward, forward, and then completing the loop at the release. As we saw in the techniques chapter, release and wrist snap may occur at very different locations for the shooter, standing pointer and squat pointer.

> For every reason cited to throw a larger boule there is an equally legitimate reason for throwing a smaller boule. The human engine is composed of an infinite number of variables. *There's no universal formula*.

A larger boule requires greater gripping force which tightens the forearm flexor muscles inhibiting wrist snap and rétro generation. A larger boule may unintentionally engage the thumb for stabilization assistance producing undesired side-spin and a non-linear rollout.

Measuring Hand Span Size

Hand span is the primary factor to determine boule diameter. Petanque stores have a template to measure an open hand with spread fingers from which basic boule size is determined. Manual hand measurement is easy. Spread your open hand and fingers as wide as possible on a flat surface, then measure the distance between the tips of the thumb and middle finger in millimeters: **1 inch = 25.4mm**.

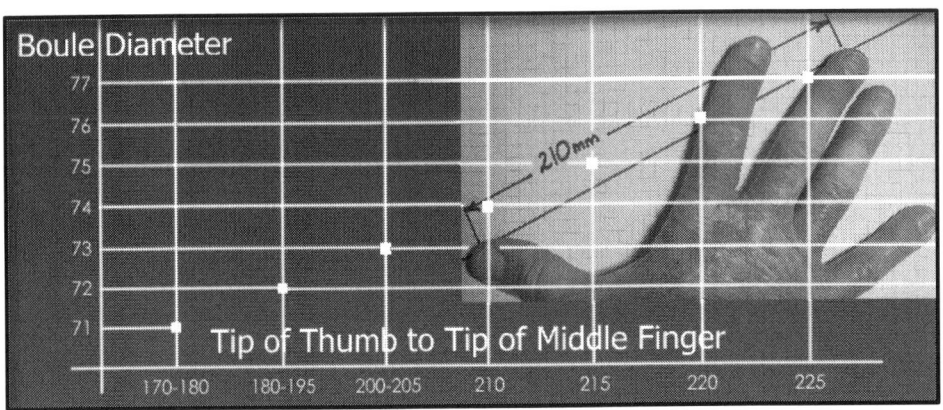

The hand in the photo measures 210mm. According to the chart this equates to a basic boule diameter of 74mm. You will find many hand-to-boule sizing charts and tables on the Internet. Basic boule size suggestions for a given hand-span fall within a one to two millimeter range.

Hand-span is a primary factor, but is not definitive. The length and thickness of fingers is not always directly proportional to palm width. People with professions or hobbies that develop hand flexibility (e.g. pianist, rock-climber, yoga practitioner) tend to have longer thumb to middle finger span than suggested by their palm width. Finger thickness is important because it provides the stability of the cradle in which the boule rests. People often have large hands with long, delicate fingers. It's hard to imagine that they would prefer the same boule size as someone with the same hand span that has thick and powerful fingers.

Consider a softball player. A regulation U.S. adult softball has a 96mm (3.8") diameter which is almost one inch larger than the average 73mm (2.9") Pétanque boule. I've seen softball players with a hand-span measurement of only 165mm, which the chart suggests a boule diameter below the 70.5mm minimum, comfortably and accurately throw a 73mm boule! When a hand is conditioned to throwing a 96mm softball, a 73mm boule probably feels quite comfortable.

Women's Hands and Boule Sizing

Membership statistics of U.S. Pétanque clubs are misleading because a significant percent of female members are non-participating spouses of active male members. My experience is that the biggest obstacle and greatest frustration to novice female petanque players (especially those with hand issues such as carpal tunnel or arthritis) is boule size. The boule size specification was created to accommodate the average French male hand-size, which puts the average woman at a tremendous disadvantage.

> **A Millimeter Makes a Difference!**
> Your hand wraps around the boule's circumference, not its diameter. Circumference is equal to diameter multiplied by the constant π (3.14).
> **A small change in diameter makes a big change in circumference.**

The minimum certified boule size is 70.5mm. According to the boule sizing chart a 71mm boule equates to the hand measurement between 170mm to 180mm. I've measured the hands of over 50 women with a variety of heights and bone structures. The average thumb to middle finger span is about 163mm which, according most sizing charts, would specify a 69mm boule!

Small boules are small targets for shooters. Allowing smaller boules would lower shooting percentages and change the game dynamics. Women Pétanque players who wish to compete must use *FIPJP* certified boules. Pétanque America carries several models of boules in a 71mm diameter which is 0.5mm larger than the *FIPJP* minimum. Generic boules are only available in a 73mm diameter. Often the manufacturing tolerances are so loose that the diameter varies from 72mm to 74mm and the weight by 10g. If a new player with small hands has release and side-spin problems, then a set of 71mm certified boules may be the answer. **For people with small hands a millimeter or two of boule diameter may be the difference between falling in love with Pétanque and finding another sport.**

Manual Sizing Method

The next best thing to going out onto a terrain and making a couple of dozen tosses is to hold a boule in your hand. If you have access to several different sized boules try this manual sizing method.

> Most boules aren't engraved with the diameter. Measure each boule with a set of metric calipers before conducting the manual sizing test.

Hold the boule in your upturned palm. Roll it out toward the finger tips and then gently grasp it, keeping the boule centered where the fingers meet the palm. Tuck your thumb against the side of your hand rather than using it to assist holding the boule. When the boule is secure extend your arm in front and rotate your palm downward into the standard back-handed grip. Your fingers should wrap a little more than half-way around the boule and a moderate grip should be sufficient to keep it from falling out of your hand.

Smaller Boules or Bigger Forearms

Many of the women whose span measurement was too small to register on the hand-to-boule size chart could grip a 71mm boule and have their hand wrap almost halfway around its circumference. The issue of oversized boules is compounded

> Developing hand and forearm strength (as detailed in the last chapter) is the only practical way to compensate for being forced to throw oversized boules.

because, on the average, a woman's hands and forearms aren't as strong as a man's. An oversized boule demands a tighter grip often engaging the thumb for additional support which produces chronic release slippage and side-spin issues. The only way to compensate for throwing oversized boules is to strengthen the forearm (as specified at the end of *Chapter 4*) or by only throwing simple roulette and low arced demi-portée.

A Petite Competition Boule

I have a friend who is a solid plombée pointer and medium-trajectory au fer shooter. Her hand is so small that it doesn't register on the sizing chart. She threw 71mm, 680g boules, but still suffered from chronic release issues. One day a visitor showed us her set of JB Junior Evolution, 70.5, 650g boules. After throwing one game with the Juniors her release issue was vanquished. *Yes, ½mm & 30g can make a huge difference*!

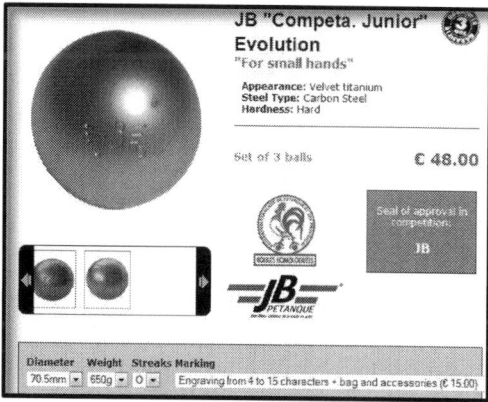

Because of lack of demand *Petanque America* no longer carries the JB Junior or any minimum sized boule. But it's a "self-fulfilling prophecy" because the frustration of throwing oversized boules makes people with small hands (especially competitive athletes who work hard to master technique) give up on Pétanque. That's why there's no market for minimum size and weight boules.

Currently JB Juniors are only available from European vendors. Originally I used Obut's La Boule Noire web-store, but the price was outrageous: €48 plus €42 shipping or $135. Discount shipping starts with a minimum purchase of 12 sets. I now use Madison Sports in Barcelona, Spain (http://www.petanque-madison.com/). They sell the JB Junior for €42 (no VAT for U.S. citizens and they accept PayPal). With a minimum purchase of two sets, they are about $96 a set – that's more like it. Isn't that *person in your life with those little hands worth it?*

When is a Boule Too Small?
A tight grip produces an awkward, hesitant and inconsistent release. Start with the smallest boule you can find. Progressively try incrementally larger boules until you have to squeeze hard to keep it from slipping or your fingers wrap less than halfway around the boule. A slightly smaller boule is preferable to one that is too large. Conceivably when a boule is more than a couple of millimeters too small there may be enough palm wiggle room that might cause the boule to hang and not cleanly release.

On the other hand, I have a friend with gigantic hands. His fingers seem to wrap ¾ of the way around his generic, 73mm boules. When a boule is resting in his open upturned palm it looks like a baseball sitting in a catcher's mitt. Even so, he's an accurate pointer, a fair shooter, generates significant retro and rarely has a bad release. I doubt that he'll go with a larger size when he purchases a set of certified boules. His wife has average size hands and she was also content with their generic 73mm, 720g boules. Then she had the opportunity to throw a set of 71mm, 680g Obut Match 115 boules and everything changed. She pointed with an ease and accuracy she hadn't imagined. Boules aren't a silver bullet but for some people the right size and weight make a huge difference. Other people could throw round rocks and have just as much fun.

Boule Size Fine Tuning
Let's review the role specific tuning criteria. Some conventional wisdom suggests that *pointers prefer slightly undersized* boules because:

- ✓ A smaller boule is a smaller target for shooters. A reduced diameter of just a few millimeters results in more clean misses and less direct hits.
- ✓ A smaller boule enables the thumb to be safely tucked to the side of the index finger or away from the hand, minimizing accidently imparted side-spin.

Disadvantages of smaller boules for pointers:

- ✓ A smaller boule is a smaller target for teammates to promote
- ✓ A smaller boule is slightly less effective as a boule-devant, blocking boule
- ✓ If one boule is 73mm and another boule is 71mm and the center of both boules are the same distance from the jack, then the edge of the larger boule is 1mm closer to the jack and wins the point!

Conventional wisdom also suggests that shooters prefer slightly oversized boules because:

- ✓ a larger boule is a bigger bullet

Boule Weight Considerations

Hand and forearm strength, endurance and chronic hand, wrist, elbow, shoulder or rotator cuff injuries are the primary boule weight selection considerations. Although the *FIPJP* allows a range of 650g to 800g, (at the time of this writing) *Petanque America* typically stocks boules in the 680g to 720g range. Many people consider 700g as a good starter weight and adjust it according to physical strength, injury limitations and specialty.

Boule Weight Issues For The Pointer:

Many contend that pointers prefer a heavier boule by 10g to 20g (0.35-oz to 0.7-oz) because:

- ✓ A heavier boule rebounds less on impact which ensures a truer rollout. However, the "hardness" property of boules also affects rebound
- ✓ Greater rolling inertia produces straighter tracking on rough and rocky terrain
- ✓ A heavier boule has more inertia. It absorbs more impact energy when shot which makes it harder to displace; especially when struck by a capping (casquette) or glancing blow.

Disadvantages of a heavier pointer boule:

- ✓ May impose a tighter grip which may cause release and retro problems
- ✓ Greater effort to throw results in less accuracy at longer distances. In advanced competition the jack is often throw long distances to reduce shooting percentages.
- ✓ Produces greater fatigue during long matches
- ✓ Limits the effective range for many squat pointers

Boule Weight Issues for The Shooter:

Conventional wisdom suggests that shooters prefer lighter boules by 10g to 20g (0.35-oz to 0.7 oz). But shooting au fer is very different than shooting palet roulant. There's no debate that shooters want bigger bullets. But weight considerations are more subtle.

- ✓ Lower weight boules are more accurate for au fer shooting at longer distances
- ✓ Less weight means less fatigue and more consistency during long matches
- ✓ Normal or heavier boules may benefit palet roulant shooting. More weight minimizes impact rebound, produces a truer rollout and packs a bigger knockout punch to displace the target.

A Little Field Testing

If you have boules and a terrain go out for a little field testing. Throw the jack to ten meters.

1. Pick a donnée about one to two meters in front of the jack. Point six full-portée pointing throws with appropriate height and rétro. Gauge the physical effort required to throw a long portée.
2. Place a few target boules around the jack. Shoot six times au fer with a lazy to medium trajectory. Did shooting au fer require more physical effort than portée pointing?
3. Now shoot pallet roulant. With a slightly lower arc hit 2m to 3m short and slide into the target. Does shooting au fer at distance require that much more effort than shooting pallet roulant?

Considering your current preferred shooting style will a lighter boule enhance your range or shooting effectiveness, producing more carreaus, fewer casquettes and glancing shots? Most competitive players throw boules in the 690g to 720g range.

Striations, Striping or Groove Patterns

Boules may be smooth (boules lisses) or striated (striage or stries). Depending on the manufacturer and model a boule may be available in one or two simple patterns or over a dozen complex patterns.

Boule Identification

For the novice the primary function of striations is to help identify boules. Eventually you'll become proficient at picking your boules out of the pile around the jack . It takes experience to learn to distinguish subtle differences in metal color, stains, bangs and bruises that make every boule unique.

From a functional perspective, experienced players cultivate the habit of observing every throw in the end. An engaged player can identify every player's boules at the completion of the end. The final arbitrator is that certified boules (in sets of three) are stamped with a unique serial number.

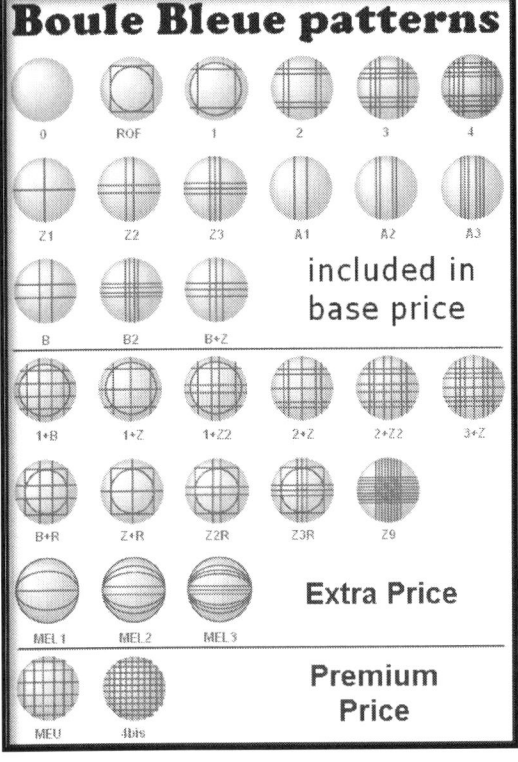

In addition to the type of metal and finish, striations affect a boule's hand-feel and release. Common wisdom asserts several criteria for choosing boule striations.

- ✓ Shooters prefer smooth boules because they provide a clean, precise release
- ✓ Pointers prefer mildly striated boules because striations are reputed to minimize rolling slippage and sliding on rough terrain, producing truer tracking.
- ✓ Deeply engraved (a.k.a. waffle iron, checker, pineapple or turtle) boules are said to improve grip and enhance ground control friction. Most serious players consider them gimmicks; others love the feel, bite and rollout control.
- ✓ Obut's Bi-Pole is a hybrid smooth/striated boule. It has variable stripe depth (0 to 8/10th mm) and the pattern doesn't span the entire boule, so it can be gripped on either the smooth or the grooved side.

Boules Identification for Guests and Novices

Generic boules are usually available in four patterns: one stripe through four stripes. Even so, they are sometimes difficult for novices to distinguish. We use permanent ink markers or even metal spray paint for customizing our generic, non-certified "guest" boules. *Petanque America* carries permanent ink boule markers. With boules "permanent" is fairly temporary, depending on the terrain, because the ink is quickly worn off through abrasion. The most important characteristic of a "permanent" boule marker is that it doesn't stain the player's hands. Experience has taught us to test boules that we've marked, least the player's hand stains last longer than the boule's markings.

> When in doubt get boules lisses or minimal patterns. They are the overwhelming choice of seasoned players.

Boule Hardness Rating

Hardness is the third most important technical boule characteristic, right behind size and weight. During manufacturing boules are tempered to a precise hardness through the process of "quenching" in which hot boules are submerged in a cooler fluid to acquire new properties. The hardness rating defines a boule's resistance to be nicked, dented or fractured when crashing into hard terrain or being savagely struck by an opponent's shot. In simple terms:

- Harder boules have long lifetimes, but absorb less impact energy so they bounce higher on hard terrains and produce fewer carreaus
- Softer boules absorb more impact energy with less rebound which benefits plombée pointers and au fer shooters, but because they get banged and dented they have shorter lifetimes
- Medium hardness (aka semi-soft) boules are a great compromise of longevity and playability

In actual game play the two most demanding occurrences of boule integrity are when a boule is struck square-on with a fast, low trajectory au fer shot or when a high plombée unfortunately lands on the sharp edge of a hard rock. I've done that many times on hard and rocky desert terrains, and my semi-soft boules have the dueling scars (i.e. "badge of honor") to prove it.

The breaking strength test is the most common. It determines the magnitude of force required to crack a boule specified in units of kg/mm^2 (kilograms of force per square millimeter). The breaking strength test roughly simulates the force experienced when a target boule is shot au fer.

The Rockwell-C Hardness (HRc) is a newer test which consists of a 120° diamond cone driven into the surface of the boule by 150kg (330-lb) of force. The depth of penetration is measured and translated into units of HRc (Hardness Rockwell-C). The Rockwell test simulates the trauma that occurs when a high plombée slams into a donnée which is an imbedded rock with a sharp edge.

Text Descriptions	Vickers Number Breaking Strength	Rockwell-C Penetration Resistance
Very Soft (Tender)	$110kg/mm^2$	35 HRc
Semi Soft (Half Tender)	$120kg/mm^2$	37 HRc
Hard	$130kg/mm^2$	40 HRc
Very Hard	$140kg/mm^2$	43.5 HRc

When in doubt, think semi-soft!

FIPJP certification specifies a minimum hardness of $110kg/mm^2$. A very-hard boule ($140kg/mm^2$ or 43.5 HRc) has the equivalent hardness of a typical axe or chisel. The two tests are so different that a direct comparison of breaking strength and penetration resistance is only approximate. Traditionally boule hardness is specified in kg/mm^2; to the best of my knowledge the only manufacturer that currently specifies boule hardness in units of HRc is Thailand's La Franc Boule.

It's true that the hardest rated boules last a very, long time. I own a set of very-hard Obut Match ID boules that are reputed to be playable for many decades! Nevertheless, for both pointers and shooters, there are many compelling reasons to sacrifice hard boule longevity for soft boule playability.

Hard Boules Characteristics:

✓ Longest life: resists nicks, dents and abrasion
✓ Tracks straighter on rough, rocky surfaces. Also a characteristic associated with heavier boules.
✓ Effective on softer terrains that absorb much of the boule's impact energy.
✓ Preferred by roulette and low arced demi-portée pointers whose throws generate minimal terrain impact.
✓ Because it doesn't absorb as much force when shot, a hard boule it is more easily displaced than a softer boule.

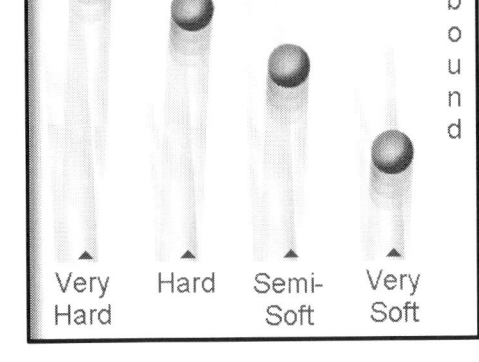

Softer Boules Characteristics:

✓ Shorter life: a couple years vs. a decade
✓ More expensive because of critical tempering process
✓ Absorbs more energy, which results in lower rebound
✓ Ideal for hard terrain plombée pointers because lower rebound produces a controlled and consistent rollout.
✓ Energy absorption results in more au fer carreaus
✓ Depending on the terrain, pointing and shooting style, soft boules are more easily scratched, scarred and pitted. Most damage is only cosmetic, but large dents affect rolling stability.

Shooters on Hard Terrains

Reliable au fer shooters prefer softer boules that theoretically absorb more impact energy and are thus more likely to produce a carreau. We discussed in the techniques chapter that new or less confident shooters tend to shoot short with the rational that, unlike a long shot, a short-shot at least has a chance to slide into the target. A short-shot can be thrown perfectly on-line, but still cleanly skip over the target boule. Although technically dependent on shooting style and trajectory, it's safe to say that on very hard terrains the reduced rebound of softer boules produce more short-shot hits.

Hybrid Hardness

The Obut Bi-Pole and Match Plus boules are examples of proprietary hybrid-hardness. Confusingly, Obut describes the Bi-Pole as "extra-hard" which is not one of the standard hardness ratings. Hybrid-hardness boules are specially tempered producing hard boule durability with soft boule reduced rebound. Obut claims that you can have the best of both worlds. Perhaps because of their premium price, proprietary hybrid-hardness boules have yet to gain significant popularity.

When in Doubt, Buy Semi-Soft Boules!!!

✓ In the absence of other factors, your first set of competition boules should be semi-soft in the range of 125 kg/mm^2 to 115 kg/mm^2.
✓ Consider a harder boule for economic reasons, extended life or to play soft terrains.
✓ Consider a very-soft boule if you are a pure shooter, portée pointer or to compensate for extremely hard terrains.

Steel Alloys

The *FIPJP* specifies that boules must be fabricated from metal. A few bronze alloy boules are on the market, but ninety-nine percent of boules are either carbon or stainless steel. The type of steel affects the boule's aesthetics, hand-feel and maintenance. Hardness is independent of the type of steel alloy; it's a function of the tempering process.

Carbon Steel

Conventional very hard carbon steel boules are the least expensive. But the high-tech, specially alloyed and tempered hybrid-hardness carbon steel boules are in the mid- to upper-price range. Because carbon steel boules oxidize (rust) they are typically finished with one to three anti-corrosion layers. Finishing materials including very glossy satin (aka nickel-chrome) or matt chrome plating, and black, blue or gold glosses. Paint glosses wear off quickly, whereas chrome plating is much more durable.

Chrome provides the most enduring finish. It consists of layers of nickel and chrome, typically with a copper base. One or more layers of nickel provide smoothness and the majority of corrosion protection. A thin layer of chrome is plated on top of the nickel. Polished satin chrome is shiny and glossy. Some people like the smooth feel, others find them slippery. Matt chrome has a titanium look, lacking contrast and gloss.

How well polished satin chrome maintains shine and smoothness is dependent on the terrain's abrasiveness and the player's throwing style. My first set of competition boules was loaned to me by a friend who had played on the simple hard dirt and light gravel terrains of Provence. The Obut Match is very-hard (140 kg/mm^2) with a polished satin chrome finish. They had been used for several seasons, but were still impressively smooth and shiny. Much to my embarrassment after two weeks of play on my summer DG (decomposed granite) terrain they became extremely scratched and pitted; in fact, they appeared as if they had been sand blasted; which is not far from the truth since DG has the abrasiveness of 60-grit sandpaper. Aesthetics aside, I much preferred the rougher grip and more positive tactile feedback. When I returned them my friend was not thrilled. My argument that her boules were better than ever because I had taken the time and effort to properly break them in did not carry the day.

Carbon Steel Maintenance

Carbon steel boules require minimal maintenance. Even scratched and pitted they are protected until the underlying carbon steel is exposed. When the finish is sufficiently compromised, then after every use the boules should be wiped clean, dried and stored in a cloth that is either lightly oiled or sprinkled with baby powder.

As previously mentioned, some people prefer the feel of a little rust on their boules. As an experiment I "cured" a couple of sets of generic boules in salt water brine for a week. After being thoroughly rinsed I preferred the feel of the newly developed slightly pitted surface. I've also sanded off the top chrome layer to expose the nickel and then spray painted the boule as an alternative identification method. So far rust has not been an issue. I don't recommend subjecting *FIPJP* certified boules to that kind of abuse.

> **Competition Spray-Paint Issues**
>
> In several countries spray paint disqualifies a boule from sanctioned tournaments. It can be used to conceal illegal tampering, such as a small hole which was drilled to inject stabilizing substances into the hollow core.

Carbon steel boules in summary:

- ✓ The least expensive steel alloy
- ✓ Beyond the various finishes, many prefer the rough feel as the surface wears
- ✓ Several new variants of special carbon steel and tempering techniques are used to produce high-tech carbon steel boules with premium prices, e.g. Obut hybrid-hardness boules.
- ✓ People with moist hands may find polished chrome slippery

Stainless Steel (Inox)

With over 10% chromium by mass stainless steel is remarkably resistant to stain, corrosion (breakdown due to chemical environmental reactions) or rusting (breakdown due to contact with oxygen). Stainless steel ("inox" in French) is an exceptional material to produce high-performance, maintenance-free, long-life boules. Unlike carbon steel, inox doesn't require protective plating. Most inox boules have a natural or polished satin finish.

Stainless Steel Boule Characteristics

- ✓ Thirty to 50% more expensive than carbon steel equivalents
- ✓ Typically available in very-hard (140-kg/mm^2) through semi-soft (120-kg/mm^2)
- ✓ No maintenance or storage requirements. After play wipe the boules clean and drop them into a boule bag or carrier

The feel of a smooth stainless steel boule is often described as "silky" providing the shooter with an exceptionally clean release. I love the feel of my stainless steel Obut (striated) and La Franc (smooth) boules, but the "silky" feel may become "slippery" in low humidly conditions. The daily use of a high quality hand moisturizer dramatically improves boule feel during the winter or while playing in the desert or at high altitudes.

> **When in doubt think semi-soft (120-kg/mm2 or 37HRc)**
>
> Semi-soft boules do it all, suitable for portée pointers and shooters on all terrains. If you're an occasional recreational player, then a semi-soft boule may enhance your game and still provide years of service. If you're a competitive, multiple times per week player, they will definitely enhance your game. Purchasing new boules every few seasons will be a joy.

U.S. Boule Purchasing Options

You can amble into a Target or Big Five and find Bocce sets in stock - not so with Petanque boules. I'm not aware of any brick and mortar store in the United States that either stocks or even special-orders *FIPJP* certified boules. At the time of this writing there are only two established, reputable and reliable U.S.-based Internet boule sources: *Play-a-Boule* and *Pétanque America*.

> As of the summer of 2011 Pétanque America carries only competition certified boules. I suggest that you visit their web site periodically to see if they've entered the generic market.

Play-a-Boule

Currently Play-a-Boule (http://www.playaboule.com/) is the leading U.S. supplier of inexpensive, generic, *non- FIPJP* certified boules. Play-a-Boule has great prices and exceptional customer service. They ship fast and cheap employing USPS flat rate priority mail. Long after you've purchased a set of certified boules your Play-a-Boule boules will continue to be useful to introduce novices to petanque, as loaner guest boules for drop-ins, for shooting practice and to construct pointing scenarios.

Pétanque America

At the time of this writing Pétanque America (http://petanque-america.com/combal.html) is the exclusive U.S. supplier of *FIPJP* certified boules. They typically stock or can acquire products from over seven manufacturers with boule sets ranging in price from the $69 La Franc Boule SM to the $342 JB Quatre X stainless steel bushed gold boule. Petanque America doesn't act as though it has a monopoly on the U.S. boule market; their product line, shipping policies and customer service are exceptional.

Let's Go Boule Shopping

To prepare you for your first online boules purchase let's examine several product listings. These prices were valid in early summer of 2011. Since most certified boules are manufactured in France the euro-to-dollar exchange rate may have a significant impact on prices. We'll quickly examine the best strategy to buy inexpensive, but still regulation weight and size boules. Then we'll examine several sets of certified boules. **But first let's see what boule purchases to avoid.**

You Don't Need Teak Box "Designer" Boules

Don't buy grossly inflated, shiny, generic boules just to get a "display quality" designer box. *The only place you want to admire your boules are sitting in the dirt and gravel closer to the jack than your opponent's.* You don't need a set of cheap designer boules nested in an endangered species teak box sitting on your desk to remind you of where you'd rather be.

Leisure Boules – Just Say "No Thanks"

Leisure boules (loisirs) are inexpensive and targeted at the "recreational" player. They are usually sold in sets of eight to support a modified two-ball version of doubles. They are much lighter than regulation boules, but have a standard 72mm diameter. Because of the large diameter they're not a good solution for children or adults with diminished hand strength and grip issues. At the time of this writing *Pétanque America* carries La Franc's Junior Boules which are 65mm and 600g; a competition grade boule which is perfect for children and people that require lighter and smaller boules. Your kids deserve proper size and weight boules - loisirs or generic boules are not the answer.

Boule Buying Mindsets

I know people who throw almost every week and are absolutely satisfied with a generic set of inexpensive boules. For them price isn't the issue - perhaps it's the sense that they'll somehow get caught up in equipment obsession and lose touch with the essence of Petanque; maybe it's performance expectations associated with throwing properly sized, competition certified boules. Their mantra is that generic, one-size-fits-all boules keep their lives simple.

Players who want an edge, especially those who have developed a specialty, are driven to acquire a set of boules to complement their game and preferred terrain. To them it is money well spent.

Refer to the fabrication process photo at the beginning of the chapter and note that the boule wall is at least twice as thick as the one pictured to the right. For some players just the thought of throwing cheap, debris filled boules diminishes the intrinsic spirit and purity which Pétanque embodies. How can something so outwardly attractive, be so ugly within?

Life is too Short to Throw Generic Boules

For less than $100 you can buy a great set of boules; for less than $185 you can own the same boules thrown by the best players in the world. Anyway you look at it Pétanque is one of the greatest bargains in the sports world. It's true that you don't need expensive boules to throw great and have a fantastic time. On the other hand, throwing a beautiful set of certified boules may be an inspiration and provide the psychological lift to elevate your game and enhance your enjoyment. For what many golfers pay for

Play-a-Boule Boules: Getting in Cheap

I've purchased several dozen of these boules and they have served me well. You might outgrow them in a couple months but every *Pétanque Evangelist* must always have several extra sets of boules on hand for friends, family and new inductees.

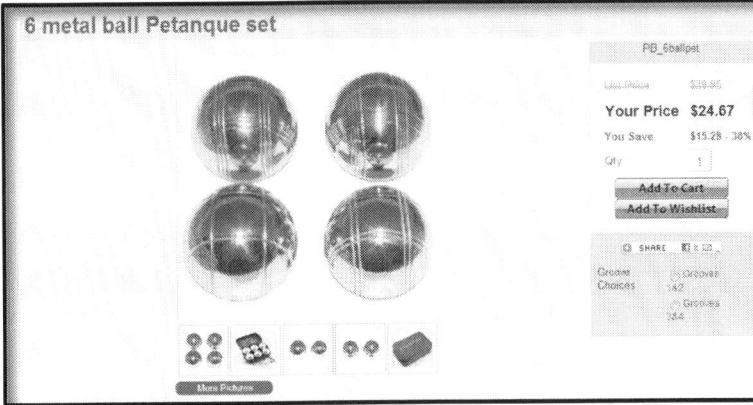

I wish that Play-a-Boules were available in a smooth version. It would make it much easier for novices to play on teams with the smooth boules verses grooved boules. To create a distinctive look the Play-a-Boules pictured below were stripped down to their nickel/copper under-layer. Novices like the weather-beaten look and feel, and they sure are easy to identify!

Size and weight estimate are the only specifications provided with generic boules – remember that they are one-size-fits-all. The following are based on my measurements of 36 generic boules:

- ✓ *Size*: 73mm (± 1.5mm)
- ✓ *Weight*: 720g (± 12g)
- ✓ *Alloy*: Thin carbon steel shell filled with manufacturing debris to provide weight
- ✓ *Finish*: Thin layer of highly polished satin chrome
- ✓ *Hardness*: Soft, thin walled boules dent easily on hard and rocky terrains
- ✓ *Striping*: Sets of 1 & 2 or 3 & 4 shallow grooves which don't provide positive tactile feedback
- ✓ *Accessories*: Six-boule carrying case, plain wooden target jack & simple measuring string

A Brief Survey of Competition Boules

This is a selection of competition boules which are stocked by Pétanque America. There is no doubt that Obut (and the other five bands that they own) represent Pétanque's gold standard. But La Franc boule has redefined the market and Pétanque America carries their three top models. La Franc Boule rivals Obut's specifications and quality at a 25% to 35% discount!

Entry Level, FIPJP Certified: La Franc SM

- ✓ Sizes: 71mm to 74mm
- ✓ Weight: 680g to 720g
- ✓ Alloy: Carbon steel
- ✓ Finish: Satin chrome
- ✓ Hardness: Very-Hard: 45-HRc (140-kg/mm^2)
- ✓ Striping: Smooth, plus five patterns
- ✓ No Accessories

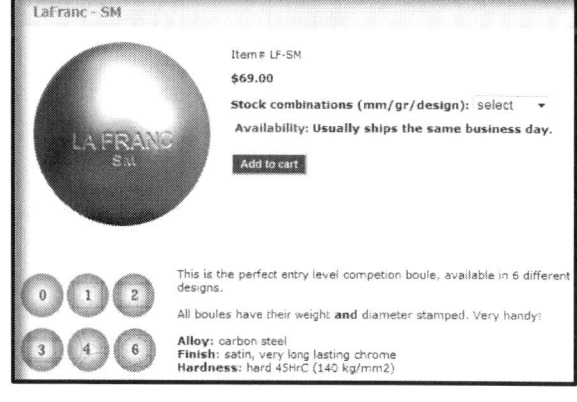

This is a great entry-level, very-hard carbon steel boule. Note that they are available in a 71mm, 680g size, which is great for players with small hands. Many people don't have to look further than the La Franc SM to find their first certified boule. La Franc provides a two-year breakage warranty. I own La Franc stainless steel (SS-01) and semi-soft carbon steel (SB) boules. There's no question of quality and durability. They may not have the status, reputation and history of Obut, but the *FIPJP* wouldn't have certified La Franc if they didn't have quality control and durability.

All-Purpose Semi-Soft: La Franc SB

- ✓ Sizes: 71mm to 74mm
- ✓ Weight: 680g to 710g
- ✓ Alloy: Carbon steel
- ✓ Finish: Matte black
- ✓ Hardness: Semi-Soft: 37-HRc
- ✓ Striping: Smooth, plus five patterns

The La Franc SB is a great all-purpose boule, suitable for shooters and plombée pointers, on hard and soft terrain. This is the best under $100 entry-level competition boule available to the U.S. Market. Many players prefer the feel of the dark matte black finish over polished satin chrome.

> I have several sets of semi-soft name brand boules that cost nearly twice as much, but the SB is my favorite all-around boule.

To the right is a photo of a La Franc SB after a week of intensive play on a hard and rocky terrain. The black matt is gone, but the underlying metal

has a surprisingly attractive titanium look and feel. The look and feel is much more characteristic of inox rather than carbon steel. Note the lack of nicks and dents, for a semi-soft it's a tough boule!

Obut's Entry Level Semi-Soft: Match 120 TR

- ✓ Sizes: 72mm to 76mm
- ✓ Weight: 680g to 730g
- ✓ Alloy: Tempered carbon steel
- ✓ Finish: Polished satin chrome
- ✓ Hardness: Semi-Soft, 120-kg/mm^2
- ✓ Striping: Smooth or 4-circle

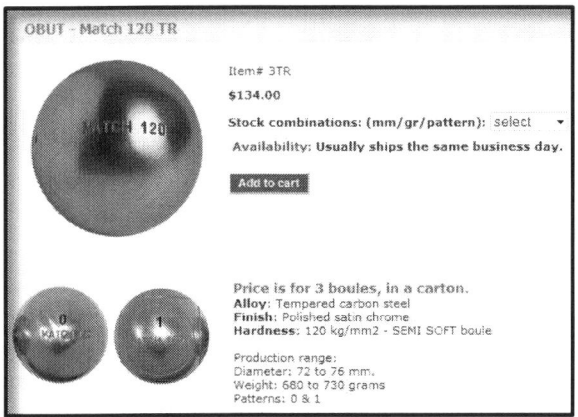

The Match 120 has similar specifications to the La Franc SB, but costs 33% more and isn't available in the 71mm diameter. On the other hand it has the prestige of Obut. This is an electroplated carbon steel boule, depending on your terrain and playing style the polished satin chrome finish will eventually take a beating. The functional difference between the Obut Match 120 TR and the La Franc SB is the hand feel of polished chrome versus matte black paint.

<table>
<tr><td>

Oxidation: Chrome vs. Matte Finish

There's no debate that the Obut polished chrome finish lasts much longer than La Franc's matte black paint as evidenced in the previous photograph. One might argue that because polished chrome provides a much more durable oxidation protection that these boules would be a better choice for wetter climates. It depends on how you feel about a little rust.

</td><td>

Boule Patterns & Baseball Stitching

An interesting observation that several players have made is the functionality of the groove patterns. Many baseball or softball players that learn Pétanque prefer the Obut Pattern-1 with the single circle on each of the six boule faces because they can place their fingertips on the grooves in a similar way to holding the seams (stitching) on a baseball.

</td></tr>
</table>

Obut's Very-Hard Stainless Steel: *Match* ID

✓ Sizes: 72mm to 76mm
✓ Weight: 690g to 730g
✓ Alloy: Stainless steel
✓ Finish: Polished satin
✓ Hardness: Very-Hard, 140-kg/mm^2
✓ Striping: smooth or two patterns

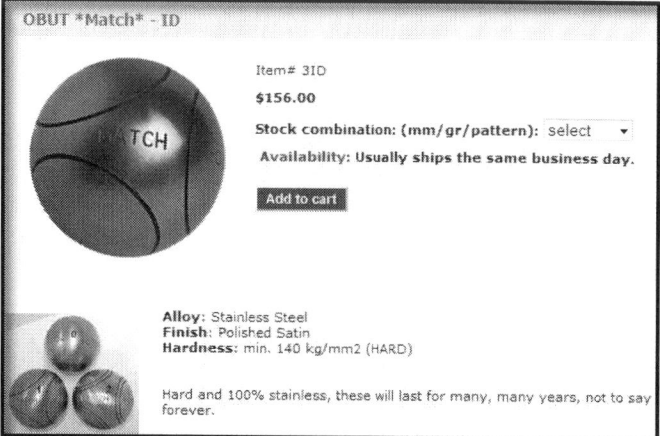

The star "★" on an Obut boule designates inox (stainless steel). The ★Match★ ID is polished satin, it's not plated. Inox maintains a much more consistent hand-feel than electroplated carbon steel boules. My set of ★Match★ IDs (pictured on the right) still look nearly new after a couple hundred hours of play on a variety of nasty and abrasive terrains.

The ★Match★ ID is very-hard (140-kg/mm^2) and should be playable for at least a decade. As previously considered, the downside of very-hard boules is high rebound. Sometimes on decomposed granite after a hard rain my ★Match★ IDs seem to bounce like tennis balls! If I shoot a few centimeters short the boule bounces right over the target. However, on medium to soft terrains they are stable and predictable.

> **Obut discontinued production of the ★Match★ ID in fall of 2010.** The La Franc SS-01 is an inexpensive, very-hard inox alternative with a warmer titanium-like feel.

Obut's Semi-Soft Inox: ★Match 115★ IT

✓ Sizes: 71mm to 76mm
✓ Weight: 650g to 730g
✓ Alloy: Special stainless steel
✓ Finish: Polished satin
✓ Hardness: Semi-Soft, 115-kg/mm^2
✓ Striping: smooth or 4-circle

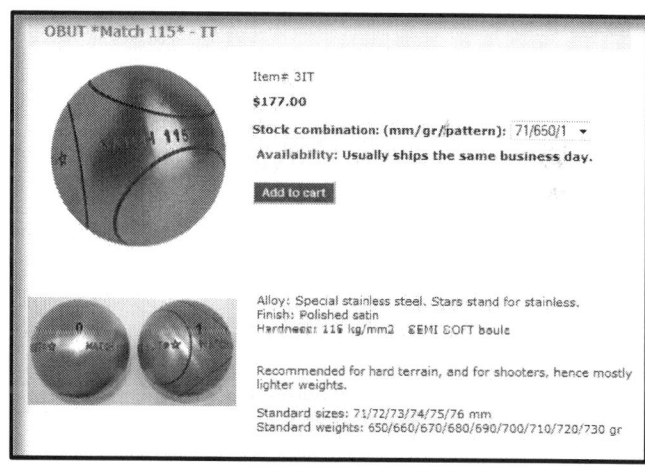

The ★Match 115★ IT semi-soft is one of the finest all-purpose stainless steel boules in production. At 115-kg/mm^2 it is between semi-soft and very-soft. The ★Match 115★ IT is sometimes available from Pétanque America in the *FIPJP* minimum 71mm, 650g size. But that's quite a premium for a beginner to pay over purchasing JB Juniors for under $100 from a European web-store. In the larger sizes and heavier weights the ★Match 115★ IT is a great all-around boule for any serious player. It's got the specifications and reputation on which to build your entire Pétanque career. This is a serious top-of-the-line competition boule. Until La Franc Boule produces an inox semi-soft, the ★Match 115★ IT will be the best all-around boule for under $200 that's directly available to the U.S. market.

Purchasing Summary

Most novices are best served to start with generic Play-a-Boule boules and accumulate several months of experience in which to find their game and preferred specialty before purchasing a set of certified boules. In this chapter we examined five models of certified boules which are available from Pétanque America.

The most frustrating situation is throwing an oversized boule that produces chronic side-spin and release issues. The only way to compensate for oversized boules is to develop exceptional hand and forearm strength. Almost equally bad is throwing a boule which is too heavy. One is forced to sacrifice technique to reach long points; it especially limits au fer shooting and high portee pointing range. And worse if you develop improper biomechanics, then chronic shoulder issues are sure to follow.

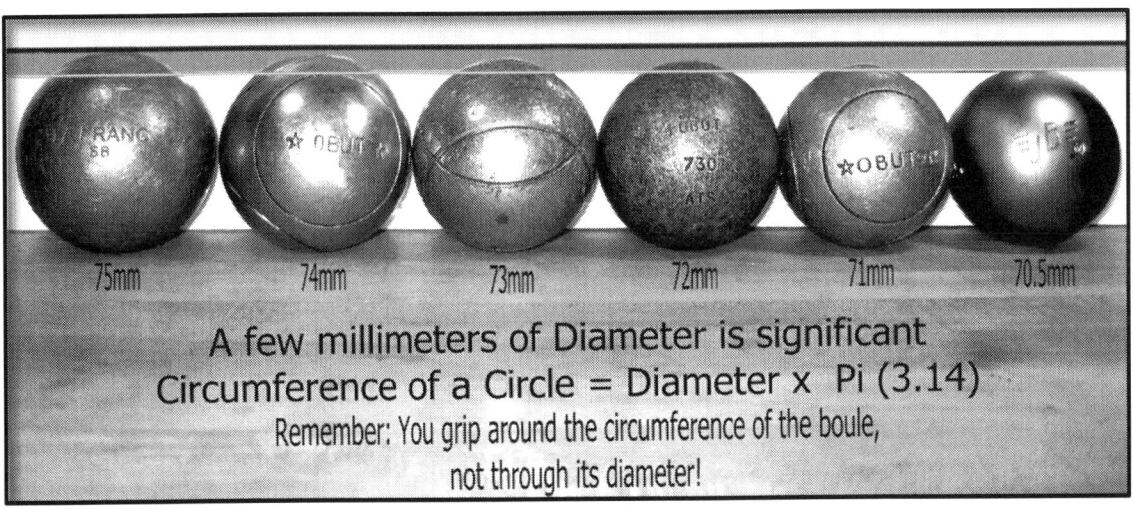

As the photo shows, even ½mm and 30g can make a huge different to a player with petite paws. If Petanque America can't order J.B. Juniors then it's worth the trouble getting them from France or Spain. Of the 12 regular women players in my summer group, eight of them throw J.B. Juniors – and they absolutely love them!

The Bottom Line:

Generic boules are a <u>one-size-fits-all proposition</u>: one size and one weight with marginal size and weight quality control. They are acceptable for introducing Pétanque to people with average sized hands and no hand or forearm issues.

FIPJP certified boules are available in a wide range of sizes and weight to accommodate hand size, arm strength and playing style. Although (*due to FIPJP/FPUSA collusion and apathy*) a significant percentage of women are still forced to throw oversized boules at 70.5mm, that's almost an 8mm reduction in circumference from 73mm generic boules. Competition boule quality control is impressive: size and weight are within 1.5% tolerances, and precise dynamic balancing standards ensure a consistent rollout. As previously state, "Life's too short to throw generic boules!"

Throwing a comfortable boule develops a consistent game. And consistency is the platform from which every advanced skill is built and perfected.

Appendix A: Rules to Remember

This is my interpretation of the *FPUSA* translation of the French language version of the *FIPJP* Official Rules. The official rules may be downloaded from the *FPUSA* and *FIPJP* websites. Most of these rules were presented in the game simulation in *Chapter Two*.

I've selected the rules which are applicable to everyday, club-level play. I may have misunderstood or misinterpreted the official rules; you often hear them debated on the terrain. And official rules change and are periodically reinterpreted and rewritten. I have changed the order of the rules to provide context and to group them into similar concepts.

One of the best features of Pétanque is its simplicity. Many people are hesitant to learn and apply rules because they feel that they are inherently oppressive and the resultant complexity diminishes the joy of the game. On the other hand, rules allow Pétanque to retain a consistent structure wherever it is played in the world. It's up to you to reasonably apply these rules to enhance your Pétanque experience, rather than letting them take on a life of their own.

Article 06: Start of play – Rules regarding the circle

- Coin toss to determine who throws the jack and first boule
- Rond is drawn (35-cm to 50-cm) or prefabricated rond (inside diameter of 50cm) at least 1m from any obstacle.
- All previous drawn ronds in the area should be erased. Club players rarely do this which inevitably produces confusion and debate about which is the current rond.
- Unlike any other area of the terrain, the inside of the rond may be cleaned of debris (pebbles, sticks, etc.) to provide solid footing, but it must be returned to the original state the completion of the end. (I've never seen a club player replace the rocks and twigs which were removed.)
- The player's feet must be entirely inside of the circle and *must not touch the inside edge of a prefabricated rond.*
- Some portion of both feet must be in constant contact with the ground until the thrown boule hits the terrain. Lifting a foot before the boule lands is a foot fault and that boule is declared dead and taken out of play.
- No part of the body can touch the ground outside of the rond. This is a concern of squat pointers who use torso torque or squat bouncing techniques.
- Wheel chair players must have the wheel of the throwing arm inside the rond

Article 16: Player Etiquette

- It is suggested that players from both teams stand just beyond the jack and at least 2m to the side (as illustrated in the photo at the top of page 72.) Everything relevant to strategy or throwing feedback happens near the donnée or the jack. In matches constrained to tournament pistes, it is common to stand near the jack and just beyond the side line markers. Players with ambulatory issues may stand behind the rond at least 2m to the side, but must be beyond the peripheral vision of the player in the rond.

- Teammates of the player preparing to throw may remain between the rond and the jack to provide guidance. However, no object may be placed or marks drawn on the terrain as aids.

- When a player is in the rond preparing to throw everyone should be silent or speak only in whispers; extend this courtesy at all levels of play, don't force the thrower to be the bad guy by having to request silence. Ask yourself, are you on the terrain to play Pétanque or socialize?

- Opponents must not walk, gesticulate or disturb the thrower in any way. For most Americans friendly competition invokes a little trash talk and teasing; although you may not care if people are talking when you're in the rond, don't assume, even in casual play, that your teammates and opponents have the same temperament.

- When playing with friends or regulars you may be lenient about player conduct. When playing with strangers or at the club level start with a strict observance of the conduct rules and relax things as the situation dictates.

Article 07: Valid jack placement

- For adult competition a valid jack throw is 6m to 10m from the outer edge of the rond.
- Like the rond (throwing circle), the jack must also be at least 1m from an obstacle or O.B. (out-of-bounds) area.
- The jack must be visible to all players. If it is hidden in a gulley or settled into a gopher hole it must be re-thrown.
- The nature of Pétanque is free form. At the completion of the end, a rond is drawn around (or a prefab rond is dropped over) the current position of the jack. This ensures that one can't manipulate play by moving the location of a rond to a position that the throwing team finds more advantageous to their skills or preferences. There are a couple of exceptions:
    - If the edge of the rond is less than 1m from an obstacle, it should be moved just enough to meet that specification
    - If the jack can't be thrown 10m in any direction, then the rond may be moved back in line with the previous end's play just far enough to accommodate a 10m jack placement.
- The team has 60 seconds and three attempts to make a legal jack throw. If they fail, the opponents have three attempts. Regardless of which team succeeds in placing the jack, the team that won the last end always throws the first boule.

Article 10: Terrain grooming

- Although Pétanque is customarily played on ungroomed terrains, *prior to play* it is permissible to perform minor grooming. This typically entails dragging a landscaper's rake around the pitch to smooth and redistribute gravel, rake out ant hills, fill gopher holes and manually remove chunks of bark, braches, palm fronds or other major natural debris.
- The terrain may be misted with a hose to minimize dust.
- Beverage containers, food wrappers and other human (and canine) relics should be cleaned-up.
- Once play commences it is forbidden to move any natural object such as leaves, acorns, twigs, bark or rocks. They are part of the terrain and important random components which usually aid the novice and frustrate the expert.
- A player must not use their foot to smooth any area or to move surface rocks with one exception. On medium to soft terrains a high lob can leave a significant divot. The divot may be the next thrower's best donnée or be in the direct path of boule rollout. The team about to throw may fill one (and only one) divot by foot before each throw.

Article 15: Throwing the first and subsequent boules

- The team that won the coin toss makes the first throw to start the game. On subsequent ends, the team that won the end or scored last (in the event of end which is declared void) makes the first throw.
- After the first throw the opposing team makes a throw. From then, until the end is complete, *the team not holding the point* throws until they hold the point or are out of boules.
- As also stated in Article 16, the terrain shall not be modified in any way which aids a player's throw. No objects may be used to aid a throw except when playing beer bottle cap Pétanque as specified in *Chapter 4*.
- A player must not "accidently" drop a boule (tâter la donnée or "feeling the donnée") as a way to evaluate rebound.
- Knowing how many boules your teammates and opponents have in hand is a mandatory component in strategy consideration and a good mental exercise to keep you engaged in the game.
- *This is not an official rule but a safety issue:* While in the rond a player with more than one boule left to throw may choose to lay the remaining boules just outside of the rond. When they have completed throwing they should pickup and hold their remaining boules; this behavior minimizes trip hazards and helps enable players on both teams to visually determine who has boules left to play.
  - Since no one should ever stand directly behind the rond, that area can be used by people with small hands or strength issues who cannot comfortably hold the boules they have left to throw.
- Except for boules that have been deflected by humans, animals, or objects (like a soccer ball) a throw may never be replayed.
  - The FIPJP rules specify that the rond is "not out-of-bounds." That means accidently dropping a boule while standing in the rond technically qualifies as a throw. This type of incident is seldom enforced except by players who love mind games, are desperate to win or want to flaunt their knowledge of Pétanque minutia.
- Spit balls are not allowed. It is forbidden to moisten a boule or jack because dirt will stick to it and stabilize its roll. This extends to the requirement of wiping boules clean of mud or dirt before throwing. *All players should hold a rag in their non-throwing hand during the entire match.* It's good practice to wipe your boules several times a game.

Article 20: Time permitted to throw

- A player has one minute to make a throw:
  - After a successful jack throw
  - Following a teammate's or opponent's throw
  - After the conclusion of a measurement
- If the opposition throws next, the player who just threw must immediately exit the rond and quickly walk to the jack area and stand with the other players as previously described.

Article 28: Equidistant Boules

This is a tricky situation which is a function of the measuring instrument, your eyes, the light and the steadiness of your hand. Although a typical metric tape measure has calibration marks to 1mm, it's only reliable to ½cm (5mm). A set of calipers may be accurate to ½mm. When it is determined that the two boules closet to the jack are equally distance and belong to opposing teams:

- If neither team has boules in hand (i.e. both teams are out of boules) the end is declared void and no points are awarded. The team that won the previous end retains jack control and makes the first throw in the next end.
- If only one team has boules in hand, those boules are played and the end is scored as normal. If the two closest boules are still equidistant the end is void as previously described.
- If both teams have boules in hand, the team that threw the last boule throws again. If the two closest boules are still equidistant, then the opposing team throws. The teams alternate until one team is holding the point or no boules are left and the end is declared void.
- If, after completion of the end, all boules are O.B. (Out of Bounds) the end is void and no points are awarded. This may happen through a combination of circumstances when the jack is very close to the O.B. and all of the boules are overthrown or shot into the O.B. - a rare case indeed.

Article 09: Dead jack

The jack is dead and declared out-of-play when:

- It is knocked O.B. even if rebounds back onto the terrain
- It is freely floating, because it must provide a stationary reference
- Although it is knocked onto a legal portion of the terrain, there is an O.B. area between the rond and the jack
- It is knocked into a location where it is no longer visible to all players (i.e. gopher hole or deep rut)
- It is further than 20m from the rond. *The Paris terrain in the photo on the right is so enormous that the jack could be knocked a couple of kilometers!*
- Playing on pistes (marked out terrains) it is knocked <u>two more</u> pistes to the side
- It is lost and isn't found within a 5 minutes

When the jack is declared dead points are awarded as specified in Article 13.

Article 13: Dead Jack Point Allocation

When the jack is declared dead:

- If <u>both teams</u> or <u>neither team</u> has boules in hand, then the end is void and <u>no points are allocated</u>
- If <u>only one team</u> has boules in hand, it is <u>awarded one point for each boule</u> it has left to throw

Article 17: Game time practice throws

- Practice or test boules may not be thrown during a game. (It's discourteous and distracting, and you should be standing beside the rond engaged in the game!)

Article 18: Dead boules

- A boule is dead when it <u>completely crosses</u> into the O.B. even if it subsequently rolls or rebounds back onto the terrain.
- Similar to the jack rule, a boule thrown or knocked outside of the piste's side marker is in-play until it crosses more than one marked lane
- A dead boule must be immediately removed from the terrain.

Article 25: Measuring of Points

- A member of the <u>team that last threw last</u> has the duty to make any measurements in question. Any member of the opposing team has the right to contest and verify the measurement.
- The measurement is best made with a metric tape measure, or any appropriate commercially available device. Whatever device is used, the measurement must be made without disturbing the location of the boules or jack (see Article 27); that precludes using the feet. See the end of *Chapter 2* for a suggestion on how to make an accurate measurement without disturbing the jack.

Article 27: Accidental displacement of boules or jack

- When the jack or a contested boule is moved during a measurement, the opposition team is award one penalty point.

Article 26: Removing boules in play from the terrain

- It is forbidden to pickup <u>any boule in play</u> until
  - the end is complete
  - points are allocated
  - both team captains are in agreement
- If a boule is picked up prior to agreement of point allocation, that boule is <u>considered dead</u> and is not considered in point allocation

Consequently it is best to only pickup your own boules. Much too frequently boules are accidently picked up or moved prior to point allocation agreement. It's up to the team captain to signal his teammates when it's safe to pick up boules. It may seem to be a silly formality, but players (and rightfully so) get frustrated when points aren't allocated properly because someone prematurely picked up boules. The truth is if you are engaged in the game and paying attention to point allocation, you won't accidently touch a boule before point allocation is concluded.

Appendix B: Two Minute Quick-Start

✓ **Equipment** 12 boules, target jack and tape measure (or a long piece of string)
✓ **Petanque means "anchored feet"** The thrower stands inside a circle with both feet on the ground. The feet don't have to be flat; the player may even squat on the balls of the feet, but neither foot may be fully lifted until the thrown boule hits the ground.
✓ **The Target Jack** Pétanque's bull's-eye is initially tossed six to ten meters from the throwing circle
✓ **Holding the Point** The team with the boule closest to the jack is "holding the point." The other team throws until they are holding the point or have run out of boules.

Four Ways to Hold the Point: Throw a boule that:

5. Stops closer to the target jack than the opponent's best boule
6. Strikes the opponent's best boule driving it away; leaving one of your boules closest to the jack
7. Strikes a teammate's boule which moves it closest to the jack
8. Hits and moves the target jack to a new location where one of your boules is closest

Number of Boules and Throwing Order In doubles each player throws three boules; in triples each player throws two boules. Any member of the team <u>which is not holding the point</u> may throw next, but each player must only throw their allocated number of boules

Winning the Game: The first team to accumulate 13 points

Scoring: Only one team scores each end. <u>The team with the closest boule to the jack</u> is awarded <u>one point for every boule</u> which is <u>closer than the opponent's best boule</u>. One to six points are allocated with the exception of a rare null end (see *Chapter 2* for details.)

Three Steps to Start the Game

1. Pick teams
2. Flip a coin
3. The winning team selects the terrain and draws a 50cm (20") diameter circle in the dirt.

Six Steps Repeated Each End

1. A member of the winning team steps into the circle and throws the target jack 6m (19.5 ft) to 10m (32.8 ft) from the circle's edge. After three failures, the opposition gets three tries to throw the jack. <u>However, the winning team always makes the first throw</u>.
2. A player from the winning team places both feet completely in the circle and throws a boule attempting to make it stop near the target jack. That team is now holding the point.
3. A player from the other team steps into the circle and throws attempting to accomplish one of the four ways to hold the point as specified above.
4. The team <u>not holding the point</u> throws until either they are holding or have run out of boules.
5. When all 12 boules have been played the end is complete and points are allocated.
6. If neither team has yet accumulated 13 points, a new end is started. The team which won the last end draws a circle 50cm (20") around the jack and play resumes at Step 1)

Appendix C: The Art of Jack Placement

The Rond and Jack: Petanque's Golden Braid

The strategic advantage of jack placement (throwing the jack) depends on several factors. Most club play is free-form, although constrained to large rectangles. To start the next end the rond is thrown over (or drawn around) the current jack position. The only exceptions are that the rond must be at least 1m from the O.B. area and a legal 10m jack placement must be possible.

- A 50cm prefabricated rond is the fairest solution because it gives people with big feet plenty of toe room.
- In club play the requirement that the rond must always be dropped (drawn) over the current jack position to start the next end is often ignored. That enables the team who controls the jack to cherry-pick the next terrain. For a thinking, engaged team that privilege provides a tremendous advantage.

Prefabbed Ronds and Irrational FIPJP Rules

At a sanctioned tournament it's acceptable to draw a non-circular circle in the dirt which vaguely has a diameter of 35cm to 50cm. But if you have the temerity to prefer a prefabricated rond it *must be rigid* (non-folding) and have an inside diameter of 50cm ±2mm. Can you imagine pedaling your bike to the terrain transporting a rigid 50cm (19.7") diameter rond?

I've been told by several club players that they consider a prefabricated rond to be a trip hazard! **By the way, those are the same guys that have no problem with the practice of players leaving their boules laying randomly about the terrain (talk about a trip hazard).** Ironically the flat prefabricated rond sold by *Petanque America* (which the worst foot dragger couldn't trip on) is not *FIPJP* approved because it folds for efficient transport.

> ### Use a Prefabbed Rond
>
> Recently I was at a mixed doublettes regional championship played on a simple dirt and gravel terrain. The scene was dominated by traditionalists, so few prefabbed ronds were employed. Within ninety minutes I witnessed three arguments resulting from a player attempting to throw from a rond that had (allegedly) been used in a previous end and not erased.
>
> *FIPJP Rules Article 6* states that the team which throws the jack must erase all previous used ronds in the vicinity. It's a sensible rule which is ignored by most club players, even at tournaments.

I've built prefabbed ronds from many types of materials. My two favorites are constructed from quarter-inch flexible tubing (less than $1) or 3/16" stainless steel cable (about $2.50) which will last a lifetime. Both types of ronds quickly and easily twist into a figure-8 and then flip into overlapping circles with about a 6" diameter.

It's the responsibility of the player that throws the last boule to pick up the prefabbed rond and carry it to the jack. When the points are awarded and agreed upon, the rond is dropped over the jack. *Any miscreant who throws last and forgets to pick up the rond is charged a $1 fine that goes into the refreshments kitty, to remind them to keep their head in the game! If they pick up the rond before the last boule is thrown, the fine is increased substantially: un pack de six bière froide*

In all seriousness, it may be impossible to precisely reposition a rond that has been picked up prior to the end's completion, but assessing a fixed penalty is difficult. (Where are the *FIPJP* bureaucrats when you need them?) The rule could state that the team whose player prematurely picked up the rond will forfeit their remaining boules in hand, but what if they don't have any boules in hand because it is the other team that still has boules left to throw?

My rule is that the offending player's team is penalized one point. Our procedure for returning the rond to the original location is based on the practice of many players (me included) who always pace the distance de jeu (distance from the rond to the jack) before throwing. Knowing the precise distance assists replacing the rond in the original position.

The real issue is that the player who prematurely picked up the rond didn't have their head in the game. At the absolute minimum every player should know the number of boules that each team is currently holding. Keep your head in the game and you'll play better and have a great time.

When Controlling the Jack Isn't Really an Advantage

As you know, the team that wins the end controls the jack. They may throw it in any direction as long as it comes to rest 6m to 10m from the outer edge of the rond and is at least 1m from any obstacle or O.B. area. To formalize what was casually stated at the beginning of this appendix, if a legal 10m jack toss can't be made, *the rond may be moved in a direct line to make the accommodation*. There are a few minor distinctions, see *FIPJP Rules, Article 7: Jack Placement for the gruesome details*.

The advantage of controlling the jack is greatest on a large, multifaceted free-form terrain such as the one pictured below. *When a terrain is consistent or constrained into pistes the advantage of controlling the jack is reduced to distance and angles of play against the O.B.* e. g. throw the jack just over 9m in the corner of the piste, very near to where the sideline and backline intersect.

The photo below is the jardin de Tuileries, adjacent to the musée du Louvre in Paris. This immense and challenging terrain consists of several kilometers of very wide dirt/gravel walking paths with leaves, twigs and human debris (including an abundance of French cigarette butts.) Executing a strategic jack placement on complex freeform public space terrains provides a significant advantage.

Freeform versus Rectangular Terrain

Non-dedicated, oddly shaped public spaces support the freest Pétanque play. A bit more constrained and usually much more consistent are the large rectangular terrains of most Pétanque clubs. *The photo above shows a small part of the beautiful and extensive Pont d'Ouilly Pétanque Club on the Orne River in Suisse Normande (Swiss Normandy).* Wooden beam backboards subdivide each terrain into 18m x 18m squares for regular play. The terrains are further subdivided by string (lignes tracées) or chalk into individual pistes to support maximum game density for large tournament play. As specified in the *FIPJP* Rules, for National and International Championships the playing surface is 15m x 4m; for club or regional tournaments it may be reduced to 12m x 3m.

How to Toss the Jack

Typically your lead pointer makes the jack toss:

- *The person who places the jack is not required to throw the first boule of the end.*
- After choosing a precise location, have a teammate use their foot as a target to specify where the jack should come to rest.
- The player throwing the jack must stand inside the rond.
- The jack should be thrown as if it were a boule. Most people use "the flick" or demi-portée.
- Carefully observe the jack as it impacts and rolls-out. Look for bounces and lurching directional changes that may indicate the presence of larger rocks or other obstructions.
- Although jack rollout is helpful in determining terrain speed, contours and breaks, ***remember that it only has a 30mm diameter and weights 2% of a boule***. Therefore, jack impact and rollout doesn't directly emulate boule rollout behavior.

The Never Be Lackadaisical List

Even when you are playing on a consistent and constrained piste take your time and find a jack placement to give your team an edge.

- Practice throwing the jack to different distances and locations. Since the jack rolls after it is thrown it takes practice to stop it at a specific spot.
- *Play to your team's strengths and your opponent's weaknesses.* If you're playing against roulette rollers and your team has plombée pointers choose the roughest, most rugged, rocky spot for the jack.
- If you team has aggressive short range (6m to 8m) shooters throw the jack short and let your opponents throw perfect points only to be instantly removed by your shooter. If your opponents can't shoot long distances, keep the jack at 9.5m and beyond – you get three jack throws within sixty seconds, don't be afraid to use them. After three failed attempts your opponents get three attempts. Regardless of which team succeeds in placing the jack, the team that won the last end always throws the first boule.
- There are also some quasi-ethical ways to throw the jack. If your team is decked out in wide brimmed hats and sunglasses and your opponents are hatless, throw the jack directly into the glaring sun to blind them.
- Where and how far to throw the jack is a team decision. You may be a great long pointer, but your shooter may not feel confident beyond 8m – find a compromise that leverages your teammate's strengths and your opponent's weaknesses.
- You can tell how much effort your opponents are investing in jack placement by observing whether they huddle before the jack toss, which team member tosses it and whether they carefully throw it like a boule or just casually flip it underhanded into the air.
- One would think that a jack measurement request must occur before the first throw of the end so *file this in the stupid tricks category for exploiting lazy people*. If the first boule is an exceptionally good pointing throw (especially a tadpole) and the jack placement was either fairly short (close to 6m) or long (close to 10m) before they throw their first boule, the opposition can call for a jack measurement. If the jack is verified to be too short or long, it must be re-thrown and that great first pointing throw is nullified. See the *FIPJP Rules, Article 8 — Validity of the Jack* for details.
- In regards to the previous issue, note that advanced players almost always pace the distance to the jack – if for no other reason than to know the precise distance in meters. Also as we've discussed, the lead pointer should always walk the line from rond to the jack to evaluate possible données, rocks and obstructions and contours before making the first throw. Sometimes you'll notice that the jack is sitting in a little dish or depression, in a patch of sandy or soft soil, or that there are larger rocks in front or behind the jack which may stop or alter the path of a slowly moving boule.

All of the effort required just to get a target in play may seem excessive, but it all depends on your reason for being on the terrain. If you're in the mood to be engaged and reinforce competitive techniques, then you should follow some or all of the jack placement observation and suggestions. If you've decided that you're just out for a casual throw and you're more concerned with enjoying the out-of-doors and a little time with friends, then flip the jack wherever your fancy leads and play it as it lies.

Appendix D: Cutthroat: a Game for Three

It's tough when only three players are on hand. If one player has six boules, then the trio can play modified doublettes with the singles player throwing six boules and the doublettes players throwing three boules each. But I look at a gathering of three as an opportunity to force people into the secretly desired, but often uncomfortable role of shooter.

Summary

Cutthroat is Pétanque singles with a *nasty twist*. Each singles player **must employ the services of a designated shooter two times each end**. The singles players score points just like a conventional singles game; the shooter accumulates points based on the effectiveness of each shot. Roles are rotated at the completion of each end.

The Designated Shooter

The singles player **not holding the point** may order the designated shooter to shoot a boule. After the shot, the shooter <u>immediately removes</u> his boule from the terrain. After either player has thrown their last boule, if that player has not yet used the services of the designated shooter twice, he must do so before play continues with the other singles player or the end is declared complete.

The Jack as a Target

The jack may be specified as the target only if it can be directly shot (not screened by a boule.)

Scoring

The two singles players are awarded points just like a regular game. The shooter accumulates points on-the-fly based on each shot's effectiveness. To score, a shot must <u>directly strike</u> the designated target; if the shooter directly strikes any other object he is assessed <u>one penalty point</u>. Rebounding off of the target into other boules is normal play and does not result in a penalty.

Exception

If the direct line between the rond and designated target boule is obscured by other boules, the shooter may declare a "combination shot" specifying that another boule will be shot first, and that boule will rebound into the designated target. The shot is declared a hit only if the combination is successful.

Per Shot Point Allocations (disputes are settled by majority vote)

🚫	0 points	<u>Clean Miss</u> doesn't hit any boule or the jack
👍	+1 point	<u>Incidental Hit</u> (tick, nick or cap) metal-to-metal contact that moves target less than 1m
👍👍	+2 points	<u>Solid Shot</u> drives the target boule more than 1m
👍 👍👍	+3 points	<u>Carreau!</u> Solid Shot and shooter's boule stops within 50cm of the original target position
👍 👍 👍	+3 points	<u>Shooting the Jack</u> and driving it more than 1m
☠	(-1 point)	Initially striking any object other than the designated target (except a declared combination)

Choosing the Initial Roles

Players stand side-by-side, the jack is thrown a legal distance and on command everyone tosses a boule. The order of the boules from the jack specifies the order in which players choose their preferred role for the first end.

Role Rotation

At the completion of the end after singles points are allocated each player verbally announces their accumulated score and roles are rotated as specified in the diagram.

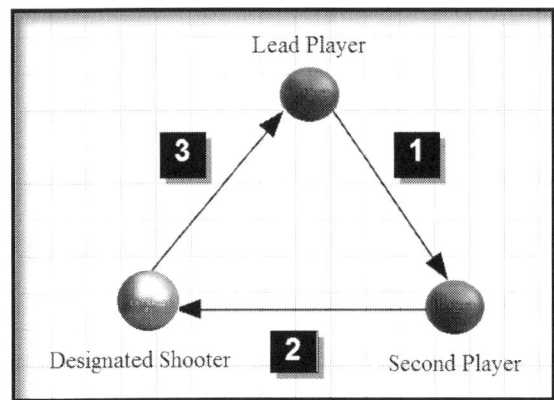

1. Lead Pointer becomes Second Pointer
2. Second Pointer becomes Designated Shooter
3. Designated Shooter becomes Lead Pointer

The Lead Pointer always tosses the jack and throws the first boule.

Strategy

The game is called "cutthroat" because players may form an ad hoc, untrustworthy alliance to attack the current leader. The shooter may purposefully miss a shot or even shoot the wrong boule and lose a point, if it has a greater negative impact on the current scoring leader.

The shooter can be neutralized by specifying a target boule that is far away, behind blocking boules and can only be shot au fer, or requires a difficult combination. Declaring the jack as a target is a gamble. It is a low percentage shot, but a solid hit yields three points. The two singles players are not restricted from shooting, but they don't accumulate points like the designated shooter. Alliances are temporary, fluid and dependent on each player's competence in their current role; alliances often terminate in back-stabbing and double-crosses. That's, Cutthroat!

Index and Glossary

R

S

V

W

Y

Z

Printed in Great Britain
by Amazon.co.uk, Ltd.,
Marston Gate.